Rich States, Poor States

ALEC-Laffer State Economic Competitiveness Index

Dr. Boettke,

Thanks for all you do!

Best Wishes,

AMERICAN LEGISLATIVE EXCHANGE COUNCIL

Rich States, Poor States
ALEC-Laffer State Economic Competitiveness Index
© 2009 American Legislative Exchange Council

Published by
American Legislative Exchange Council
1101 Vermont Ave., NW, 11th Floor
Washington, D.C. 20005

Phone: (202) 466.3800
Fax: (202) 466.3801

www.alec.org

For more information, contact
the ALEC Public Affairs office

Dr. Arthur B. Laffer, Stephen Moore
and Jonathan Williams, Authors

Designed by Freerayn Graphics

ISBN: 978-0-9822315-2-4

Rich States, Poor States: ALEC-Laffer State Economic Competitiveness Index has been published by the American Legislative Exchange Council (ALEC) as part of its mission to discuss, develop and disseminate public policies, which expand free markets, promote economic growth, limit the size of government, and preserve individual liberty. ALEC is the nation's largest nonpartisan, voluntary membership organization of state legislators, with 2,000 members across the nation. ALEC is governed by a Board of Directors of state legislators, which is advised by a Private Enterprise Board representing major corporate and foundation sponsors.

ALEC is classified by the Internal Revenue Service as a 501(c)(3) nonprofit and public policy and educational organization. Individuals, philanthropic foundations, corporations, companies or associations are eligible to support ALEC's work through tax-deductible gifts.

Table of Contents

About the Authors

Dr. Arthur B. Laffer

Arthur B. Laffer is the founder and chairman of Laffer Associates, an economic research and consulting firm, as well as Laffer Investments, an institutional investment firm. As a result of Dr. Laffer's economic insight and influence in starting a worldwide tax-cutting movement during the 1980s, many publications have named him "The Father of Supply-Side Economics." He is a founding member of the Congressional Policy Advisory Board, which assisted in forming legislation for the 105th, 106th and 107th Congresses. Dr. Laffer served as a member of President Reagan's Economic Policy Advisory Board for both terms. In March 1999, he was noted by *Time Magazine* as one of "the Century's Greatest Minds" for his invention of the Laffer Curve, which has been called one of "a few of the advances that powered this extraordinary century." He has received many awards for his economic research, including two Graham and Dodd Awards from the Financial Analyst Federation. He graduated from Yale with a Bachelor's degree in economics in 1963 and received both his MBA and Ph.D. in economics from Stanford University.

Stephen Moore

Stephen Moore joined *The Wall Street Journal* as a member of the editorial board and senior economics writer on May 31, 2005. He splits his time between Washington, D.C., and New York, focusing on economic issues including budget, tax and monetary policy. Moore was previously the founder and president of the Club for Growth, which raises money for political candidates who favor free-market economic policies. Over the years, Moore has served as a senior economist at the Congressional Joint Economic Committee, as a budget expert for The Heritage Foundation, and as a senior economics fellow at the Cato Institute, where he published dozens of studies on federal and state fiscal policy. He was also a consultant to the National Economic Commission in 1987 and research director for President Reagan's Commission on Privatization.

Jonathan Williams

Jonathan Williams is the director of the Tax and Fiscal Policy Task Force for the American Legislative Exchange Council (ALEC), where he works with state legislators and the private sector to develop free-market fiscal policy in the states. Prior to joining ALEC, Jonathan served as staff economist at the Tax Foundation, authoring numerous tax policy studies. His work has been featured in many publications including *The Wall Street Journal, The Los Angeles Times, Forbes* and *Investor's Business Daily*. Williams is a contributor to *The Examiner* (Washington, D.C.) and writes a syndicated column for the Flint Hills Center for Public Policy in Wichita, Kan., where he also serves as an adjunct fiscal policy fellow. He is a contributing author to the Reason Foundation's

Annual Privatization Report and has written for *Tax Analysts*, a scholarly journal dedicated to tax issues. Williams has also appeared on numerous television outlets, including *FOX Business News*. A Mid-Michigan native, Williams graduated magna cum laude from Northwood University in Midland, Mich., majoring in economics, banking/finance, and business management. While at Northwood, he was the recipient of the prestigious Ludwig von Mises Award in Economics.

Acknowledgements

We wish to thank the following for making this publication possible: First, the Searle Freedom Trust and the Claude Lamb Foundation for their generous support for the research and promotion of this book. Next, we wish to thank Alan Smith, Michael Bowman, Jeff Reed, Jonathan Moody, Don Sheff, Myles Butler, Daniel Chasen, Anthony P. Campau and the professional staff of ALEC for their assistance in publishing this in a timely manner. We also appreciate the research assistance of Tyler Grimm, Ford Scudder, Mark Wise, Jeff Thomson, Amy Kjose, Michael Hough and Allison Moore. Richard Vedder and Wayne Winegarden also provided us with a catalog of high-quality studies on the impact of immigrants on state economies. We hope these research findings help lead to the enactment of pro-growth economic policies in all 50 state capitals.

Foreword

Dear ALEC Member,

In an economic climate as troubling as the one we currently face, it is vital to understand the environment in which we operate. We must be willing to adapt and adjust if we want to remain competitive in the global marketplace.

Throughout the past four years serving as the Governor of the great state of Utah, I have made reforming our state's antiquated tax system a top priority of my administration. This reform is essential to ensure the long-term strength and economic competitiveness of our economy. As a result of these efforts, our state has been able to drop our top marginal tax rate by 40 percent. Our state's tax system is now more transparent, fair, efficient and simple.

Since 1973, ALEC has provided information and analysis to lawmakers throughout the country. Its members provide much needed leadership in state legislatures. We value ALEC's expertise and ability to help articulate critical economic data.

The second edition of *Rich States, Poor States* is a valuable resource to those charged with understanding fiscal policy and enacting change. In times of change, it is essential to understand the perspectives from which other states are making decisions, especially as policy-makers determine the best path forward for their respective states.

I commend those who have worked to produce this invaluable report.

Sincerely,

Jon M. Huntsman, Jr.
Governor of Utah

Executive Summary

This second edition of *Rich States, Poor States* by the American Legislative Exchange Council is yet another invaluable resource ALEC has provided for state lawmakers and citizens to evaluate their state's fiscal and economic policies, as well as the results and ramifications of those policies.

Authors Arthur Laffer, Stephen Moore and Jonathan Williams provide an in-depth analysis of policies, some of which foster economic growth and prosperity in states like Utah, Arizona and Texas, others of which cause economic malaise in states like California, New York and Michigan.

Our introduction focuses on some of the most critical issues facing lawmakers today, with more than 40 states struggling with budget deficits. As our elected officials think about beginning the annual task of budget writing, we remind lawmakers that levying tax increases is not a sustainable answer for budget problems. Especially during an economic downturn, states need to be doing everything they can to become more competitive, not less.

Chapter one presents our most recent state rankings with a number of brief commentaries. Prior to entering the depths of just how we calculate our state rankings, a quick demonstration of the power of these rankings is in order. In the following table, we compare the economic performances of the top 10 states – according to our 2009 Economic Outlook Rankings – with the bottom 10 states. The results are shocking. Look for yourself.

ECONOMIC OUTLOOK RANKINGS

The methodology for the 2009 Economic Outlook Rankings has changed from 2008.

Therefore, the 2008 Economic Outlook Rankings have been revised using the 2009 methodology and are listed in Appendix B. Please refer to the updated Rankings for an accurate comparison between the 2008 and 2009 Economic Outlook Rankings. All factors of the 2009 methodology are explained in detail in Appendix A.

This year's book on state competitiveness focuses on California. The Golden State is not only our nation's largest state in most every economic metric, it also has a highly volatile political climate. California can move from Karl Marx to Adam Smith and back again in what seems to be the blink of a political eye. California's experiences from its radical shifts in policy are the very essence of what we mean when we write "policy matters." Chapter two compares California's recent experiences with those of another populous state, Texas. The results may surprise you.

Chapter three compares California's present with the "Ghosts of California's Past." The history of California – centered on the tax revolt crystallized in Proposition 13 – shows a laboratory experiment in which the state went from

RELATIONSHIP BETWEEN POLICIES AND PERFORMANCE:
ALEC-Laffer State Economic Outlook Rank vs. 10-Year Economic Performance: 1997-2007

State	Rank	Gross State Product Growth	Personal Income Growth	Personal Income Per Capita Growth	Population Growth
Utah	1	86.7%	82.3%	45.6%	26.3%
Colorado	2	77.8%	84.9%	52.1%	20.0%
Arizona	3	93.9%	101.4%	47.9%	33.1%
Virginia	4	80.7%	78.4%	56.4%	12.6%
South Dakota	5	71.3%	73.8%	63.9%	7.8%
Wyoming	6	111.4%	114.6%	103.4%	8.5%
Nevada	7	112.3%	114.6%	48.4%	40.3%
Georgia	8	67.0%	74.4%	38.5%	23.2%
Tennessee	9	59.0%	64.8%	46.5%	11.6%
Texas	10	90.5%	89.8%	55.8%	20.7%
10 Highest Ranked States*	-	**85.1%**	**87.9%**	**55.9%**	**20.4%**
Florida	11	87.6%	87.9%	55.0%	18.3%
Arkansas	12	61.1%	67.5%	55.8%	8.7%
North Dakota	13	69.9%	71.1%	75.3%	-0.9%
Idaho	14	79.4%	87.4%	53.5%	21.7%
Oklahoma	15	78.6%	81.1%	69.3%	7.0%
Alabama	16	61.9%	64.0%	54.6%	5.8%
Indiana	17	46.6%	51.6%	40.9%	6.3%
Louisiana	18	90.8%	68.0%	74.4%	-0.7%
Mississippi	19	52.8%	61.6%	52.8%	4.8%
South Carolina	20	56.9%	68.9%	47.3%	14.3%
North Carolina	21	74.5%	69.3%	41.8%	18.1%
Washington	22	74.5%	76.9%	55.8%	13.5%
Missouri	23	45.0%	53.7%	43.1%	7.1%
Kansas	24	62.8%	59.9%	51.5%	5.3%
New Mexico	25	60.6%	72.4%	55.8%	10.6%
Massachusetts	26	58.5%	66.9%	61.4%	3.6%
Wisconsin	27	53.3%	57.3%	46.5%	6.2%
Maryland	28	74.3%	77.3%	61.1%	8.2%
Nebraska	29	58.5%	58.3%	51.6%	5.2%
Montana	30	78.9%	79.5%	66.1%	8.4%
Delaware	31	69.4%	74.1%	48.8%	14.4%
Connecticut	32	57.1%	67.3%	58.2%	4.0%
West Virginia	33	48.8%	51.6%	52.4%	-0.1%
Michigan	34	27.7%	39.0%	33.8%	1.6%
Iowa	35	57.5%	52.2%	47.5%	3.4%
Kentucky	36	45.8%	58.4%	46.8%	7.1%
New Hampshire	37	56.8%	68.2%	50.1%	9.1%
Alaska	38	77.9%	66.4%	49.5%	10.7%
Oregon	39	63.8%	62.3%	42.9%	13.1%
Minnesota	40	63.5%	65.9%	50.7%	8.5%
Hawaii	41	63.9%	61.7%	54.4%	6.0%
Pennsylvania	42	54.7%	54.6%	50.9%	1.7%
California	43	77.9%	76.6%	56.0%	11.4%
Illinois	44	50.9%	55.6%	47.1%	5.1%
Ohio	45	40.4%	42.3%	38.4%	1.5%
New Jersey	46	54.7%	62.4%	52.5%	4.8%
Maine	47	55.8%	60.7%	52.1%	4.6%
Rhode Island	48	64.5%	61.7%	55.4%	1.9%
Vermont	49	61.8%	69.3%	61.2%	3.5%
New York	50	68.5%	61.7%	55.3%	3.9%
10 Lowest Ranked States*	-	**59.3%**	**60.7%**	**52.3%**	**4.4%**
U.S. Average*	-	**66.8%**	**69.5%**	**53.6%**	**9.9%**

Net Domestic in-Migration as % of Population	Non-Farm Payroll Employment Growth	2007 Unemployment Rate
0.3%	25.9%	2.7%
4.6%	17.7%	3.8%
12.2%	34.4%	3.8%
2.2%	16.4%	3.0%
0.2%	15.2%	3.0%
2.1%	28.3%	3.0%
17.2%	45.0%	4.8%
6.7%	14.7%	4.4%
4.4%	8.3%	4.7%
3.4%	20.3%	4.3%
5.3%	**22.6%**	**3.8%**
7.8%	25.5%	4.0%
2.6%	9.0%	5.4%
-5.4%	13.9%	3.2%
8.5%	29.7%	2.7%
0.4%	11.9%	4.3%
1.6%	7.5%	3.5%
-0.4%	4.6%	4.5%
-7.4%	3.9%	3.8%
-0.9%	4.0%	6.3%
6.9%	13.5%	5.9%
7.0%	13.7%	4.7%
3.5%	16.6%	4.5%
0.8%	6.0%	5.0%
-2.7%	8.6%	4.1%
0.6%	19.0%	3.5%
-5.6%	5.3%	4.5%
0.1%	8.5%	4.9%
-1.5%	15.0%	3.6%
-2.6%	12.4%	3.0%
3.9%	21.2%	3.1%
5.7%	12.7%	3.4%
-3.0%	5.6%	4.6%
0.5%	7.0%	4.6%
-4.8%	-4.0%	7.2%
-1.7%	7.8%	3.8%
2.0%	9.2%	5.5%
4.0%	13.8%	3.6%
-2.3%	18.1%	6.2%
4.8%	12.7%	5.2%
-0.3%	10.9%	4.6%
-4.0%	17.3%	2.6%
-0.9%	7.2%	4.4%
-4.0%	15.5%	5.4%
-5.4%	3.6%	5.0%
-3.5%	0.6%	5.6%
-5.3%	9.4%	4.2%
3.1%	11.5%	4.7%
-3.7%	9.6%	5.0%
0.1%	10.2%	3.9%
-9.5%	8.3%	4.5%
-3.3%	**9.3%**	**4.5%**
0.9%	**13.3%**	**4.3%**

* Equally-weighted averages.

fiscal malaise to fiscal health and then back to malaise again. By showing the current class of legislators the ghosts of California's past, we hope they can begin picturing the ghosts of California's future – identified by much lower taxes and much higher economic growth.

The 15 policy factors included in the 2009 ALEC-Laffer State Economic Outlook Index:

- Highest Marginal Personal Income Tax Rate
- Highest Marginal Corporate Income Tax Rate
- Personal Income Tax Progressivity
- Property Tax Burden
- Sales Tax Burden
- Tax Burden From All Remaining Taxes
- Estate Tax/Inheritance Tax (Yes or No)
- Recently Legislated Tax Policy Changes
- Debt Service as a Share of Tax Revenue
- Public Employees Per 1,000 Residents
- Quality of State Legal System
- State Minimum Wage
- Workers' Compensation Costs
- Right-to-Work State (Yes or No)
- Tax or Expenditure Limits

The final section of this book is a state-by-state detailed description of the key economic variables. The 2009 ALEC-Laffer State Economic Competitiveness Index offers two rankings. The first, the Economic Performance Rank, is a historical measure based on a state's performance on three important variables: Personal Income Per Capita, Absolute Domestic Migration, and Non-farm Payroll Employment — all of which are highly influenced by state policy. This ranking details states' individual performances over the past 10 years based on this economic data.

The second measure, the Economic Outlook Rank, is a forecast based on a state's current standing in 15 state-policy variables. Each of these factors is influenced directly by state lawmakers through the legislative process. Generally speaking, states that spend less — especially on income-transfer programs — and states that tax less — particularly on productive activities such as working or investing — experience higher growth rates than states which tax and spend more. There are 50 fascinating stories here to read. Enjoy!

Introduction

When we set out to write the first edition of ALEC's *Rich States, Poor States* in early 2007, state revenues were booming. At the time, news reports from across the nation beamed the exciting news that more than 40 states were reporting budget surpluses.[1] Boy, how times can change.

At the time of writing this second edition of the book – just 18 months later – state revenue growth is flat for the first time since 2002,[2] state coffers have dried up, and more than 40 states either faced budget deficits for fiscal year 2009, or are projecting deficits for fiscal year 2010, which starts July 1 in all but four states.[3] Few remain hopeful that state coffers will recover anytime soon, since the worst state budget deficits generally follow national economic downturns.[4]

There is little question many states are in dire financial straits today. However, in the face of state budget pressures, we are convinced that the work of ALEC becomes even more important. ALEC is dedicated to providing innovative solutions for lawmakers to solve budget problems – without increasing taxes. In the subsequent pages, this second edition of *Rich States, Poor States* will give you more than ample evidence to protect the American taxpayer during these difficult times.

Analysts are projecting cumulative deficits anywhere from $97 billion to $200 billion for the states through fiscal year 2010.[5] Even more concerning is the colossal problem of state unfunded liabilities. A recent study conducted for ALEC by Dr. Barry Poulson of the University of Colorado found that state pension systems alone are now more than $350 billion in debt.[6] Furthermore, the Governmental Accounting Standards Board (GASB) recently issued a guideline that requires states to report the full actuarial contributions needed to meet their other post-employment benefit (OPEB) obligations.[7] Of the 40 states that have complied with the guideline, total unfunded liabilities in this category are estimated at nearly $400 billion.[8]

During the early months of 2008, many states that were able to avoid the sub-prime mortgage crisis were in comparatively good shape financially. In their respective 2008 state-of-the-state addresses, only 36 percent of governors talked about substantial budget problems, while 58 percent described their state's economy as good or strong.[9] However, their good times are now coming to a halt.

Even some of the states with strong natural resource production that were hoping to be immune from the recent national downturn are starting to feel the pain. As the price of oil and other commodities fell dramatically in the last half of 2008, the natural resource and agricultural states are now under the gun. "We are clearly in stiff-drink territory," said George Hammond, an economist with West Virginia University. "But just one stiff drink. The national economy is in the two-or-three-stiff-drinks stage."[10]

In the words of Yogi Berra, this is like déjà vu all over again.

The "dot-com" boom of the late 1990s fueled large surpluses in the states. Some states took the course of fiscal restraint and returned the money back to the taxpayers, while others ratcheted up spending levels, in many cases spending every last dime! Then we suffered through the devastating attacks of 9/11, and the resulting economic downturn caused states to find themselves in a world of hurt.

Of course, the only reason many of these states faced budget shortfalls was because they spent beyond their means during the good years of the late 1990s. In an attempt to remedy this situation, some state officials conducted a lobbying effort to get Uncle Sam to bailout the states in 2003.

This all seems strangely similar to the situation states find themselves in today, as state budgets have once again ballooned over the past few fiscal years. Let's take the recent example of FY 2008. Even though overall growth in state spending had begun to decline as a result of the national downturn, some state budgets don't appear to have felt much pain.[11]

LARGEST STATE SPENDING INCREASES
2007-2008

2008 State General Fund Budget Growth	
Oregon	27.9%
Montana	21.9%
North Dakota	19.0%

Source: National Association of State Budget Officers

With state spending increasing at rates like these, it is really no surprise that many states are facing significant budget shortfalls. In the good times over the past few fiscal years, states again had no trouble finding ways to spend the soaring tax revenues that came their way. In the fat years for state budgets, expenditures for education, transportation and health care grew at astonishing rates in many cases. With

the economic downturn worsening in the last half of 2008, tax revenues are beginning to slide and the so-called "structural deficits" are back. Predictably, voices from the political left have already begun talking about the "need to raise taxes."[12] As the following pages outline, if states wish to remain competitive in the 21st century, they need to avoid tax increases by living within their means. From Saginaw, Mich. to Prescott, Ariz., and from Cumberland, Md., to Umatilla, Fla., hard-working families and businesses are required to live within their means each month.

Why on earth should we hold state governments to a lower standard?

Today, some states have learned their lesson in dealing with budget problems, while others have clearly not. According to the National Association of State Budget Officers (NASBO), "31 states have reported budget gaps totaling $29.7 billion for fiscal year 2009 since budget enactment." Out of these states, 22 have already cut their enacted budgets for fiscal year 2009, with more reductions on the horizon.[13] But even if states manage to make it through FY 2009, the much larger challenge will be finding solutions for budgets in FY 2010. According to recent reports, more than 20 states are expected to face budget shortfalls, which will cumulatively exceed $65 billion next year.[14]

Should the Feds Bailout the States?
As in any time of crisis, Washington is suffering from a predictable case of the "do something" disease. Many state and local elected officials want instant solutions to the budget problems they are facing. Although ALEC led the opposition to the federal bailout of the states in 2003, Congress nevertheless approved Uncle Sam's $20 billion bailout check. Proponents of the last federal bailout said it would save states from having to raise taxes. These experts were wrong;[15] 35 states passed net tax increases in FY 2004, as did 24 states in FY 2005.[16]

Like we said, this is like déjà vu all over again.

Just recently, the National Conference of State Legislatures (NCSL) and several other groups called on Congress to approve a new federal bailout of the states – as a part of the current bailout mania in Washington. First it was $700 billion for the financial sector, and then executives from the auto industry pounded a path from Detroit to Washington, seeking billions in taxpayer dollars to assist their ailing companies. Most recently, the National Governors Association (NGA) convened a meeting with President Barack Obama in Philadelphia to discuss the economic downturn and lobby for a federal bailout of the states. Unfortunately for taxpayers, the price tag could be significantly higher than the 2003 bailout, as the governors asked for a cool $176 billion from Uncle Sam.[17] Not to be outdone, the Democrat governors of New York, New Jersey, Massachusetts, Ohio and Wisconsin have asked President Obama for a staggering $1 trillion to aid their states.[18]

Their attempt to persuade the former state senator from Illinois seemed to get results almost overnight. President Obama outlined his broad ideas for the largest increase in spending on "public works" programs since President Dwight D. Eisenhower built the interstate highway system in the mid-1950s.[19] For those who believe that government should be in the business of "creating jobs" by increasing spending on infrastructure and public works, we suggest they go back and read the history of the Great Depression.[20]

In response to the idea of a federal bailout, ALEC and the National Taxpayers Union led a coalition of roughly 60 taxpayer groups in opposition to the state bailout. The ALEC-NTU coalition letter to Congress hit the nail on the head. It concluded, "[Approving the federal bailout of the states] would set a horrible precedent, discourage responsible budgeting in the future, and place a greater strain on America's hard-working families and businesses."[21]

While the rosy fiscal times enjoyed by states over the past few years have clearly disappeared, important questions need to be addressed before rubber stamping a multi-billion dollar bailout of the states: 1) What were the causes of the current budget problems in the states? 2) Should the federal government spend taxpayer dollars to bailout the states in this economic downturn?

States are not facing budget deficits because they don't tax enough. The real problem facing states is the fundamental issue of overspending taxpayer dollars. State spending has grown at an unsustainable rate over the past decade. In fact, state spending is up 124 percent over where it was just 10 years ago, and state debt increased by 95 percent during that same period.[22]

In many cases, states facing the worst fiscal climates are the very same states that engaged in reckless spending. During his recent testimony before the House Ways and Means Committee in Washington, South Carolina Gov. Mark Sanford noted: "California increased spending 95 percent over the past 10 years (federal spending went up 71 percent over the same period). To bail out California now seems unfair to fiscally prudent states."[23]

Gov. Sanford's point is quite germane. Why should taxpayers who live in states that were fiscally responsible subsidize states like California that were not? ALEC member Sen. Curtis Bramble of Utah complained that California and other states were "asking for a bailout from their bad spending habits." He continued, "they're asking for a loophole to violate living within their means."[24] Over the past few years, many states like California have spent money like drunken sailors on a 48-hour furlough. It's not right to expect the American taxpayer to pick up the tab. The federal government should not be in the business of rewarding states that have overspent taxpayer dollars. Furthermore, with new estimates from the Congressional Budget Office (CBO) showing Uncle Sam's own budget deficit reaching $1.2 trillion, Washington is not in the best financial position itself.[25]

In last year's edition of this book, we found

countless instances of states engaging in reckless spending. In fact, we devoted an entire chapter to warning state lawmakers that the spending binge states had enjoyed couldn't last forever. For example, we highly doubt New Mexico will be able to continue funding projects like their recent endeavor to create a "space launch pad for future commuter orbital excursions."[26] To the surprise of no one, some of the very same suspects are now racking up frequent flier miles traveling to Washington, D.C. to lobby for a state bailout. The real problem may have been described best by Nobel Laureate (and one of our heroes), Milton Friedman: "Governments never learn. Only people learn."

Whenever the government bails someone out of trouble, it always puts someone else into trouble. In this case, a bailout for the states means big-time trouble for taxpayers. In reality for taxpayers, the talk of a federal bailout of the states is just a slight of hand. As Brian Riedl from The Heritage Foundation recently penned, "Hiking federal taxes to keep state taxes from rising is like running up your VISA card to keep the MasterCard balance from rising. Either way, you'll pay. All that changes is where you send your payment."[27]

There is another very important reason why state officials should be worried about a federal bailout. When has the federal government ever given money to the states without countless strings attached? ALEC's 2009 National Chairman, Speaker Bill Howell of Virginia, recently stated his objections to a federal bailout of the states:

"At a time when federal spending and debt are soaring, the federal government should not put taxpayers on the hook for yet another bailout. Furthermore, a federal bailout could have dire implications on the proper role of federalism. A more effective approach to help the states would be to free them from costly federal mandates.

In my home state of Virginia, we are dealing with our own budget shortfall. Even though it is tempting to accept a short-term federal handout, I am deeply concerned about the long-term implications a federal bailout would have on state sovereignty."[28]

Further, a study conducted by ALEC during the post-9/11 economic downturn estimated that "every one dollar more of federal assistance increases state and local budget deficits by over 62 cents."[29] It is clear the many strings accompanying federal dollars impose significant burdens on the states.

During his testimony, Gov. Sanford urged Congress to "accept that there may be better routes to recovery than a blanket bailout, including offering states ... more in the way of flexibility and freedom from federal mandates instead of a bag of money with strings attached."[30]

One disastrous federal mandate that should be eliminated immediately is the equivalent of the Holy Grail to big labor: The Davis-Bacon Act. This burdensome federal law requires states to pay the "prevailing wage" for all federally supported construction projects. While that may sound reasonable to some, studies have estimated that this arduous regulation is responsible for adding up to 38 percent to the cost of construction in some states.[31]

State budgets have faced financial duress many times before because of overspending, and certainly will again in the future. History suggests federal bailouts are not the answer as they decrease state sovereignty, incentivize future fiscal irresponsibility, and reward fiscally imprudent states at the expense of fiscally responsible states. Economist Richard Vedder said it best: "In short, federal bailouts are not a solution. They are the equivalent of giving booze to alcoholics – providing at best some temporary respite, but aggravating fundamental problems, in this case overspending."[32]

Unfortunately, the "do something" disease

that plagues Washington will probably do so for the foreseeable future. If this results in spending additional taxpayer dollars to rescue states who mismanaged taxpayer dollars in the first place, it will only spiral them into a cycle of federal dependency, further encouraging fiscal irresponsibility. Let's hope that is not the case.

Taming the Beast

"If men were angels, no government would be necessary. If angels were to govern men, neither external nor internal controls on government would be necessary. In framing a government which is to be administered by men over men, the great difficulty lies in this: you must first enable the government to control the governed; and in the next place oblige it to control itself."

- Federalist Paper No. 51

Relying on government to control itself and stop the state fiscal roller coaster can be a bit naive today in most states. However, in our experience, constitutionally limiting the government's ability to grow – through a tax or expenditure limit (TEL) – has proven to be a very effective approach. Colorado, for example, was able to restrain government spending and tax burdens through the Taxpayers' Bill of Rights (TABOR) beginning in the early 1990s, limiting the growth of government to a reasonable formula of population plus inflation growth. Taxes could be increased, but it took a vote of the people to do so.

For years, the political left has attempted to define the taxpayer protection movement by twisting the record of Colorado's Taxpayers' Bill of Rights, for the very reason that TABOR was an effective deterrent to the unbridled growth of government. Following the low-tax plus limited-government formula, TABOR gave Colorado one of the most competitive business climates in the nation, not to mention giving taxpayers back some of their hard-earned money. The economic growth followed, as

Colorado boasted one of the fastest growing economies in the nation.

Some suggest that Colorado enjoys economic growth simply because of the beautiful terrain, tourism and abundant natural resources. However, let's take a look at that theory. Colorado decided to earnestly pursue free-market policies of tax relief and spending restraint in the early 1990s, and the state's economic boom didn't occur until those pro-growth reforms had been implemented. Colorado's economy had not experienced nearly that level of growth in the preceding decades, and believe it or not, the ski slopes full of tourists and natural resources were just as abundant in the 1980s as they are today.

The historical evidence is clear: States that keep spending and taxes low exhibit the best economic results, while states that follow the tax-and-spend path lag far behind. The recent evidence suggests that if you tax and spend enough, you might even end up like California.

Budget Transparency:
A Shiny New Tool to Curb Government Waste

One of the best new tools to shine the light on wasteful government spending is budget transparency. ALEC members have taken the lead, promoting legislation across the country to accomplish this task. You will find ALEC's highly-acclaimed model legislation in Appendix C.

Thomas Jefferson hoped that one day, "we might hope to see the finances of the Union as clear and intelligible as a merchant's books, so that every member of Congress and every man of any mind in the Union should be able to comprehend them, to investigate abuses, and consequently to control them." Today that vision can be a reality for states. With the advance of computer and network technologies, states now have the capacity to publish their yearly budgets on the Internet, providing taxpayers with a searchable, manageable report of all state expenditures from year to year. This is the central principle behind budget transparency legislation.

Budget transparency's ultimate aim is to see all information on state budget expenditures provided in a readily accessible and structured format so that any interested party can access this information. In the past, government budgets were available in print, but the time necessary to mull through thousands of pages to track down relevant information was very prohibitive. Budget transparency legislation solves this problem by providing taxpayers the ability to see where their tax dollars are going in a detailed, item-by-item manner, across all departments, from any computer, free of charge.

While all budget transparency legislation shares this basic goal, the specifics of the legislation vary among different models. The most basic formulations call on government to do little more than publish budget expenditures online in some format and update the data every year. Stronger models go a few steps further, such as requiring states to publish performance results for state expenditures, listing funding sources per agencies and programs, mandating item-by-item listings, and integrat-

ACTIVE SPENDING TRANSPARENCY WEB SITES LAUNCHED SINCE 2007
as a result of legislative or gubernatorial action

■ Web sites launched
■ Executive Orders/Passed Legislation

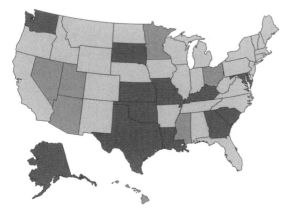

Source: Center for Fiscal Accountability

ing advanced search functionality for ease of research and cross-referencing.

Over the last two years, budget transparency legislation has been enacted in numerous states and has enjoyed widespread support on a bipartisan basis.

In 2007, six states enacted legislation (or executive orders) which began implementing budget transparency, starting the process of establishing searchable online databases accessible to the general public. One such example is the Missouri Accountability Portal, which was created by an executive order of Gov. Matt Blunt. On the Web site, one can search by agency, category, contract and vendor to track down state expenditures.[33] The portal also contains data on state employee salaries and tax credits issued. The site is easily navigable and lists all expenditures per fiscal year, down to items that cost only a few dollars.

Another fine example is Oklahoma's OpenBooks Web site.[34] This site was created as a result of the Taxpayer Transparency Act, unanimously passed by the Oklahoma Legislature in 2007, and signed into law by Gov. Brad Henry. In addition to expenditure data on agencies, payroll and vendors, this site also lists the funding sources for government agencies and programs. Lawmakers in Kansas created yet another effective budget transparency Web site, which you can peruse at: www.kansas.gov/kanview. In the first few months of operation alone, sites like these have streamlined the process of budget research, reduced the burden of paperwork on state agencies, and generated millions of hits, demonstrating real public interest in such a service.

In 2008, ALEC members in 30 states fought for increased budget transparency. Washington serves as a fine example for 2008, unanimously passing bipartisan legislation that will dramatically improve budget transparency. Mississippi gives us yet another model of enacting comprehensive budget transparency in 2008.[35] Guided into law by ALEC member

Sen. Alan Nunnelee the Mississippi Accountability and Transparency Act of 2008 was enacted with the steadfast support of Gov. Haley Barbour. Given the tremendous success of the budget transparency movement, we expect a significant number of states will consider legislation to establish working databases of their own in 2009.[36]

Although the success of these sites is impressive, it should be noted that many of the states that recently mandated budget transparency are still in the process of creating their Web sites. Some of the current state budget sites have not implemented keyword search functionality, and some suffer from user interfaces that are difficult to navigate. Nevertheless, it is encouraging to see such progress in such a short time period. Improved functionality will be implemented in the near future on each of the current sites, as well as expanded databases to include all state funding and expenditure information. These examples prove that budget transparency sites can be established within only a few months time after the passage of transparency legislation and can be further upgraded in the future.

One innovative upgrade is applying transparency to K-12 budgets at the school district level. In 2007, legislation was introduced in Texas to require all school districts to post their check registers online. Although this legislation failed in the senate, more than 200 school districts are already posting their records online voluntarily. In 2008, Collin County, Texas, became the first school district in America to post records online in a searchable PDF format.[37]

Unfortunately, the movement for increased transparency and accountability has suffered some defeats as well. South Dakota Gov. Mike Rounds vetoed budget transparency legislation in his state in 2008 on the basis of its estimated cost of $600,000. ALEC member Rep. Hal Wick introduced the South Dakota transparency legislation and led a valiant effort to override the

governor's veto. Supporters pointed out that $600,000 was an exceedingly high estimate of what the real costs would likely be, given the experience of other states.[38] The override was hugely successful in the South Dakota House, but failed in the Senate by a margin of only two votes. However, in a dramatic turnaround of events, Gov. Rounds unveiled his own budget transparency Web site in September. This resource makes more than 180,000 pages of information available to the public in a searchable format.[39] The site includes more than 106,000 financial records and information about revenue and budget information, as well as vendor and state payroll data.[40]

On the issue of cost, time and again the fiscal impact has been shown to be minimal. The fiscal impact statement from the legislation passed in Oklahoma last year estimated the total outlay for programming and implementation at $300,000, but it turned out to cost only $8,000 plus staff time. Missouri's budget office said its site was created "within existing resources."

Technology companies are often able to help set up transparency sites, and there remains the possibility of free assistance with programming and source coding from companies like Microsoft and Google. By partnering with the private sector, lawmakers can further defray the costs associated with these projects. When opponents of transparency talk about the high costs of a budget Web site, their argument is usually a red herring. Time and time again, the actual cost of budget transparency is vastly overstated. And, as ALEC member Sen. Randy Brogdon of Oklahoma stated, "Any cost for implementation is far less than the cost of not knowing where tax dollars are being spent."[41]

Taxpayers should be able to easily access and track how their state is spending their tax dollars. Enabling this will act as a cost-effective measure to protect taxpayers and limit the size of government by holding lawmakers accountable for wasteful spending. Judging by the wave of states that have passed legislation in the past two years, it is encouraging to see there are many throughout the United States who share this belief. In 2009, we are optimistic that ALEC members will continue to support efforts to open government spending records to the general public through budget transparency legislation. Having millions of American taxpayers reviewing state spending projects will be a tremendously valuable asset for cash-strapped states looking to eliminate wasteful spending.

The Great Debate:
Increase Taxes or Reduce Spending?

In the face of today's budget pressures, many states are not talking fiscal restraint or budget transparency, but misguidedly looking to target businesses and individuals alike as a strategy to balance the books. As our elected officials think about beginning the annual task of budget writing, it is important they remember that levying tax increases is not a sustainable answer for budget problems. In fact, it comes at a great cost. Whenever a state changes its tax and fiscal policies, it directly and immediately influences that state's competitive position for personal and business investment.

Especially during an economic downturn, states need to be doing everything they can to become more competitive, not less. Policymakers across the nation should be very aware that changes to policy are not created in a vacuum. Today, business capital is increasingly liquid and can easily be shifted between competing opportunities throughout the international marketplace.

Today, many states stand at a crossroads, and it will soon become apparent if lawmakers choose to use history as a guide for their actions. Because states cannot simply print money like Uncle Sam, they are left with two basic choices to solve budget shortfalls: 1) raise taxes, or 2) decrease spending. Of course, many states regularly issue debt, but in reality this simply repre-

sents the potential of a future tax increase – and don't forget the interest on the principal. As we outline in chapter two, choosing your state's future is as easy as a case study of two theories in practice (California vs. Texas).

As we describe in much greater detail in chapter three, Sacramento is in complete disarray, facing more than a $40 billion budget shortfall over the next 18 months. The Golden State has so mismanaged state finances that a recent *Los Angeles Times* headline asked, "Is California too unwieldy to govern?"[42] Of course, even dreadful situations can bring about good – providing others use them as an example of what not to do. Such is the case with liberalism run amok in Sacramento. We devote chapter three to the unfortunate tale of the Golden State's financial decay.

The citizens of California are clearly facing a frightening budget deficit, but it's naïve to think increasing taxes will solve the fundamental problem of overspending in Sacramento. The truth of the matter is California doesn't have a budget problem – it has a severe spending problem. California is already behind the proverbial eight ball in terms of economic competitiveness. Increasing taxes would be the worst thing California lawmakers could do today.

Despite the dubious distinction of having both the highest statewide personal income tax *and* the highest state sales tax in the nation, California still finds itself with far and away the largest budget deficit of any state. If simply spending money were the solution to all of government's problems, there wouldn't be a problem left in California today. The Golden State provides us all with a great lesson: You can't tax your way to prosperity.

On the other hand, Texas has proved that (contrary to the opinions of our friends on the left) any state can do without a personal income tax – in fact, they can do so and prosper. Texas Gov. Rick Perry's approach is one worth noting. Not only has he taken an active opposition to the idea of a federal bailout, Gov. Perry is adamantly opposed to increasing taxes during this economic downturn.[43]

Today, it is encouraging to note that other states are taking the responsible approach as well, and are looking for ways to balance their budgets by reducing overspending. For instance, Utah Gov. Jon Huntsman, Jr., has proposed a budget that is $1 billion smaller than the previous year's.[44] Newly-minted Kansas Speaker Mike O'Neal optimistically remarked: "The good news is we have a two-year window of opportunity to look at doing things fundamentally differently. If we don't have the will to do it now with the budget situation the state is in, then we will have missed a golden opportunity."[45]

Gov. Butch Otter of Idaho recently wrote state agency directors, stating budget cuts "should involve eliminating entire programs if they are not in furtherance of or required by your statutory mission."[46] This obviously raises the question of why the spending was justified in the first place. However, the governor's action is a worthwhile attempt to correct past overspending and move towards a more priority-based budget.[47] Sadly, many state agencies across the country are not even required to produce mission statements – let alone observe them.

Former director of the federal Office of Management and Budget (OMB) Indiana Gov. Mitch Daniels has a keen eye for responsible budgeting. In a speech to ALEC members in late 2008, he suggested that the current economic downturn "is a terrific time to shrink government. This is a great time to do those things that probably should have been done before but are easy to let slide or to beat back when times are flush."[48] Subsequently, Daniels called on Hoosier State lawmakers to decrease state spending by more than $750 million to balance the budget without a tax increase.[49] If only more lawmakers followed that approach! Regrettably, it appears that many states will take a vastly different approach to budgeting in 2009.[50]

New York to Taxpayers: Drop Dead

Today states fall into one of two categories. On one hand you have the tax hikers, who are making their states less competitive. On the other hand you have the innovators, who are protecting taxpayers by learning to live within their means. New York may be the worst example of the former, as Gov. David Patterson astonishingly proposed an overall increase in the state's budget, while supporting massive tax increases for New Yorkers.[51] Not surprisingly, Gov. Patterson is also one of the biggest supporters of a federal bailout of the states (New York is estimated to face a budget shortfall exceeding $15 billion). Additionally, the New York governor just might have broken the record for the number of bad ideas he put forward during a recent 17-minute budget address – most notably, his 137 proposed tax increases come to mind (see box on page 10).[52]

Patterson's abysmal proposals have given us an unfortunate example of predatory tax policy. (As if New York didn't already have the reputation of a tax purgatory.) Another egregious example from Albany is their new (and almost certainly unconstitutional) "Amazon Tax." This 2008 law looked for revenue outside of New York's borders and imposed the burden of sales tax collection on catalog and online retailers across the nation – with no physical presence in the state.[53] The "Amazon Tax" is clearly detrimental to interstate commerce, which puts it at odds with the U.S. Supreme Court's ruling in *Quill Corp. v. North Dakota* (1992). New York's "tax adventurism" has already driven Overstock.com away from doing business in the Empire State while several lawsuits are pending.[54] This should both reaffirm the importance of protecting interstate commerce in the 21st century and give every New York resident clear evidence of why taxes matter. Not coincidentally, New York earns the dubious distinction of having the worst economic outlook of any state in our ALEC-Laffer 2009 Economic Competitiveness Index.[55]

A SMALL SAMPLE OF NEW YORK GOVERNOR DAVID PATTERSON'S TAX INCREASES

"iTunes tax" of 4% on videos, music or pictures downloaded from the Internet

4% tax on taxi, limo and bus rides

Sodas and other fruit drinks containing less than 70% real fruit juice will be taxed at 18%

The tax per cigar will rise 16 cents

The taxes for beer and wine will both more than double to 51 cents per gallon of wine and 24 cents per gallon of beer

Elimination of the sales tax exemption on clothing and footwear priced under $110

A 4% entertainment tax on tickets to movies, concerts and sporting events

A 4% tax on cable TV and satellite services

Hiking the cost of personal services – including haircuts, manicures, pedicures, massages and gym memberships – by 4%

Elimination of the law that caps the state sales tax on gasoline at 8 cents per gallon

Increase the tax on rental cars from 5% to 6%

A new 5% "luxury tax" on the price of cars that cost more than $60,000, boats and yachts that cost more than $200,000, jewelry and fur that cost more than $20,000, and noncommercial aircraft that cost more than $500,000

Sources: *Tax Analysts, New York Post, PolitickerNY*

We undoubtedly won't make Gov. Patterson's Christmas card list, but things are so bad in the Empire State that we just can't make this up. However, we do see a ray of hope for New York – the voters. Maybe it's the appalling "iTunes tax," or the prospect of paying more for their favorite soft drinks, but sky-high taxes are finally beginning to wear on residents. Recent polling clearly shows that New Yorkers are extremely opposed to increasing taxes to balance the budget. The recent poll from Siena College asked respondents about desired solutions to the budget shortfall in Albany. While a full 75 percent supported spending reductions, only 10 percent were willing to consider a tax increase.

Predatory Taxes

Unfortunately, New York is not the only state looking to increase taxes in an attempt to balance its books. One of the perennial favorite targets for tax increases during bad budget times is "big tobacco." Many states have proposed or are considering new taxes on tobacco products in an attempt to solve their budget deficit. Unfortunately for the tax hikers, increasing taxes on smokers is one of the least effective ways to raise long-term revenue for states.

On paper, tobacco taxes always look attractive to lawmakers as revenue forecasters often show a windfall of projected receipts from the taxes. However, in the real world people respond to incentives, and cigarette taxes have been shown to encourage smokers to avoid high-tax jurisdictions. As state after state has learned, the promise of substantial cigarette tax revenue often goes up in smoke.

Take Maryland, for example. State lawmakers recently doubled the state's cigarette tax to $2.00 per pack to pay for additional health care and balance the budget. Of course they expected a revenue boom to help fix their state's unstable finances. However, they were sorely mistaken, as *The Wall Street Journal* reports that cigarette sales are down 25 percent.[56] In fact, nearly 30 million fewer cigarettes have been sold in Maryland since the tax increase this year. Therefore, the cigarette tax, which was supposedly the panacea for the state's budget woes, has come up short, and lawmakers in Annapolis are back to the drawing board.

Retailers in Maryland have seen their cigarette sales plummet because of good old fashion competition – and in this case, specifically tax competition. Just across the Potomac River, Maryland residents can take full advantage of the lower taxes in Virginia. Maryland's neighbor to the south has one of the lowest cigarette taxes in the nation at 30 cents per pack. Such a cost difference with a bordering state has made it profitable for Maryland drivers to venture down Interstate 95 into the Old Dominion, saving $1.70 a pack in cigarette taxes alone. Maryland has responded with hopeless attempts to control out-of-state cigarette purchases with investigations and searches of suspected "tax evaders" on the border.

As lawmakers in Maryland have painfully learned, states cannot expect that cigarette taxes will raise enough revenue to solve budget problems. Furthermore, states cannot expect smokers to ignore the incentive to purchase their cigarettes in bordering states, especially when that incentive is high enough. The case study of Maryland is not an isolated example, as states across the nation have experienced similar outcomes when they tamper with the law of incentives. New Jersey lawmakers found this out the hard way in 2007, losing revenue when they enacted the nation's highest cigarette tax, and tax revenues fell by $23 million the next year.[57] Back in 2005, Washington lawmakers recognized this phenomenon of tax competition and actually *lowered* tobacco taxes to raise revenue and help in-state businesses.[58]

Unfortunately, with politically charged topics such as these, it is easy for some public-policy leaders to lose sight of basic economic realities. However, history has clearly shown us that tobacco tax increases will fail to raise the revenue suggested. Not only will consumers have a greater incentive to purchase their cigarettes across state lines, today they can evade the increased taxes in the comfort of their own home through the Internet.[59] Politically, tobacco taxes are an easy sell because they target a fraction of society and involve a socially unpopular activity. However, they are strikingly bad public policy.

Tobacco isn't the only industry with a target on its back in difficult revenue times. During the 2008 presidential campaign it seemed like "big oil" was one of the favorite targets of the class warriors – especially as gasoline prices were front page stories for several months in the first half of the year. Even though prices have drastically retreated, the Obama Administration is supporting the idea of a "windfall profits tax." This tired policy would take us right back to the disastrous energy policy of the 1970s under Jimmy Carter. Of course, the oil industry is an easy political target for tax increases, but historical studies have shown that "big oil" has paid more in taxes than it has earned in profits – in fact, nearly three times more![60]

Some states have also looked to capitalize on public scorn and target oil companies with predatory taxes at the state level.[61] Pennsylvania, Wisconsin and California are among the states that have considered such a disastrous policy. As state budget deficits worsen, it will only add to the ill-fated populist temptation to target "big oil." We could add countless examples of lawmakers hitting a particular industry with discriminatory taxes; however, during tough budget times, being profitable can be a deadly sin.

Conclusion

As budget problems become more severe, states must utilize every cost-saving measure possible to avoid economically damaging tax hikes. Increasing taxes during the current downturn is a non-starter for states that wish to remain competitive. Instead, we hope states will use their current financial problems to put their fiscal houses in order and say no to profligate spending and irresponsible budget practices, which have caused many of the current difficulties.

As lawmakers return to session in 2009, many will be faced with a budget crisis. A handout from Washington, D.C., might seem to help in the short-term, but as many seem to overlook, dollars from Washington rarely come without costly strings attached. Furthermore, a federal bailout would do nothing to address the fundamental problem of a decade's worth of state overspending. If anything good comes out of the budget problems in the states, maybe it will highlight the key to good budgeting: having the ability to say "no." Hopefully the next time we face an economic downturn, states will have policies in place to avoid another crisis of their own making.

In this second edition of *Rich States, Poor States* you will find countless examples of how tax and budget policy really do matter for states. This year we have added an appendix with a sample of tools that ALEC's Tax and Fiscal Policy Task Force has developed to protect the taxpayers of this great nation. In Appendix C you will find ALEC model legislation designed to improve budget transparency, accountability, and to protect the hardworking taxpayers in your state.

As Supreme Court Justice Louis Brandeis famously declared, "States are the laboratories of democracy." In the following pages we will highlight what states are doing right – and what they're not.

Rich States, Poor States supplies ample evidence for lawmakers to avoid the mistakes that have caused economic malaise in so many states today. It is our hope that ALEC members across the country will continue to be powerful advocates in the battle to keep their states and our nation competitive in the 21st century.

ENDNOTES

1   Prah, Pamela. "41 States Posting Surpluses." *Stateline.* April 19, 2007.

2   The Nelson A. Rockefeller Institute of Government. "State Revenue Flash Report." November 6, 2008.

3   National Association of State Budget Officers. "Fiscal Survey of the States." December 2008.

4   Boyd, Donald and Dadayan, Lucy. "The Damage is Just Beginning." The Nelson A. Rockefeller Institute of Government. State Revenue Report Number 73. October 2008.

5   Prah, Pamela. "Budget gap could widen to $200 billion." *Stateline.* December 15, 2008.

6   Poulson, Barry. "Is There a Gorilla in Your Backyard? Pension and Other Post Employment Benefit (OPEB) Liabilities." The American Legislative Exchange Council. December 4, 2008.

7   For additional information see: Mattoon, Rick. "OPEB: The 800 Pound Gorilla in the Room." The Federal Reserve Bank of Chicago. February 17, 2008.

8   Poulson, Barry. "Is There a Gorilla in Your Backyard? Pension and Other Post Employment Benefit (OPEB) Liabilities." The American Legislative Exchange Council. December 4, 2008.

9   Nodine, Thad. "The Governors Speak – 2008." The National Governor's Association. April 2008.

10 StateNet. "Capitol Journal" December 15, 2008.

11 National Association of State Budget Officers. "Fiscal Survey of the States." December 2008.

12 Fehr, Stephen. "States Warned Tax Hikes May Be Needed." *Stateline*. December 15, 2008.

13 National Association of State Budget Officers. "Fiscal Survey of the States." December 2008.

14 Prah, Pamela. "State budget gaps balloon to $97 billion." *Stateline*. December 5, 2008.

15 Fitzgerald, Thomas. "Despite Federal Windfall, Pennsylvania Governor Still Backs Income Tax Hike." Tax Analysts, *State Tax Today*. June 2, 2003.

16 National Association of State Budget Officers. Fiscal Survey of the States. 2003 and 2004 editions. Available at http://www.nasbo.org.

17 Lee, Carol. "Cash-strapped governors ask for aid." *The Politico*. December 2, 2008.

18 Hurdle, Jon. "U.S. governors seek $1 trillion federal assistance." *Reuters*. January 2, 2009.

19 Montgomery, Lori. "Obama Team Assembling $850 Billion Stimulus." *Washington Post*. December 19, 2008.

20 Our friend, Amity Shlaes has written a wonderful new book "The Forgotten Man: A New History of the Great Depression", which exposes many of the myths surrounding FDR's New Deal. Also, the Mackinac Center for Public Policy offers a terrific resource on this subject: "Great Myths of the Great Depression," written in 1998 and revised in 2005 by President Emeritus Lawrence W. Reed. Available at: http://www.mackinac.org/archives/1998/sp1998-01.pdf.

21 Full PDF available at http://www.alec.org.

22 Sanford, Mark. Testimony before the United States House Committee on Ways and Means. October 29, 2008.

23 *Ibid*.

24 Fehr, Stephen. "States Warned Tax Hikes May Be Needed." *Stateline*. December 15, 2008.

25 Sunshine, Robert. Testimony before the United States Senate Budget Committee. January 8, 2009.

26 Laffer, Arthur and Moore, Stephen. "Rich States, Poor States: The ALEC-Laffer Economic Competitiveness Index (first edition)." December 2007.

27 Riedl, Brian. "Don't Bail Out the States: Spendthrifts Made Own Mess." The Heritage Foundation. October 31, 2008.

28 Howell, William. ALEC Issue Alert. December 12, 2008.

29 Vedder, Richard. "Should the Feds Bail Out the States?" The American Legislative Exchange Council. February 2003.

30 Sanford, Mark. Testimony before the United States House Committee on Ways and Means. October 29, 2008.

31 Williams, Jonathan. "Paying at the Pump: Gasoline Taxes in America." Tax Foundation Background Paper Number 56. October 2007.

32 Vedder, Richard. "Should the Feds Bail Out the States?" *Washington Times*. March 3, 2003.

33 See: http://mapyourtaxes.mo.gov.

34 See: http://www.ok.gov/okaa/.

35 Nunnelee, Alan. "Budget Transparency in Mississippi." *Inside ALEC*. January 2009.

36 It should be noted that constitutional officers in many states have set up budget transparency Web sites for their agencies, or in some cases, overall state spending. Additionally, numerous State Policy Network (SPN) groups have initiated budget transparency sites of their own. To learn more about these efforts, see: http://www.fiscalaccountability.org.

37 Center for Fiscal Accountability.

38 Wick, Hal. "Open Records Essential in Honest Government." *Inside ALEC*. January 2009.

39 See: http://open.sd.gov/.

40 Wick, Hal. "Open Records Essential in Honest Government." *Inside ALEC*. January 2009.

41 Quoted in: Coburn, Tom and Dutcher, Brandon. "State Spending Website Needed." *The Oklahoman*. October 18, 2006.

42 Halper, Evan and Rothfeld, Michael. "Is California too unwieldy to govern?" *Los Angeles Times*. December 15, 2008.

43 "Perry warns of need to keep taxes, spending low." *The Associated Press*. December 17, 2008.

44 Gehrke, Robert. "Huntsman proposes budget $1B smaller." *The Salt Lake Tribune*. December 5, 2008.

45 LaCerte, Phil. "Speaker urges Legislature to start examining consolidation of school district administrators." *Kansas Liberty*. January 9, 2009.

46 "Gov. Butch Otter calls for 2010 cuts of $169 million." *The Associated Press*. December 17, 2008.

47 For additional information, see the excellent work of the Evergreen Freedom Foundation's Stewardship Project. Available at: http://www.effwa.org/projects/stewardship_series.php.

48 Smith, Sylvia. "Daniels: It's time to shrink." *Fort Wayne Journal Gazette.* December 6, 2008.

49 Olson, Scott. "Daniels floats tight budget plan." *Indianapolis Business Journal.* January 6, 2009.

50 Lambro, Donald. "States Ring in the New Year with Increased Taxes." Townhall.com. January 1, 2009.

51 Henchman, Joseph. "State Budgets: New York Plans to Raise Taxes and Fees." Tax Foundation. December 28, 2008.

52 Scott, Brendan. "Govs Tax & Spend Shocker." *New York Post.* December 17, 2008.

53 Cooper, Seth and Williams, Jonathan. "An Unconstitutional Internet Sales Tax." *Forbes.* May 14, 2008.

54 Cooper, Seth. "Government Killed the Internet Star: How State Sales Taxes Threaten the Online Commerce." *Inside ALEC.* July 2008.

55 Spector, Joseph. "New Yorkers say cut spending, don't raise taxes." *The Rochester Democrat and Chronicle.* November 17, 2008.

56 "Cigarette Tax Burnout." *The Wall Street Journal.* August 11, 2008.

57 "Dope Smokers." *The Wall Street Journal.* September 7, 2007.

58 "Cigarette Tax Burnout." *The Wall Street Journal.* August 11, 2008.

59 For additional information see: LaFaive, Michael, Fleenor, Patrick and Nesbit, Todd. "Cigarette Taxes and Smuggling: A Statistical Analysis and Historical Review." The Mackinac Center for Public Policy. December 2008.

60 Williams, Jonathan and Hodge, Scott. "Oil Company Profits and Tax Collections: Does the U.S. Need a New Windfall Profits Tax?" Tax Foundation Fiscal Fact No. 41. November 9, 2005.

61 Williams, Jonathan. "Why a windfall profits tax on oil companies won't work." *Northeastern Pennsylvania Business Journal.* April 6, 2007.

Chapter One
State Winners and Losers

State Winners and Losers

The geographical center of economic and political power in America is shifting right before our very eyes – and in a more dramatic fashion than at any time in a century. Americans are uprooting themselves and moving to places where there is economic vitality, opportunity and a high quality of life. In short, they are going to where the action is. And over the past 25 years, tens of millions of Americans (and immigrants) have voted with their feet against anti-growth policies that reduce economic freedom and opportunity in states mostly located in the Northeast and Midwest.

The big winners in this interstate competition for jobs and growth have generally been the states in the South and West, such as Nevada, Arizona, Texas and Florida, while the big losers have been in the Rust Belt regions of the Northeast and Midwest. The demoralizing symptoms of economic despair in declining states like New York, Michigan, Pennsylvania, Illinois and New Jersey include lost population, falling housing values, a shrinking tax base, business out-migration, capital flight, high unemployment rates, and less money for schools, roads and aging infrastructure.

What's new is that California has joined the ranks of the "has been" states. Despite all of its natural geographical advantages – ports of entry to the Pacific region, balmy weather, relaxing beaches, idyllic mountains and as the Beach Boys sang, those gorgeous "California Girls" – years of redistributionist economic policies (liberalism run amok in Sacramento) have resulted in more U.S. residents now leaving California than arriving.

The decline of California is probably the best evidence we can present as to the impact of poor state policy-making on the economic pulse of a state. Table 1 shows that in the 10 years leading up to 2007, California had the second largest domestic population outflow of any state in the nation.

Defenders of the high-tax and high-spending conditions that precipitated this fall into the economic cellar argue that big government policies and taxes on the wealthy are neces-

TABLE 1
NET DOMESTIC MIGRATION, 1998-2007

Top 10		Bottom 10	
State	**Inflow**	**State**	**Outflow**
Florida	+1,579,704	Connecticut	-113,892
Arizona	+817,169	Pennsylvania	-148,979
Texas	+736,903	Massachusetts	-335,391
Georgia	+679,420	Louisiana	-390,998
North Carolina	+646,284	Ohio	-397,899
Nevada	+481,534	Michigan	-419,961
South Carolina	+295,074	New Jersey	-468,024
Tennessee	+278,698	Illinois	-735,768
Colorado	+248,322	California	-1,438,480
Washington	+206,168	New York	-1,936,127

Source: U.S. Census Bureau

sary to protect the poor and the disadvantaged. Yet when flight occurs away from an area, it is always the highest achievers and those with the most wealth, capital and entrepreneurial drive who tend to "get out of Dodge" first, leaving the middle class, and then eventually only the poor and disadvantaged behind. In fact, it is only those individuals with wealth who have the means and thus the ability to choose where they will reside. Consequently, the poor are left victims of the misguided liberal policies that were enacted to assist them. The governmental hand, which sought to lift up the poor, in turn holds them down. The result is fewer taxpayers and a heavier tax burden for those who remain.

There's an old saying that high taxes don't redistribute income, they redistribute people. That is precisely what we have found in the research that went into writing this book. When California faced its last deficit in 2003, one of the major causes for the red ink was the stampede of millionaire households out of the state.

The July 2008 survey of 281 corporate executives by Development Counselors International revealed California, New York and Michigan as the three states with the least favorable business climates. Seventy-two percent of executives surveyed listed California as having the worst business climate, followed by New York (42.4 percent), and Michigan (16.8 percent). The most common complaints included high taxes and anti-business regulations.[1]

The five least favored states – California, New York, Michigan, New Jersey and Massachusetts – hold combined projected budget deficits of nearly $65 billion. This figure accounts for approximately 50 percent of the combined deficits that states are facing in fiscal years 2009-2010. In contrast, respondents elected Texas, North Carolina, Georgia, Tennessee and Florida (none of these being extremely high-tax states), as the top five business environments. Texas, Georgia, Tennessee, North Carolina and Florida face combined deficits of roughly $15 billion.[2]

America's Economic Black Hole: The Northeast

The center of America has grown more fiscally conservative, more dismissive of big government command-and-control policy prescriptions, and more economically prosperous. Meanwhile, the heavily unionized, economically exhausted, industrial Northeast has edged ever further to the left. "In the rest of the country, liberal is a dirty word; in the Northeast it isn't," notes Darrel West, a political science professor at Brown University.[3]

The result: an ever widening ideological Grand Canyon between what truly are now two Americas. Let's start by defining the geographical boundaries of this "other America."

Michael Barone, editor of the indispensable *Almanac of American Politics*, calls this peculiar region the "New England-Metro-liner Corridor."[4] The issue starts in Washington, D.C., a city with no manufacturing and no industry (outside of influence-peddling), in which one out of every three households receives a government paycheck or a welfare payment. Its aid per capita has surged to among the highest of any metro-area in the United States. For the most part, Washingtonians extract wealth, they don't create it.

If you were to drive north from Washington, you would travel directly through each of the Northeast corridor states. Welcome to Blue State America.

You would first hit affluent Montgomery County, Md. (eighth richest county in the United States[5]), with its herds of upscale federal employees and "Beltway Bandits." Then, in succession, you would pass through America's modern-day Rust Belt: Eastern Pennsylvania, New Jersey and New York. The shared experience of these states is oppressive tax rates, mindless and meddlesome regulation, obese social welfare programs, slumping real estate markets, and a steady stampede of outward migration. *Wall Street Journal* political writer John Fund best summarized the climate of New York by saying, "I've had friends who fled from here to Eastern Europe in search of freedom."[6] And this is the politically conservative section of the Northeast. The rest of this "other America" encompasses the New England states of Connecticut, Maine, Massachusetts, Rhode Island and Vermont. These states are systematically anti-free, culturally left-wing enterprises. One of the most popular politicians in the region is Bernie Sanders, the Harvard professor turned Mayor of Burlington, and now Vermont Senator – and an avowed socialist. Enough said.

However, there is a tiny foothold of low taxes and free markets in this sea of statism: New Hampshire. We would add that Delaware is also more free-market oriented than its Northeastern neighbors. Its growth rates in recent years underscore its more business-friendly policies.

Mr. Fund refers to the Live Free or Die state as "the Orange County of the East Coast."[7] With no state income tax on wages or state sales tax, and the fifth lowest overall tax burden in the nation, New Hampshire has enjoyed the fastest growth rate in all of New England. New Hampshire is an aberration; its growth in a sea of big government neighbors is a monument to the power of free markets and low taxes. It's not the cold weather that is causing the Northeast to atrophy. We worry, however, that increasingly New Hampshire is catching the Northeast diseases. As more and more Massachusetts refugees move there, the politics of the state are shifting to the left.

The politics of the region are solidly Democratic, but "there is one conservative issue that plays well in the Northeast these days," explains political strategist Jeff Bell, the Republican Senate candidate in New Jersey in 1978. Northeastern voters are suffering from severe tax fatigue. For good reason. Six of the 10 states dubbed as

tax hells by *Money Magazine* are in the Northeast: Maryland, Massachusetts, Maine, Rhode Island, Washington, D.C., and New York. A typical family of four living in Maryland, for example, can save close to $2,500 on its taxes by simply packing the U-Haul trailer and moving across the Potomac River to Virginia. (One of us, Moore, knows this, because he did it.)[8] The average tax premium for the privilege of living in New England is more than $4,000 – for schools, police protection, and other state and municipal services that are arguably equal to, or even inferior to those in most other areas.[9]

Yet even on the tax issue, there is a quintessential free-lunch quality to the sentiments of contemporary Northeastern voters. They gripe continuously about over-taxation, but when even modest budget restraint is suggested, the media, unions, and "poverty industry" begin invoking dark visions of the apocalypse. When Gov. Martin O'Malley of Maryland and former Gov. Elliot Spitzer of New York proposed expansive state-run health care systems, "free" child care centers, pay raises for teachers, government-subsidized sports stadiums, or some other gold-plated government scheme, Northeasterners salivated.

The governments in the Northeast are already about one-fifth more expensive than in the rest of America – $6,400 versus $5,200 of state spending per resident.[10] Only in recent years has the gap between the New England states and the rest of the nation been narrowing (see Table 2). However, an average-income family of four still saves $4,000 a year by moving to just an average tax state and more like $6,000 a year by moving to Florida.[11] Because the Northeastern states tend to have highly progressive tax systems, the incentive for wealthy families to relocate is greater.

Meanwhile, the Northeast is becoming increasingly inhospitable for employers. Labor costs are about 30 percent above the national average in this region.[12] Of the 22 right-to-work states, a grand total of zero are in the

TABLE 2
STATE SPENDING PER CAPITA IN THE NORTHEAST

2006	
New England	
Connecticut	$5,898.93
Maine	$5,943.43
Massachusetts	$6,195.30
Rhode Island	$6,515.36
Vermont	$7,449.37
Extended Northeast	
Delaware	$7,639.27
Maryland	$5,158.01
New Jersey	$6,197.83
New York	$7,399.36
Pennsylvania	$5,218.15
New England Average	**$6,400.48**
Extended Northeast Average	**$6,322.52**
Rest of United States	**$5,221.06**

Source: U.S. Census Bureau

Northeast.[13] Other than taxes, this is arguably the greatest factor impeding economic competitiveness in the region.

When Ed Rendell became Mayor of Philadelphia in the mid-1990s, city employees received 14 paid holidays a year – compared to eight for most private sector workers. With sick leave and vacation time, some workers got up to 40 paid days off a year. Furthermore, in several school districts in New York, teachers have gone on strike despite salaries and benefits exceeding $75,000 a year.

In isolation, none of these anti-growth public policies would cripple a state's economic competitiveness. But in the Northeast, each new piece of special-interest-driven legislation is encrusted upon layers and layers of existing anti-business rules, regulations, edicts and laws. The compounding effect has been to convert the entire region into a kind of businessman's purgatory.

For years, Northeastern politicians and academics have responded to critics with a self-delusional mantra: Taxes don't matter. Regulatory costs don't matter. Minimum wage and pro-union laws don't matter. Reminiscent of the pampered nomenclature in the final days of the Soviet Union, Northeastern elites pretend that what they have built is a modern day worker's paradise. That fantasy is losing credibility as workers rush out of the area.

The lesson of the last 50 years, especially from Eastern Europe, is that statism is difficult to sustain without a captive citizenry. There is no Berlin Wall around the Northeast. Workers, businesses and capital have freedom of exit and entry. For three decades now, Americans have been voting with their feet against the high taxes and debilitating policies of the Northeast, creating a massive brain drain from the region.

Over the past 30 years, the domestic flight from the Northeast into the Sun Belt, Southeastern, and Mountain states has begun to resemble a stampede. Rhode Island has experienced negative domestic migration over the last 10 years, which prompted the *Providence Journal* to once quip, "Will the last person in Rhode Island please turn off the lights."

New York, New Jersey, Massachusetts, Connecticut and Pennsylvania have had almost no growth in population – and without an influx of foreign immigrants, they would be suffering population losses as well.[14] The 10 Atlantic states, plus Washington, D.C., have experienced a piddling population gain of less than five million, or just 5.6 percent from 1970 to 1995 (see Table 3). The rest of the nation grew six times faster. The 10 largest cities of the Northeast, once the centers of America's industrial muscle, lost a combined 1.6 million people during that same period.[15]

Employers are abandoning the East Coast even faster than workers. A Dunn & Bradstreet study found that, in the 1990s, New York lost more businesses than any other state. In

TABLE 3
POPULATION GROWTH TRENDS AND PROJECTIONS: NORTHEAST VS. THE REST OF THE UNITED STATES

	1970-1995	1990-2007	2000-2030
New England			
Connecticut	8%	7%	8%
Maine	25%	7%	11%
Massachusetts	7%	7%	10%
Rhode Island	4%	5%	10%
Vermont	31%	10%	17%
Extended Northeast			
Delaware	31%	30%	29%
Maryland	28%	18%	33%
New Jersey	11%	12%	16%
New York	0%	7%	3%
Pennsylvania	2%	5%	4%
Washington, D.C.	-26%	-3%	-24%
New England Average	**9%**	**7%**	**11%**
Extended Northeast Average	**6%**	**11%**	**10%**
Rest of United States	**38%**	**25%**	**29%**

Source: U.S. Census Bureau

the '90s, the net employment number in the Northeast decreased by nearly half a million – mostly high-paying manufacturing jobs – while the rest of the states gained 8.5 million jobs.[16] This is a long-term trend. For the past 25 years, the non-Northeastern states have gained new jobs at three times the pace of the Northeastern states.

Northeasterners complain disdainfully of the "war between the states" for jobs and businesses. It's not surprising. This is a war they cannot win. Southern and Western states are literally cherry picking companies from the North Atlantic states. One Southern governor recently told us that his state had closed its economic development offices in Europe. "Why search for factories overseas when we can plunder high-tax areas like Connecticut and New York?," he reasoned. Why indeed? Forty years ago, the Northeast was the global capital of manufacturing. Today, manufacturing jobs are still being created in America – but down south in Alabama, North Carolina and even Mississippi.

Other statistics only would add to the depressing tale of regional sclerosis. Incomes in the Northeast grew 20 percent slower than in the rest of the nation in the 1990s. Business start-up and bankruptcy rates in the Northeast reveal less vitality and investment in the region.

Also, despite such punitively high tax rates and overly progressive tax structures, between 1989 and 2004, New England states witnessed the highest increase in income disparity in the nation.[17] This change in income distribution is not only counterintuitive to such redistributive taxation, but is a direct reflection of the above discussion. What was once a thriving manufacturing and industrial center complete with a strong and prospering middle class is now a hollowed out region whose population is dwindling by the year. What was designed as a "fairer" tax system actually backfired. Its anti-business implications ended up driving good manufacturing jobs from the region.

The Gini coefficient, a commonly used benchmark for gauging income inequality, has increased nationally over the last 15 or so years, but nowhere more dramatically than in New England. But what is even more telling of the negative impacts of a punitive tax system is the change in inequality within the different New England states. Not surprisingly, Vermont, Massachusetts and Connecticut, three states that rank rather low on the ALEC-Laffer State Economic Competiveness Index, witnessed some of the steepest increases in income inequality. New Hampshire, the one shining star of supply-side policies in New England, maintains the third lowest Gini coefficient in the country.[18]

With respect to the economic importance of the Northeast, all the data point to one conclusion: It is dying. The Atlantic states are suffering from a slow-motion version of the economic paralysis now affecting much of Europe, particularly France and Sweden with their state-of-the-art, massive welfare systems.

In 2007, the Northeast was home to a smaller share of the U.S. population than ever before;[19] it had a smaller industrial base and produced a smaller percentage of America's total value added than at any time in the nation's history. For the rest of the United States – which has impressively restructured its economy for the challenges of the productivity-driven information age – the Northeast is not so much unnecessary as it is irrelevant. Today, most of America – competitive, capital-

ist and confident – observes the Northeast through its rearview mirror. In the mid-1990s it appeared that the Northeast might have finally awakened to the error of its ways and become ready to heal itself. In New York, Gov. George Pataki and Mayor Rudy Giuliani took some bold steps to stop the bleeding. The crime rate was down by nearly half during Giuliani's tenure as mayor, and taxes were cut more than 20 times.[20] Manhattan is visibly cleaner and safer and more vibrant than 15 years ago. In New Jersey, Christine Todd Whitman was elected governor and slashed income tax rates, which caused a mini-rally in the state.[21] Tom Ridge did the same in Pennsylvania.

But for the most part, it's back to big government normalcy in these states. Govs. Jon Corzine of New Jersey, Ed Rendell of Pennsylvania, and Jodi Rell of Connecticut have proposed giant tax increases in the last two years.[22] Today, most Northeastern states have a personal income tax rate well above the national average and every

TABLE 4
TOP INCOME TAX RATES IN THE NORTHEAST

	Personal Income Tax	Corporate Income Tax
New England		
Connecticut	5.00%	7.50%
Maine	8.50%	8.93%
Massachusetts	5.30%	9.50%
Rhode Island	9.90%	9.00%
Vermont	9.50%	8.50%
Extended Northeast		
Delaware	5.95%	8.70%
Maryland	6.25%	8.25%
New Jersey	8.97%	9.00%
New York	6.85%	7.10%
Pennsylvania	3.07%	9.99%
Washington, D.C.	8.50%	9.98%
United States Median	**6.00%**	**7.30%**

Source: Tax Foundation and Laffer Associates

one of them has a corporate tax rate above the norm (see Table 4).

There is an old Wall Street adage: Sell a falling stock. Economically, the Northeast is exactly that: a falling stock.

Under normal circumstances, domestic migration would be expected to mitigate the economic and ideological distinctions among different regions. But the culturally based migration of the past decade is making the Northeast more rock-solid liberal and the rest of the nation more conservative. The Northeast's political culture is repellent to the very human capital that is the life blood of a prospering region: college graduates, entrepreneurs, conservative-oriented families with children, and the wealthy. What has been left behind in the Northeast has been a residual of welfare recipients, government workers, senior citizens and university professors.[23]

State Political Winners and Losers
"At some point, the political balance in New England will tip irretrievably in favor of the redistributionists, business-bashers, anti-growth preservationists, the swelling ranks of government employees and retirees living on tax-exempt bonds," notes John McClaughry, president of the Ethan Allen Institute in Vermont.[24] "These people, whose policies have driven out those who create wealth, will be permanently in charge." The wipeout of Republicans in the Northeast in the 2006 and 2008 elections suggests this process is well under way. Today, Republicans control a grand total of zero U.S. House seats in all of New England.

And what are they in charge of? A region consisting almost solely of tax consumers sows the seeds of its own destruction.

The good news is that the left's monopoly status in this region is almost inconsequential. The political clout of the Northeast hit its high watermark long ago, and with every year it continues to recede. The very demographic trends that are draining the region of economic energy are working against the Yankee states in terms of their political clout as well. In the 1950s, the Northeastern states had 141 House seats.[25] Now they are down to 92. They will lose four or five more seats after 2010. This slow drip, drip, drip of lost political power will continue at least through 2030, as Table 5 shows. Between 1970 and 2030, the Northeast will have lost about one-third of its political power and relevance. New York and Pennsylvania will have lost 40 percent of their congressional seats.

TABLE 5
CHANGE IN APPORTIONMENT OF HOUSE SEATS IN THE NORTHEAST

	Apportioned Reps Based on 1970 Census	Apportioned Reps Based on 2000 Census	Apportioned Reps Based on Census Projection 2030	Seat Gain/Loss 1970-2030
New England				
Connecticut	6	5	4	-2
Massachusetts	12	10	8	-4
Rhode Island	2	2	1	-1
Extended Northeast				
New Jersey	15	13	12	-3
New York	39	29	23	-16
Pennsylvania	25	19	15	-10

Source: House of Representatives, Office of the Clerk and the U.S. Census Bureau

FIGURE 1
CONGRESSIONAL SEAT APPORTIONMENT: 1970-2030

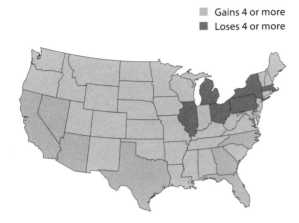

Gains 4 or more
Loses 4 or more

Source: House of Representatives, Office of the Clerk and the U.S. Census Bureau

Figure 1 shows the shrinking political influence of the Northeast and Midwest as well. Political power has shifted steadily to the perimeter states in the South and West. The red states are gaining muscle as the Northeast corridor surrenders its command of national politics. As with every failing institution in the world today, the Northeast now confronts a clear choice: Change or die. At the time of this writing, it is not clear that the political class in the region will choose the right course.

The ALEC-Laffer
Economic Competitiveness Model

Of course, every state aspires to be a high-octane, high-growth state – a place of destination, not a place where people say with nostalgia that they are "from." The Economic Performance Rankings in chapter four didn't just happen by chance. It is not a random occurrence that people move from Connecticut to Florida or from California to Nevada. They are driven by the law of supply and demand: High-growth states supply jobs, high incomes, and opportunities that Americans demand.

In this ALEC book, we investigate what policy levers state legislators control that can make their state a desired location. Many of the most important factors that make a place attractive – such as the climate, accessibility to beautiful beaches or mountains, or the mineral resources in the ground – are of course, beyond the control of politicians. No one should think that Newark, N.J. will ever compete on equal footing with Malibu, Calif., or that Flint, Mich. will ever be as desirable a destination as Palm Beach, Fla.

But the central premise of this publication is that the economic policy decisions made by state legislators don't just matter in terms of how a state performs financially, they matter a whole lot. We know that national leaders can impact the desirability of living or investing in a nation. Likewise, state officials can also influence these factors – the economic, fiscal, and social policy legislation that contribute to, or in all too many cases against, the desirability of a state. If you don't believe that economic policies matter, then why is it that thousands upon thousands of people in East Germany risked their lives and fortunes every year to get through the Berlin Wall to move to West Germany? Or why has the population of South Korea increased four times faster than the population of North Korea? Why is it that Mexicans line up at the U.S. border to get into this nation and live and work here by whatever means they possess, and yet few Americans sneak over the border to get into Mexico?

A logical extension of firms setting up operations in economically friendly countries is that companies based in the United States also place their operations in states within the United States that offer the best business environment. Earlier this year, *Fortune* published the 2008 edition of the Fortune 500, their ranking of the country's top 500 companies based on gross revenue. While there were no big surprises in terms of winners and losers or entries and exits, we did notice an interesting change in the geographical distribution of this year's

Fortune 500. Texas posted 58 companies on the Fortune 500, up from 56 last year, overtaking New York, which dropped from 57 to 55, as the state home to the most Fortune 500 headquarters.[26] This shift in corporate headquarters is merely the latest example of the pivotal role that fiscal policy, especially tax rates, plays in the economic competitiveness and attractiveness of a state.

When you consider the economic rationale, it comes as no surprise to us that companies are moving to low-tax, right-to-work states like Texas at the expense of high-tax, high-regulation states like New York. Not only does New York state have a corporate income tax of 7.1 percent, but for companies in the New York City metropolitan region there is an additional mass transit surcharge of 17 percent, which brings the overall rate to 8.3 percent. And if that's not enough, New York City imposes its own non-deductible corporate tax rate that brings the rate up to an astounding 17.63 percent! Now it's one thing for people to "vote with their feet" in response to high personal marginal tax rates, but when a Fortune 500 company decides to relocate its headquarters, it takes with it a multitude of resources, hundreds if not thousands of jobs, and millions in tax revenue.

In this study, we have identified 15 policy variables that have a proven impact on the migration of capital – both investment capital and human capital – into and out of states. They are the basic ingredients of our 2009 Economic Competitiveness Rankings of the states. Each of these factors is influenced directly by state lawmakers through the legislative process. Generally speaking, states that spend less – especially on income transfer programs, and states that tax less – particularly on productive activities such as working or investing – experience higher growth rates than states which tax and spend more. The 15 factors are as follows:

- Highest Marginal Personal Income Tax Rate
- Highest Marginal Corporate Income Tax Rate
- Personal Income Tax Progressivity
- Property Tax Burden
- Sales Tax Burden
- Tax Burden From All Remaining Taxes
- Estate Tax/Inheritance Tax (Yes or No)
- Recent Tax Policy Changes 2007-08
- Debt Service as a Share of Tax Revenue
- Public Employees Per 1,000 Residents
- Quality of State Legal System
- State Minimum Wage
- Workers' Compensation Costs
- Right-to-Work State (Yes or No)
- Tax or Expenditure Limit

Based on these factors, we rank the competitiveness of the states in Table 6.

In the following pages, we provide a more in-depth look into the policy variables that make up the ALEC-Laffer State Economic Competitiveness Index. We also will provide a primer on how and why taxation, over-spending, regulation, excessive litigation, and other factors in our index inhibit a state's capability to generate economic growth and jobs. Because taxation is one of the most heavily weighted factors in our index, let's start by reviewing why higher tax rates inhibit the economic performance of states. And also, let us establish some basic rules for state policy-makers to live by regarding the effect of taxes on economic performance. Later, we will address the importance of the remaining policy variables.

The 10 Principles of Effective Taxation

Principle #1:
Tax something and you get less of it.
Tax something less and you get more of it.
Tax policy is all about reward and punishment. Most politicians know instinctively that taxes reduce the activity being taxed – even if they

TABLE 6
2009 STATE ECONOMIC OUTLOOK RANKINGS
based upon equal-weighting of each state's rank in 15 policy variables

Rank	State	Rank	State
1	Utah	26	Massachusetts
2	Colorado	27	Wisconsin
3	Arizona	28	Maryland
4	Virginia	29	Nebraska
5	South Dakota	30	Montana
6	Wyoming	31	Delaware
7	Nevada	32	Connectiut
8	Georgia	33	West Virgnia
9	Tennessee	34	Michigan
10	Texas	35	Iowa
11	Florida	36	Kentucky
12	Arkansas	37	New Hampshire
13	North Dakota	38	Alaska
14	Idaho	39	Oregon
15	Oklahoma	40	Minnesota
16	Alabama	41	Hawaii
17	Indiana	42	Pennsylvania
18	Louisiana	43	California
19	Mississippi	44	Illinois
20	South Carolina	45	Ohio
21	North Carolina	46	New Jersey
22	Washington	47	Maine
23	Missouri	48	Rhode Island
24	Kansas	49	Vermont
25	New Mexico	50	New York

don't care to admit it. Congress and state law-makers routinely tax things that are "bad" like cigarettes, alcohol consumption and gambling to discourage the activity. We reduce, or in some cases, entirely eliminate taxes on behavior that we want to encourage, such as home buying, going to college, investing in energy efficient appliances and giving money to charity. By lowering the tax rate (in some cases to zero), we lower the after-tax cost, in the hopes that this will lead more people to engage in that activity.

This is why it is wise to keep taxes on work, savings and investment as low as possible in order not to deter these activities.

Case Study:
The Empire State: Taxed to Death
No state better exemplifies the impact of over taxation on work and investment than New York. New York economist and professor Steve

Kagann found that between 1975 and 2000, there was a clear inverse relationship between New York's job creation and its tax burden. Here is how Kagann describes these results:

"History demonstrates that the ability of the upstate [New York] economy to provide opportunity, prosperity, and stability for New Yorkers is directly and inversely related to the propensity of the state government to spend and tax. More government means fewer jobs and less growth. When government becomes a growth industry, the private sector heads South – in New York's case, figuratively and literally."

After adjusting for wage and cost-of-living differences, the average New Yorker can expect to keep slightly more than 65 cents of every $1.00 earned – and this is before the impact of the federal income tax has been calculated. Because of this confiscatory rate, New York has the worst income incentive rate in the country. The state also imposes the largest property tax burdens on its citizens as well as a highly progressive tax code that further discourages innovation and economic activity.

Between 1995 and 1998, New York cut taxes under Gov. George Pataki.[27] The result was a temporary revival and the best private economy performance in decades. New York raised more money in the eight years after George Pataki chopped tax rates than did Mario Cuomo in the eight years after he raised taxes. But taxes rose again in the late 1990s and early 2000s, and the upstate region is again one of the most depressed areas in the nation.

Principle #2:
Individuals work, and produce goods and services to earn money for present or future consumption.

Workers save, but they do so for the purpose of husbanding their resources so they or their children can consume in the future. A corollary of this proposition is that people do not work to pay taxes – though some politicians seem to think they do.

Case Study:
The Supply-Side Version of Robin Hood

Don't believe for a moment that highly progressive tax structures in California or New York help the poor, minorities, or the disenfranchised. They don't. Just on an intuitive level, it should be self-evident that if a government taxes people who work to pay people who don't work, there will be more people who don't work and fewer people who do.

All of us understand the importance of helping those who have difficulty helping themselves. The question is not whether you want to help the poor. The question is, how can you make the poor better off.

If the rich are taxed and the money is given to the poor, do not be surprised if the number of poor people increases and the number of rich subsides. People respond to incentives; it is the way the world works. If you make an activity less attractive, people will do less of it. If you make an activity more attractive, people will do more of it. Taxes make an activity less attractive and subsidies make an activity more attractive.

Let's retell the story of Robin Hood through the supply-side lens. Robin Hood and his band of merry men would start their days hiding among the trees in Sherwood Forest waiting for hapless travellers on the trans-forest throughway.

If a rich merchant came by, Robin Hood would strip him of all his belongings. Before you feel sorry for the guy, remember he is so rich that by the time he gets back to his castle there will be an abundance of jewels and wealth waiting for him. He'll be just fine, none the worse for the wear.

If just a prosperous merchant came through the forest, Robin Hood would take almost everything the guy had, but not all. Of a normal, everyday businessman's belongings, Robin Hood would seize just a moderate chunk. And if a poor merchant came through the forest, one who could barely make it, he would be deprived of a little token.

In the vernacular of our modern day society, Robin Hood had a progressive stealing structure. You recognize the model, don't you? Doesn't it sound like the California government to you or other tax systems used in this country?

At the end of the day, Robin Hood and his men would take their contraband back to Nottingham to "help" the poor. They would distribute their treasures to citizens, based on their destituteness.

Using today's words, the more a person makes, the less Robin Hood gives him, and the less a person makes, the more he gives him. You follow the model: He stole from the rich and gave to the poor. The richer you were, the more he'd steal from you, the poorer you were the more he'd give to you. This is the story of Robin Hood.

Now, put on your supply-side economics hat and imagine for a moment you are a merchant back in the ancient days of Nottingham: How long would it take you to learn not to go through the forest?

Those merchants who couldn't afford armed guards would have to go around the forest in order to trade with the neighboring villages. Of course the route around the forest is longer, more treacherous, and as a result, more costly.

Those merchants who could afford armed guards (and by the way, today we call these armed guards lawyers, accountants and lobbyists) would go through the forest and Robin Hood couldn't rip them off. As a result, he had no contraband to give to the poor. All he had succeeded in doing was driving up the cost of doing business, which meant the poor had to pay higher prices and were literally worse off. By stealing from the rich and by giving to the poor, Robin Hood made the poor worse off.

And so it is in high-tax states. The poor who rely on the state for their sustenance are having their benefits cut to the bone. Because of some state's business-unfriendly policies, unemployment rates rise. We could go on, but the point is simple enough and its significance cannot be overstated: progressive tax structures do not benefit the truly needy.

In its attempts to redistribute income, government never, ever succeeds. What it does accomplish is the destruction of the volume of income. Government cannot change the distribution of income with taxes, but it can – and does – lower the volume of income with taxes. As we look across the world at the progressive tax structure of California and other economies, it's amazing to see how the distribution of income, if anything, is made worse.

Principle #3:
Taxes create a wedge between the cost of working and the rewards of working.

To state this in economic terms: the difference between the price paid by people who demand goods and services for consumption, and the price received by people who provide these goods and services – the suppliers – is called the wedge. Income and other payroll taxes, as well as regulations, restrictions and government requirements, separate the wages paid by employers from the wages received by employees. If a worker pays 15 percent of his income in payroll taxes, 25 percent in federal income taxes, and 5 percent in state income taxes, his $50,000 wage is reduced after-tax to $27,500. The lost $22,500 of income is the tax wedge. The wedge is the difference, or some 45 percent. Large as the wedge seems in this example, it is just part of the total wedge. The wedge also includes excise, sales and property taxes plus an assortment of costs such as the market value of the accountants and lawyers hired to maintain compliance with government regulations. As the wedge grows, the total cost to the firm of employing a person goes up, but the net payment received by the person goes down. Thus, both the quantity of labor demanded and quantity supplied fall to a new, lower equilibrium level, and a lower level of economic activity ensues. This is why all taxes ultimately affect people's incentive to work and invest, though some taxes clearly matter more.

Principle #4:

An increase in tax rates will not lead to a dollar-for-dollar increase in tax revenues, and a reduction in tax rates that encourages production will lead to less than a dollar-for-dollar reduction in tax revenues.

Lower marginal tax rates reduce the wedge and thus lead to an expansion in the production base and improved resource allocation. Thus, while less tax revenue may be collected per unit of tax base, the tax base itself increases. This expansion of the tax base will therefore offset some (and in certain cases, all) of the loss in revenues because of the now lower rates.

Tax rate changes also affect the amount of tax avoidance. It is important to note that legal tax avoidance is differentiated throughout this report from illegal tax evasion. The higher the marginal tax rate, the greater the incentive to reduce taxable income. Tax avoidance takes many forms, from workers electing to take an improvement in nontaxable fringe benefits in lieu of higher gross wages, to investment in tax shelter programs. Business decisions, too, are increasingly based on tax considerations as opposed to market efficiency. For example, at a 40 percent tax rate, which taxes $40 of every $100 earned, the incentive to avoid this tax is twice as high as when the tax rate is 20 percent and the worker forfeits $20 for every $100 earned.

An obvious way to avoid paying a tax is to eliminate market transactions upon which the tax is applied. This can be accomplished through vertical integration: Manufacturers can establish wholesale outlets, retailers can purchase goods directly from the manufac-

turer, and companies can acquire suppliers or distributors. The number of steps remains the same, but fewer and fewer steps involve market transactions and thereby avoid the tax. If states refrain from applying their sales taxes on business-to-business transactions, they will avoid the numerous economic distortions caused by tax cascading. Michigan, for instance, should not tax the sale of rubber to a tire company, then tax the tire when it is sold to the auto company, then tax the sale of the car from the auto company to the dealer, and then tax the dealer's sale of the car to the final purchaser of the car, or else the rubber and wheels will be taxed multiple times. Additionally, the tax costs embedded in the price of the product would remain hidden to the consumer.

Principle #5:

If tax rates become too high, they may lead to a reduction in tax receipts. The relationship between tax rates and tax receipts is a proposition known as the Laffer Curve.

The Laffer Curve (see Figure 2) summarizes a series of these diagrams. We start this curve with the undeniable fact that there are two tax rates that generate zero tax revenues: a zero tax rate and a 100 percent tax rate. (Remember Principle #2: People don't work for the privilege of paying taxes, so if all their earnings are taken in taxes, they don't work, or at least they don't earn income that the government knows about, and thus the government gets no revenues.)

Now, within what is referred to as the "normal range," an increase in tax rates will lead to an increase in tax revenues. At some point, however, higher tax rates become counterproductive. Above this point, called the "prohibitive range," an increase in tax rates leads to a reduction in tax revenues and vice versa. Over the entire range, with a tax rate reduction, the revenues collected per dollar of tax base falls. This is the arithmetic effect. But the number of units in the tax base expand. Lower tax rates lead to higher levels of personal income,

FIGURE 2
THE LAFFER CURVE

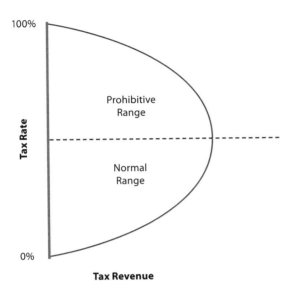

Principle #6:
The more mobile the factors being taxed, the larger the response to a change in tax rates. The less mobile the factor, the smaller the change in the tax base for a given change in tax rates.

Taxes on capital are almost impossible to enforce in the 21st century because capital is instantly transportable.

For example, imagine the behavior of an entrepreneur or corporation that builds a factory at a time when profit taxes are low. Once the factory is built, the low rate is raised substantially without warning. The owners of the factory may feel cheated by the tax bait and switch, but they probably do not shut the factory down because it still earns a positive after-tax profit. The factory will remain in operation for a time even though the rate of return, after tax, has fallen sharply. If the factory were to be shut down, the after-tax return would be zero. After some time has passed, and equipment needs servicing, the lower rate of return will discourage further investment, and the plant will eventually move where tax rates are lower.

One recent study by the American Enterprise Institute found that high corporate income taxes at the national level are associated with lower growth in wages.[28] Again, it appears a chain reaction occurs when corporate taxes get too high. Capital moves out of the high-tax area, but wages are a function of the ratio of capital to labor, so the reduction in capital lowers the wage rate.

The distinction between initial impact and burden was perhaps best explained by one of our favorite 20th century economists, Nobel winner Friedrich von Hayek, who makes the point as follows:

"The illusion that by some means of progressive taxation the burden can be shifted substantially onto the shoulders of the wealthy has been the chief reason why taxa-

employment, retail sales, investment and general economic activity. This is the economic or incentive effect. Tax avoidance also declines. In the normal range, the arithmetic effect of a tax rate reduction dominates. In the prohibitive range, the economic effect is dominant.

Of course, where a state's tax rate lies along the Laffer Curve depends on many factors, including tax rates in neighboring jurisdictions. If a state with a high employment or payroll tax borders a state with large population centers along that border, businesses will have an incentive to shift their operations from inside the jurisdiction of the high-tax state and into the jurisdiction of the low-tax state.

Economists have observed a clear Laffer Curve effect with respect to cigarette taxes. States with high tobacco taxes that are located next to states with low tobacco taxes have very low retail sales of cigarettes relative to the low-tax states. Illinois smokers buy many cartons of cigarettes when in Indiana, and the retail sales of cigarettes in the two states bear this out. The same is true of high gas taxes. Motorists, especially truckers, "fill 'er up" before they enter the state.

tion has increased as fast as it has done and that, under the influence of this illusion, the masses have come to accept a much heavier load than they would have done otherwise. The only major result of the policy has been the severe limitation of the incomes that could be earned by the most successful and thereby gratification of the envy of the less well off."[29]

Case Study:
Taxes and Housing Prices

The least mobile factors of production are land and housing. If the tax burden becomes excessive in a state or city, we could expect capital to leave, followed by businesses and families. But it's hard, if not impossible, to take your house and land with you. It is left behind and thus in theory, land values and housing prices will bear the ultimate burden of higher taxes.

Several years ago we tested this proposition with Dr. Richard Vedder of Ohio University.[30] We examined the 10 states with the largest increases in state and local tax burden as a percentage of income, 1980-1990, and compared them with the 10 states with the smallest increases – actually, decreases – in tax burden for the same time period. Correcting for inflation, *real housing prices fell significantly – more than 12 percent – in the big tax-increase states, while real housing prices on average rose dramatically – almost 58 percent – in the big tax-reduction states.* For the continental United States as a whole, real housing prices experienced a modest increase of about eight percent.

This conclusion was not some sort of statistical fluke arising from one or two extreme values. Of the 10 states with the biggest percentage increase in tax burdens, nine of them saw a decline in housing values after allowing for inflation (Ohio, Indiana, Washington, West Virginia, Idaho, Texas, Iowa, Oregon and Oklahoma). Only one state with significant tax increases had a rise in housing prices – South Carolina – and even there the increase in hous-

ing prices was in the single digits, and far less than in its neighbors to the north – North Carolina – or south – Georgia.

We also found that it wasn't just higher property taxes that held down housing prices. Changes in all forms of taxation have a negative effect on variations in housing prices. Although property tax changes have the biggest impact on housing price changes, other forms of taxation exhibit the same effects. This negative relationship was observed throughout the '70s, '80s, and '90s.

One example of this tax-substitution effect was the response to the steep increases in income taxes on the rich in New Jersey in the early 1990s. The new tax was only intended to impact the wealthiest families in the Garden State. But taxes were raised so high that many of the tax-targeted families moved out of the state. This outmigration caused a reduction in property values at the high end of the market, but the slump eventually invaded the middle-class housing market. The middle class paid the taxes levied on the rich, in part through depressed home prices. That was one reason the taxes on the rich caused a middle class revolt.

Once known for its high levels of economic growth and low levels of taxation, New Jersey has lost its competitive advantage. Public sector unions have won billions in massive wage and benefit packages, leaving the state with a $4.5 billion deficit in 2006, despite a national economic boom. This lies in stark contrast to the state's economic history. At one time, New Jersey's tax burden ranked 40th among states, 13 percent below the national average. It was once one of only two states that did not levy a sales or an income tax.[31]

Recently, however, New Jersey has embraced the restrictive tax policies of its Northeastern neighbors at a seemingly ever faster clip. From 2002 to 2004, the state increased taxes and fees more than 30 times to the tune of $3.6 billion. They implemented an estate tax, which kicks in at $675,000 – a threshold significantly lower than the $3.5 million federal level. Taxes on individuals and corporations have also increased dramatically. New Jersey's anti-growth policies are succeeding in shifting resident behavior. From 1998 to 2007, the state lost 468,000 more residents than it gained.[32]

Principle #7:
Raising tax rates on one source of revenue will reduce the tax revenue from other sources. Reducing the tax rate on one activity will raise the taxes generated from other activities.

For example, an increase in the corporate profits tax rate would be expected to lead to a diminution in the amount of corporate activity, and hence profits, within the taxing district. That alone implies less than a proportionate increase in corporate tax revenues. Such a reduction in corporate activity also implies a reduction in employment and personal income. As a result, personal income tax revenues would fall. This decline, too, would offset the increase in corporate tax revenues. Conversely, a reduction in corporate tax rates would lead to a less than expected loss in revenues and an increase in tax receipts from other sources.

Principle #8:
An economically efficient tax system has a sensible, broad tax base and a low tax rate.

Ideally, the tax system of a state, city or nation will minimally distort economic activity. High tax rates alter economic behavior. Ronald Reagan used to tell the story that he would stop making movies during his acting career once he was in the 90 percent tax bracket because the income he received was so low after taxes were taken away. If the tax base is broad, tax rates can be kept as low and nonconfiscatory as possible. This is one reason that we favor a flat tax with minimal deductions and loopholes. It is also why 24 nations now have adopted the flat tax around the world.[33] (We would add that ALEC has great model legislation for

states considering a flat tax.)

Principle #9:
Income transfer payments (welfare) create a de facto "tax" on working and thus have a high impact on the vitality of a state's economy.

Unemployment benefits, welfare payments, and subsidies represent a redistribution of income. For every transfer recipient, there is an equivalent tax payment or future tax liability. Thus, income effects cancel. In many instances, these payments are given to people only in the absence of work or output. Examples include food stamps (income test), Social Security benefits (retirement test), agricultural subsidies, and of course, unemployment compensation itself. Thus, the wedge on work effort is growing at the same time that subsidies to nonwork are increasing. Transfer payments represent a tax on production and a subsidy to leisure. Their automatic increase in the event of a fall in market income leads to an even sharper drop in output.

In some high-benefit states such as Hawaii, Massachusetts and New York, the entire package of welfare payments can pay people the equivalent of a $10-an-hour job – and don't forget welfare benefits are not taxed, but wages and salaries are. Because these benefits shrink as income levels from work climb, welfare can impose very high marginal tax rates – 60 percent or more – on low-income Americans. And those tax rates have a deleterious effect. We found a highly significant negative relationship between the level of benefits in a state and the percentage reduction in case-loads.[34]

The 10 states with the lowest benefit levels slashed their caseloads by 58 percent between 1993 and 1998. The 10 states with the highest benefit levels only trimmed their caseloads by half that much. Hawaii, which offered the most generous welfare benefits of any state, totaling more than $30,000 a year, recorded the smallest reduction in caseloads in the nation in the 1990s.[35] Conversely, Mississippi, whose welfare package provided less than $11,000 a year, reduced its rolls by an impressive 70 percent. High benefit levels reduce the attractiveness of a normal 40-hour-a-week job.

In sum, high welfare benefits increase the tax wedge between effort and reward. As such, output would be expected to fall as a consequence of making benefits from not working more generous. Thus, an increase in unemployment benefits is expected to lead to a rise in unemployment.

And finally, and most important of all for state legislators to remember:

Principle #10:

If there are two locations, A and B, and if taxes are raised in B and lowered in A, producers and manufacturers will have a greater incentive to move from location B to location A.

Our favorite real life example of this principle comes from Tennessee, which is location A in our example above, and Kentucky, which is location B.

Case Study:

Tennessee vs. Kentucky

Tennessee borders eight states, but Kentucky has the longest border and is probably the state most similar to the Volunteer State in many respects. The two states have similar histories and have comparable economic bases. In 1980, per capita income in the two states was just $8 (0.1 percent) apart.[36]

One big way in which Kentucky sets itself apart from Tennessee is tax policy. In 1980, state and local taxes as a percentage of personal income were about 10 percent higher in Kentucky than in Tennessee, with the critical difference being that Kentucky levied a personal income tax, and Tennessee did not. From 1980 to 1996, Tennessee maintained its low-tax climate with taxes as a percentage of personal income actually falling slightly. By contrast, Kentucky went in the opposite direction, raising taxes more than Tennessee

and its eight bordering states. Its income tax burden expanded enormously. By 1996, taxes per $1,000 in personal income were $117.29 in Kentucky, but only $90.42 in Tennessee. The Kentucky tax burden was nearly 30 percent higher than in the Volunteer State.

What happened to the economies of the two states? Both grew, but Tennessee's percentage growth in real output per capita was more than one-third larger than Kentucky's. Whereas Tennessee's income per capita was a minuscule $16 higher than Kentucky's in 1980 (in 1999 dollars), by 1998 the income disparity had grown 129-fold to $2,064. It now takes the typical Kentuckian 13 months to make the income that a resident of Tennessee makes in a year.

Kentucky's income tax was a key factor in its relative stagnation for two reasons. First, as stated above, dollar for dollar, income taxes are worse than other taxes since they are a direct burden on production and income. Second, income tax revenues typically rise faster than incomes over time. Therefore, the overall tax burden tends to rise automatically in states relying on income taxes, unlike with states where sales, property and other forms of taxation dominate. Since, dollar for dollar, private sector activity is more efficient and growth-inducing than public sector spending, the effect of income taxes on increasing the size of the public sector also retards economic growth in the long run. If Kentucky hopes to pick up ground lost to Tennessee, it will almost certainly have to lower its income tax, if not eliminate it altogether.

Taxes and Growth: Academic Studies

Now we examine the real world evidence of the impact of taxes on relative state economic performance. Does the evidence match our taxation principles listed above? Do taxes have the "power to destroy?"

Some of the most persuasive studies on the relative economic competitiveness of states examine a cross section of states to systematically determine the impact of tax policies on growth rates among states. In their analysis of the probable impact of the passage of Proposition 13 in California, Kadlec and Laffer examined the relationship between changes in the level of state and local tax revenues as a percentage of personal income and growth in personal income.[37] Observations from the 20 states with the largest property tax revenues in 1965 and 1975 were used. Taxes were disaggregated in property taxes and all other taxes. The results showed a statistically significant negative relationship between increases in each tax burden and the rate of growth in personal income.

A more extensive study by Genetski and Chin (1978) performed a cross sectional analysis on all 50 states and the District of Columbia. Again, changes in relative economic growth were related to changes in relative tax rates, this time between 1969 and 1976. The study concluded that during this time period, economic growth rates of particular states were not associated with relative levels of state and local tax burdens. A weak relationship was found based on changes in the states' relative tax burden. Those states that had above average increases in their tax burdens tended to experience below average economic growth, and vice versa. However, once allowance was made for a three-year period of adjustment, a strong negative relationship was evident between above average increases in tax burdens and economic growth. The study concludes, in part, that "much of the slower than average economic growth experienced in many of the Northeastern states, such as New York, Connecticut, Rhode Island, Vermont, New Jersey and Massachusetts, appears to be related to the sharp increases in relative tax burdens in those states. In contrast, New Hampshire's relative tax burden was lowered during this period, and its economic growth was above the national average. Similarly, the above average economic growth experienced

in many Western and Southern states during this period is associated with decreases in their relative tax burdens."

Newman (1979) analyzed the relative growth rate in employment in the South relative to the non-South in 16 manufacturing industries and six other industries. The impact of three variables – corporate income taxes (changes in the corporate tax rate relative to the national average lagged behind by 10 years), business climate (as indicated by "right-to-work laws") and unionization (union membership as a fraction of nonagricultural work force) – were quantified. Newman's empirical results indicate that changes in relative corporate tax rates over this period, as well as the extent of unionization and the existence of right-to-work laws, were major factors influencing the shift of industry to the South from the non-South. Moreover, the evidence suggests that capital intensive industries are more sensitive to changes in the tax rate differentials, and less sensitive to labor cost differentials than are relatively labor intensive industries.

In a 1982 study, economist Robert Genetski of the Harris Bank in Chicago compared taxes as a percentage of income in a state with income growth in the state between 1963 and 1980. Although he did not find a systematic relationship between average tax burden and income growth, he did uncover "an inverse relationship between changes in state relative tax burdens and state relative economic growth." According to Genetski, "Those states with decreasing relative tax burdens tend to experience subsequent above average income growth. Those states with increasing relative tax burdens tend to experience subsequent below average growth."

The Joint Economic Committee (JEC) of Congress has further substantiated this finding. In a 1982 study, the JEC compared the tax policies in the 16 fastest income-growing states and the slowest income-growing states from 1970 to 1979. The results demonstrated that income growth in a state is inversely related to 1) the level of state and local tax burdens, 2) the changes in state and local tax burdens, 3) the amount of income taxes levied in the state and 4) the progressivity of the income tax rates in the state. These relationships were found to be statistically significant. The conclusion of the study was as follows:

> *"The evidence is strong that tax and expenditure policies of state and local governments are important in explaining variations in economic growth between states far more important than other factors frequently cited such as climate, energy costs, the impact of federal fiscal policies, etc. It is clear that high rates of taxation lower the rate of economic growth, and that states that lower their tax burdens are rewarded with an enhancement in their economic growth. Income taxes levied on individuals and corporations are particularly detrimental to growth, more so than consumption based taxes or user charges that do not reduce incentives to work or form capital. Progressive taxation not only lowers the rate of economic growth compared with proportional or regressive taxation, but in the process hurts the very persons that progressive taxes are designed to help: The poor."*

The JEC study determined a special sensitivity of a state's economy to changes in income taxes. The JEC discovered that the top 10 income-tax-hiking states experienced a loss of 182,000 jobs, a 2.3 percentage point increase in the unemployment rate, and a $613 real decline in personal income per family of four. The top 10 income-tax-cutting states saw 975,000 new jobs, an increase in the unemployment rate of only 0.3 percentage points, and a $148 real increase in personal income per family of four.

In a 1985 study, economists Michael Wasylenko and Therese McGuire, found that be-tween 1973 and 1980, the overall tax effort (taxes as a percentage of income) in a state had "a negative and statistically significant effect on overall employment growth and on employment growth in manufacturing, retail trade and services." They also found that sales taxes, which are traditionally thought not to impair employment opportunities "had a negative and statistically significant effect on wholesale trade employment." The single stipulation to this general finding was that when the increased taxes were used to fund education, the effect on growth of taxes was positive.

Economist Robert Newman (1983), examining state employment growth between 1957 and 1973, also concluded that taxes have a significant negative effect. High corporate taxes were found to be particularly important in reducing state employment in "capital intensive industries."

Businesses flee and avoid states with high relative tax burdens. In 1985, Timothy Bartik of Vanderbilt University reported that the plant location decisions between 1972 and 1978 of Fortune 500 companies were significantly influenced by state tax policies. According to Bartik:

> *"A 10 percent increase in a state's corporate income tax rate (for example, from 4.0 percent to 4.4 percent) is estimated to cause a 2-3 percent decline in the number of new plants. A 10 percent increase in a state's average business property tax rate (for example, from 2.0 percent to 2.2 percent) is estimated to cause a 1-2 percent decline in the number of new plants... These changes in business location patterns put some limitations on the ability of states to redistribute income away from corporate stockholders, both in state and out of state, and toward other state residents."*

In some cases, state and local governments have so appreciably shrunk their corporate tax base due to high tax burdens that higher taxes have even produced lower – not higher – revenues. The classic case of this was in high-tax New York during the 1970s when more than half-a-million people left the state, causing a loss of state and local tax revenues of $640 million. According to a 1976 New York State Special Task Force on Taxation to investigate the flight of people and capital:

> *"There is evidence that the present tax structure is, in many respects, counterproductive, fostering as it has an exodus of business, industry, and individuals, eroding the tax base, and shifting the burden of taxation relentlessly down the income scale. Either New York reduces tax levels now, or New York, by inaction, will suffer an even greater revenue loss through further erosion of its tax base."*

That was a prescient prediction, given the continued decline of New York in the 1970s and '80s.

Progressive Income Taxes: The Worst

One recent study designed to document an inverse relationship between state tax burden and economic performance was published in 1996 by economists at the Federal Reserve Bank of Atlanta.[38] The Atlanta Fed study examined personal income growth in the states over the period of 1961-92. The study was pioneering in the sense that it examined the impact of average tax rates and marginal tax rates on income growth. The Fed study concluded that "relative marginal tax rates have a statistically significant negative relationship with relative state growth." It further found that state and local tax rates "have temporary growth effects that are stronger over shorter intervals and a permanent growth effect that does not die out over time. This finding supports the inference that part of growth is endogenous and susceptible to policy influence."

As such, states with progressive income taxes that tax productive activity the most will have less economic growth. And furthermore, the power of incentives does not stop at our country's borders. Because of the relative incentive differences between the United States (especially the most pro-growth states within the country) and the rest of the world, America truly is the only country that is both a developed economy and a growth economy.

Case Study:
What about "Fairness"

Pro-tax income-redistributionists argue that high tax rates on the rich are necessary to help the poor and promote a just and equitable sharing of the tax burden, based on ability to pay. In fact, one liberal think tank in the early 1990s ranked states on the "fairness" of their tax systems. "Fair" was defined as imposing a heavy tax burden on the wealthy, relative to the tax burden on the poor. States with high income tax rates tended to be labeled "fair" and states without income taxes were generally labeled the least fair.

So we used the index created by this liberal group, Citizens for Tax Justice, and we examined the migration patterns in and out of these states. We found that states with the highest tax rates on the richest one percent had much lower population growth than states with no income tax or flat rate income taxes. The highly progressive income tax states had average population growth from 1980 to 1990 that lagged 2.4 percent below the national trend. The non-income tax states had population growth on average nine percent above the U.S. average. It appears that millions of Americans vote with their feet against "tax fairness."

The Most Recent Evidence on State Taxes and Growth

We recently examined the economic evidence for the most recent 10-year period (1997-2007), for which official government data is available.

TABLE 7
STATES WITH LOWEST AND HIGHEST PERSONAL INCOME TAX (PIT) RATES:
10-YEAR ECONOMIC PERFORMANCE, 1997-2007 unless otherwise noted

State	Top PIT Rate	Gross State Product Growth	Personal Income Growth	Personal Income Per Capita Growth	Population Growth
Alaska	0.00%	77.9%	66.4%	49.5%	10.7%
Florida	0.00%	87.6%	87.9%	55.0%	18.3%
Nevada	0.00%	112.3%	114.6%	48.4%	40.3%
New Hampshire	0.00%	56.8%	68.2%	50.1%	9.1%
South Dakota	0.00%	71.3%	73.8%	63.9%	7.8%
Tennessee	0.00%	59.0%	64.8%	46.5%	11.6%
Texas	0.00%	90.5%	89.8%	55.8%	20.7%
Washington	0.00%	74.5%	76.9%	55.8%	13.5%
Wyoming	0.00%	111.4%	114.6%	103.4%	8.5%
9 States w/o PIT*	**0.00%**	**82.38%**	**84.12%**	**58.70%**	**15.62%**
9 States with Highest Marginal PIT Rate*	**9.17%**	**62.35%**	**63.82%**	**52.65%**	**6.33%**
Ohio	8.24%	40.4%	42.3%	38.4%	1.5%
Hawaii	8.25%	63.9%	61.7%	54.4%	6.0%
Maine	8.50%	55.8%	60.7%	52.1%	4.6%
New Jersey	8.97%	54.7%	62.4%	52.5%	4.8%
Oregon	9.00%	63.8%	62.3%	42.9%	13.1%
Maryland	9.30%	74.3%	77.3%	61.1%	8.2%
Vermont	9.50%	61.8%	69.3%	61.2%	3.5%
California	10.30%	77.9%	76.6%	56.0%	11.4%
New York	10.50%	68.5%	61.7%	55.3%	3.9%

*Equally-weighted averages.
Note: Highest marginal state and local personal income tax rate imposed as of 1/1/08 using the tax rate of each state's largest city as a proxy for the local tax. The effect of the deductibility of federal taxes from state tax liability is included where applicable. New Hampshire and Tennessee tax dividend and interest income only.

It revealed that the inverse relationship between state taxes and state economic performance continued to hold true. We compared the economic results of the nine states with the highest income tax rates to the economic results of the nine states without an income tax. The results fully confirm the earlier research: High income tax rates deter economic growth and job creation in states.

Major findings include the following:

- Employment Growth: Business and jobs migrated to low-tax states from 1997 to 2007. The non-income tax states had 21 percent job growth compared to 11 percent job growth in the high income tax states.

- Incomes: Personal income grew by 84 percent in the non-income tax states, versus 64 percent in the high income tax states.

- Population Growth: More than twice as high in the non-income tax states as the high income tax states.

Sales Taxes and Growth
In a static-revenue-estimating world, a higher sales tax rate will simply collect exactly the additional revenue in proportion to the increase in

Net Domestic in-Migration as % of Population	Non-Farm Payroll Employment Growth	Unemployment Rate: 2007
-2.3%	18.1%	6.2%
7.8%	25.5%	4.0%
17.2%	45.0%	4.8%
4.0%	13.8%	3.6%
0.2%	15.2%	3.0%
4.4%	8.3%	4.7%
3.4%	20.3%	4.3%
3.5%	16.6%	4.5%
2.1%	28.3%	3.0%
4.47%	21.23%	4.23%
-2.20%	11.17%	4.41%
-3.5%	0.6%	5.6%
-4.0%	17.3%	2.6%
3.1%	11.5%	4.7%
-5.3%	9.4%	4.2%
4.8%	12.7%	5.2%
-1.5%	15.0%	3.6%
0.1%	10.2%	3.9%
-4.0%	15.5%	5.4%
-9.5%	8.3%	4.5%

the sales tax rate. So, for example, increasing the sales tax from five percent to six percent is a 20 percent increase in the tax rate, and hence static analysis would assume a 20 percent increase in revenues. But we know the higher sales tax rate will lead to lower revenues than the static model predicts for at least four reasons:

1. Higher sales tax rates in one state encourage people to purchase major expenditure items across state borders in lower sales tax states. This effect is especially pronounced for those who live near state borders.

2. Higher sales tax rates encourage more evasion and nonpayment.

3. Higher sales tax rates encourage more internet and catalog sales, which can often be transacted with no sales tax.

4. Higher sales tax rates encourage less consumption and more savings, thus reducing the sales tax base.

A shining example from 2008 of the above-mentioned fiscal folly comes from Chicago. Facing a deficit of some $238 million, Cook County approved a measure that more than doubles its component of the total sales tax rate from 0.75 percent to 1.75 percent. Coupled with the recent 0.25 percent increase in the Regional Transportation Authority's portion of the county sales tax from 0.75 percent to 1 percent, Chicago's combined sales tax rate jumped to 10.25 percent, effective November 2008 – the highest in the nation. Shockingly, the Cook County Board of Commissioners fell just one vote short of raising the combined sales tax rate to 11.25 percent!

Actively making itself significantly less competitive – especially when the nation's economy is weakening – is precisely the wrong move for Cook County and Chicago to make. Does the Cook County government really believe they'll generate the $400 million they expect from this tax increase, especially in the current environment? When tax rates on an activity are raised, the volume of that activity shrinks, leading to a revenue offset. Actual revenue will fall far short of government's static revenue estimates as consumers and retailers adjust their behavior. In addition, the tax increase will only serve to worsen the current economic downturn for the county's 5.3 million residents. Piling on more taxes only exacerbates the problems faced by businesses and residents, and in some cases might represent the final straw, leading to lay-offs or relocations. Unemployment then rises, along with its associated costs to government. It can quickly become a downward spiral, and it wouldn't be a pretty one.

TABLE 8
STATES WITH LOWEST AND HIGHEST CORPORATE INCOME TAX (CIT) RATES:
10-YEAR ECONOMIC PERFORMANCE, 1997-2007 unless otherwise noted

State	Top CIT Rate	Gross State Product Growth	Personal Income Growth	Personal Income Per Capita Growth	Population Growth
Nevada	0.00%	112.3%	114.6%	48.4%	40.3%
South Dakota	0.00%	71.3%	73.8%	63.9%	7.8%
Washington	0.00%	74.5%	76.9%	55.8%	13.5%
Wyoming	0.00%	111.4%	114.6%	103.4%	8.5%
Alabama	4.23%	61.9%	64.0%	54.6%	5.8%
North Dakota	4.23%	69.9%	71.1%	75.3%	-0.9%
Colorado	4.63%	77.8%	84.9%	52.1%	20.0%
Mississippi	5.00%	52.8%	61.6%	52.8%	4.8%
South Carolina	5.00%	56.9%	68.9%	47.3%	14.3%
Texas*	5.00%	90.5%	89.8%	55.8%	20.7%
10 States with Lowest Marginal CIT Rate**	**2.81%**	**77.95%**	**82.04%**	**60.95%**	**13.48%**
10 States with Highest Marginal CIT Rate**	**10.92%**	**56.92%**	**57.96%**	**48.03%**	**5.71%**
Michigan***	9.01%	27.7%	39.0%	33.8%	1.6%
New Hampshire	9.25%	56.8%	68.2%	50.1%	9.1%
Alaska	9.40%	77.9%	66.4%	49.5%	10.7%
Massachusetts	9.50%	58.5%	66.9%	61.4%	3.6%
Minnesota	9.80%	63.5%	65.9%	50.7%	8.5%
Iowa	9.90%	57.5%	52.2%	47.5%	3.4%
Oregon	10.25%	63.8%	62.3%	42.9%	13.1%
Ohio	10.50%	40.4%	42.3%	38.4%	1.5%
Pennsylvania	13.97%	54.7%	54.6%	50.9%	1.7%
New York	17.63%	68.5%	61.7%	55.3%	3.9%

* Texas imposes a Franchise Tax, known as the margin tax, of 1.0%, this equates to a CIT rate of 5.0%
** Equally-weighted averages.
*** Michigan imposes the Michigan Business Tax (MBT) which equates to an effective CIT rate of 9.01%.
Note: Highest marginal state and local personal income tax rate imposed as of 1/1/08 using the tax rate of each state's largest city as a proxy for the local tax. The effect of the deductibility of federal taxes from state tax liability is included where applicable.

The best evidence of this is the difference between retail sales in Portland, Ore. and Seattle, Wash. Oregon has no sales tax but does have a 9 percent income tax, while Washington has no income tax but does have a combined state and local sales tax average of 8.26 percent. How does this affect retail sales? According to a famous *Wall Street Journal* investigation a number of years ago, one startling result of Seattle's high sales tax is that residents of Washington voted with their automobiles. Portland ranks first among all of the top 50 metropolitan areas in the nation in retail sales per capita. Here is how *The Wall Street Journal* put it:

> "There is 18 percent more money to spend per person in Seattle than Portland, and yet 69 percent more is spent in Portland than Seattle. It's not that Portland residents are living high; it's that others are coming here to shop. Washington shoppers freely admit they travel to Portland to avoid the sales tax.

Net Domestic in-Migration as % of Population	Non-Farm Payroll Employment Growth	Unemployment Rate: 2007
17.2%	45.0%	4.8%
0.2%	15.2%	3.0%
3.5%	16.6%	4.5%
2.1%	28.3%	3.0%
1.6%	3.0%	3.5%
-5.4%	13.9%	3.2%
4.6%	17.7%	3.8%
-0.9%	4.0%	6.3%
6.9%	13.5%	5.9%
3.4%	20.3%	4.3%
3.32%	**17.74%**	**4.23%**
-1.99%	**8.08%**	**4.96%**
-4.8%	-4.0%	7.2%
4.0%	13.8%	3.6%
-2.3%	18.1%	6.2%
-5.6%	5.3%	4.5%
-0.3%	10.9%	4.6%
-1.7%	7.8%	3.8%
4.8%	12.7%	5.2%
-3.5%	0.6%	5.6%
-0.9%	7.2%	4.4%
-9.5%	8.3%	4.5%

Portland and Seattle are about two-and-a-half hours apart on I-5. Said one man: 'The savings on a $700 television is almost $60. You bet it's worth crossing the river.'"

Washington shoppers are blazing a new Oregon Trail.

Arthur Laffer found the same phenomenon to be true when he authored a tax study for Pete du Pont, then-governor of Delaware, in 1978. Delaware had the highest income tax rate in the nation and no sales tax. Delaware also had the highest retail sales per dollar of income in the United States.

Dying to Tax You: The Deadly Estate Tax

The estate tax is an immoral double tax on income that was already taxed when it was earned by the person who leaves an estate for his family. The joke in Washington, D.C., and many state capitals is that there ought to be a policy of "no taxation without respiration."

But the estate tax is not just wicked; it is a killer of jobs and incomes in states. Many studies indicate that the death tax is so inefficient, so adverse to saving and capital investment, and so complicated, that the states and the federal government would actually recoup much if not all of the revenues lost from this tax with higher tax receipts resulting from long term economic growth. Other studies suggest that the states and federal government will recapture between 30 and 50 percent of the static revenue losses. A recent study for the American Council for Capital Formation in Washington, D.C., co-authored by Douglas Holtz-Eakin and Donald Marples at Syracuse University, highlights the negative impact of the estate tax:

> *"Entrepreneurs are particularly hard hit by the estate tax as they face higher average estate tax rates and higher capital costs for new investment than do other individuals."*

The estate tax causes distortions in household decision making about work effort, saving and investment (and the loss of economic efficiency) that are even greater in size than those from other taxes on income from capital. This has led ALEC's Tax and Fiscal Policy Task Force to pass a model resolution asking Congress to permanently kill the death tax.

Case Study:
Yankee Doodle Went to ... Florida

State estate taxes are especially unwise because old people move to avoid them. In 2005, Connecticut Gov. Jodi Rell, a Republican, did a big favor for the state of Florida by enacting a 16 percent estate tax for the privilege of dying in Connecticut. *The Wall Street Journal* joked that then-Gov. Jeb Bush of Florida "should have sent her a thank-you note with a box of chocolates and a ribbon tied around it." Why? Because Ms. Rell signed into law an estate tax that might as well be called the Palm Beach Economic Development Act.

The legislators in Hartford hope the tax will raise $150 million in revenue each year – money that will come in only if the legislators in Hartford are also planning to build a Berlin Wall around the state. If not, high income people will leave for Florida or Texas with constitutional prohibitions against an estate tax. Thanks to the Connecticut death levy, a successful small business owner with a $10 million estate can save about $1 million by packing up and heading south. "The Connecticut legislature can't seem to comprehend that it is taxing away the very wealth-producing people that this state is dependent upon for an economic revival," says economist Dowd Muska of the state's Yankee Institute think tank.

Alas, at last count 22 states had estate taxes in hopes of "soaking their rich." Washington state imposes a 19 percent death tax, the most onerous in the nation.

Since Americans build up estates in part so that their legacies can be left to their children and grandchildren – and definitely not to politicians – seniors with medium and large estates are likely to shop around for low-tax venues.

A 2004 National Bureau of Economic Research study entitled, "Do the Rich Flee from High State Taxes?" found that states lose as many as one of every three dollars from their estate taxes because "wealthy elderly people change their state of residence to avoid high state taxes." And that was when states imposed effective estate tax rates that were only one-third as high as they are enacting now. Under these new soak-the-rich schemes, some states could lose so many wealthy seniors that they may actually lose revenue over time. Not surprisingly, it is generally the liberal, tax-and-spend blue states that are frantically reinstating punitive taxes on death. Will they ever learn? Over the past 20 years, about 1,000 people every day have been fleeing these high-tax blue states for low-tax red states. It's one reason the Northeast has suffered economically, and declined politically in terms of electoral votes.

In New York, about one in three tax dollars comes from those with earnings of $1 million or more, according to the Manhattan Institute. A rational policy out of Albany would be to lay down a red carpet to encourage more rich people to move in, or at least to stay there. Instead, with the current 16 percent estate tax, Albany politicians have effectively declared: "Invest anywhere but in New York."

Summing Up:
Why and How State Tax Policies Matter
The conclusion, which is getting to be nearly inescapable, is that states with high and rising tax burdens are more likely to suffer through economic decline, while those with lower and falling tax burdens are more likely to enjoy robust economic growth. Here is a quick synopsis of the results:

- The overall level of taxation has an inverse relationship to economic growth in the state;

- The change in the level and rate of taxation impacts state economic performance;

- High tax rates are especially harmful;

- Some state taxes have a more negative impact than others.

Case Study:
Bush Tax Cuts Stimulate the Economy
One of the best contemporary examples of how tax policy can affect economic behavior is the federal tax rate reductions of the last 25 years.

In the 1980s, President Ronald Reagan

TABLE 9: **ALEC-LAFFER STATE ECONOMIC PERFORMANCE INDEX: 1997-2007**

Rank	State	Absolute Domestic Migration	Per Capita Personal Income	Employment
1	Texas	3	14	8
2	Florida	1	19	6
3	Wyoming	24	1	4
4	Montana	21	5	7
5	Washington	10	13	13
6	Virginia	11	11	14
7	Idaho	13	22	3
8	Arizona	2	36	2
9	Nevada	6	35	1
10	Colorado	9	27	11
11	South Dakota	28	6	16
12	Oklahoma	22	4	26
13	New Mexico	27	16	9
14	North Dakota	35	2	19
15	Arkansas	15	15	33
16	Vermont	26	8	29
17	Maryland	39	9	17
18	South Carolina	7	38	22
19	New Hampshire	17	32	20
20	Georgia	4	48	18
21	Hawaii	38	21	12
22	Utah	23	43	5
23	North Carolina	5	46	21
24	Maine	20	26	27
25	Alaska	31	33	10
26	Alabama	16	20	39
27	California	49	12	15
28	Delaware	19	34	24
29	Oregon	12	45	23
30	Rhode Island	34	17	30
31	Kentucky	14	40	32
32	Tennessee	8	41	37
33	Nebraska	36	28	25
34	Minnesota	30	31	28
35	Louisiana	44	3	47
36	Massachusetts	43	7	44
37	Connecticut	41	10	43
38	West Virginia	29	25	41
39	Mississippi	33	23	46
40	New Jersey	47	24	31
41	Wisconsin	25	42	35
42	Kansas	40	29	34
43	New York	50	18	36
44	Missouri	18	44	42
45	Iowa	37	37	38
46	Pennsylvania	42	30	40
47	Indiana	32	47	45
48	Illinois	48	39	48
49	Ohio	45	49	49
50	Michigan	46	50	50

chopped the highest personal income tax rate from the confiscatory 70 percent rate that he inherited when he entered office to 28 percent when he left office. The resulting economic burst caused federal tax receipts to almost precisely double: from $517 billion to $1,032 billion.

In the early 2000s, the U.S. economy was on its back thanks to the stock market collapse after the dot-com bubble burst and the liquidation of some $6 trillion in wealth.[40] The jewel of the Bush economic plan was the reduction in tax rates on dividends from 39.6 percent to 15 percent, and on capital gains from 20 percent to 15 percent. These sharp cuts in the double tax on capital investment were intended to reverse the 2000-01 stock market crash and to inspire a revival in business capital investment, which had also collapsed during the recession. The tax cuts were narrowly enacted despite complaints of "tax cuts for the rich."

The Congressional Budget Office released its Budget and Economic Outlook in January of 2008. The numbers were an eye-popping vindication of the Laffer Curve and the Bush tax cut's real economic value. Federal tax revenues surged by $785 billion in the four years after those tax cuts, the largest increase in tax receipts adjusted for inflation in American history. Thanks to strong economic growth from the tax cuts, the federal budget deficit fell from a high of $413 billion or 3.6 percent of GDP in 2004, to a low of $163 billion or 1.2 percent of GDP in 2007, a drop of about $250 billion. From 2003 to 2007, individual income tax receipts soared more than 46 percent. The numbers for corporate income tax receipts are uncanny. Over the same time period, corporate income tax receipts exploded like a cap let off a geyser, up 180 percent. This represents a larger increase in four years than over the previous decade. Once again, tax rate cuts have created a virtuous chain reaction of higher economic growth, more jobs, higher corporate profits and finally more tax receipts.

Other Policy Variables

Which Affect State Competitiveness

Taxes are not the only way state policy determines the economic attractiveness of one state versus another. Our competitiveness index includes seven non-tax variables. To recap, these include:

- Debt Service as Share of Tax Revenue
- Public Employees Per 1,000 Residents
- Quality of State Legal System
- State Minimum Wage
- Workers' Compensation Costs
- Right-to-Work State (Yes or No)
- Tax or Expenditure Limitations

The Size of the Public Payroll

States and localities have been on a hiring binge of late. Moreover, a Cato Institute study shows that in 2005, public pay rose substantially faster than private pay. States with high government payrolls have a hard time downsizing because of the power of the bureaucracy and the unions behind them. Contracting out and competitive bidding lowers costs and provides greater flexibility in getting key personnel, but only when they are needed. States with big public sector payrolls are often the most inefficient in their spending, so this variable provides us with a government efficiency measure.

During the economic boom in the 1990s, local governments experienced massive increases in revenue. State tax collection rose by 86 percent, or approximately $250 billion, from 1990 to 2001. At the same time, local property-tax revenue increased by 60 percent. This dramatic rise in government revenue was accompanied by an equally dramatic increase in government spending. From 1990 to 2001, state general-fund spending increased by 85 percent.[41] Unions and social-service groups were thus in a prime position to expand public employee membership.

Over the last 50 years, unions have sought to organize the public sector to the point that, in some states, 60 to 70 percent of public employees are now union members. Increased union influence is straining government budgets across the country. A prime example is the inflated wage and benefits packages of public employees. The average public sector wage is now 37 percent higher than the average private sector wage. At the same time, local governments spend 128 percent more on average to fund public employee health care benefits than do private employers. Similarly, local government financing of retirement benefits averages 162 percent higher than that of the private sector.[42]

As a means of financing rising debt burdens, some states are abandoning pro-growth policies. For instance, according to the Rhode Island Public Expenditure Council, Rhode Island ranks fourth in average pay for public sector employees but 23rd in average private-sector wages. To finance public sector wages, Rhode Island has continually raised taxes, achieving the 10th highest total state and local tax burden in the country. As a result, businesses located in the state exhibit low rates of investment, with investment capital per employee dropping to 30 percent below the national average. Coincidentally, Rhode Island has one of the highest rates of public sector unionization, (62 percent), compared to the national average of 37 percent.

The State Legal System
The annual static cost of America's tort system is estimated to be around $328 billion. The dynamic costs are said to reach $537 billion, a total annual cost of $865 billion a year – the equivalent of an annual "tort tax" of about $9,827 on a family of four.[43] The Tillinghast division of consulting firm Towers-Perrin, calculates that the cost of excessive litigation in America is about two cents for every dollar of production. This includes everything from car accident claims, to investor lawsuits, to class-action suits. From 1997 to 2003, the average jury verdict in a medical malpractice case doubled from $500,000 to over $1 million, accord-

ing to the Manhattan Institute.[44] The average small business earning $1 million per year has to spend $20,000 each year on legal costs associated with lawsuits. When the legal system becomes a system of jackpot justice, with huge awards not related to the negligence or misbehavior of the company being sued, the biggest winners are trial lawyers. Businesses and citizens hoping to work in the state are the losers. Firms move out of states whose legal systems do not treat businesses fairly.

Mississippi recently enacted meaningful legal reform to ensure that businesses are not punished for appropriate behavior. Immediately following the passage of this legislation, Toyota announced the opening of a new plant in Mississippi. Medical malpractice premiums are already down at least 30 percent. Lawsuits against doctors are down 90 percent. The passage of what some have dubbed the "Mississippi Miracle" was essential to the survival of Mississippi's economy, businesses and health care system.

States that have enacted common sense reforms – such as malpractice insurance limits and proper venue reforms to discourage litigation tourism – have enjoyed greater economic success. A 2002 study by the U.S. Chamber Institute finds that per capita state product rises by about 0.75 percent for every 10 percent improvement in a state's legal climate.[45] This is why we include the state legal environment in our state ranking system.

Minimum Wage
Study after study shows that states with minimum wage or living wage requirements have fewer employment opportunities for those at the lower rungs of the economic ladder. Service jobs often flow to areas with the least onerous wage requirements. States with high minimum wages also have higher and more enduring unemployment rates. This variable is also a good measure of the relative power and influence of unions in a state. Union boss policies

are generally inimical to growth and bad for business.

Workers' Compensation

Workers' compensation costs vary widely among states. Workers' compensation is a qua-si-tax on businesses for hiring workers. Those states that have reformed their workers' compensation system have much lower employer costs, which allows businesses to pay workers more. In the early 2000s, California's workers' comp costs were sometimes three times higher than in states like Arizona and Nevada. States that reduce workers' compensation costs and payouts are generally more economically healthy and independent of union control and trial lawyer control.[46]

Right-to-Work

The Labor Department reported in early 2008 that union membership in America is at near all-time lows. Unions lost 15,000 members between 2006 and 2007, and the percentage of working Americans who belong to a union stands at 12.1 percent – significantly lower than the all time high of 34 percent in the 1950s. Today, only one in 13 private sector workers is a member of a labor union – the tiniest percentage in at least 60 years. There are four Americans who are stock holders for every one American union member.[47]

States are divided into two broad categories with respect to their union organizing laws. They are either right-to-work, which means workers have the right to not join the union, or non-right-to-work which means that workers have to join the union and pay dues if they work in a unionized industry. Ranking far and away at the top of non-right-to-work states are California and New York. Nearly half, (7.8 million) of the 15.7 million union members in the United States live in six states: California (2.5 million), New York (2.1 million), Illinois, Michigan and Pennsylvania (0.8 million each) and New Jersey (0.7 million).[48] As we have dem-

onstrated and will continue to demonstrate, the evidence points overwhelmingly to the fact that right-to-work states have much greater employment growth than non-right-to-work states.

Case Study:
Union Power Play in Iowa
After the 2006 midterm elections, union bosses were feeling their oats from big Democrat victories in state legislatures. To regain lost power, they sought to overturn right-to-work laws that had been on the books for years in some states. These laws prohibit employers from requiring workers to join a union as a condition of employment. They also protect workers from having to pay the union dues withholding tax extracted from their members' paychecks.

Iowa is one state where unions are flexing their muscles. Iowa has been a right-to-work state for 60 years. Now, for the first time in 40 years, the Democrats control both chambers of the legislature and the governorship. Though neither the new Gov. Chet Culver, nor the legislative candidates, campaigned on overturning right-to-work, the unions are demanding a vote to overturn the popular law. If their scheme succeeds, thousands of Iowa workers, who don't want to pay union dues, would be forced to do so if they work in a union shop. Those union dues can be used for political purposes, so many workers would be required to bankroll causes they don't believe in.

If the Iowa legislature were intentionally trying to chase jobs and employers out of the state, they couldn't come up with a better plan. Leo Troy, an economist at Rutgers University, finds that "right-to-work laws are strongly correlated with faster growth in jobs and personal income." Many international and domestic companies won't even consider locating a plant in a non-right-to-work state, which is why almost all the new foreign auto plants owned by Mercedes, Nissan, BMW and Honda are locating in southern states like Alabama, South

Carolina, Tennessee and Texas. One survey recently found that between 1986 and 2006, 11 right-to-work states added 104,000 auto manufacturing jobs, a 63 percent increase. The non-right-to-work states *lost* 130,000 auto jobs, or 15 percent of their total, over the same period. One leading plant selection consultant, Bob Goforth, put it this way: "If you're not a right-to-work state, you're not in the game."

Ironically, for years Iowa politicians have been searching for ways to reverse the state's population losses and its lethargic economic performance. If Iowa joins Rust Belt states like New Jersey, Pennsylvania, Michigan and Ohio and adopts forced unionism, the politicians might as well ask the last Iowa employer to turn off the lights before leaving.[49]

State Tax or Expenditure Limits

One successful strategy employed by some states to prevent squandering budget surpluses during times of economic expansion is a state Tax or Expenditure Limitation (TEL). One popular form of a TEL is a cap on taxes at some predetermined rate of growth. The most famous TEL was Proposition 13 in California, which capped property taxes in the state and ignited a nationwide tax revolt.

Colorado and Missouri each have constitutional tax limitations that restrict the growth of revenues to the rate of population growth plus inflation. Colorado's Taxpayers' Bill of Rights (TABOR) has been a boon to the economy of the state as shown in Figure 3.[50] Those states generally require that any revenue in excess of that amount be rebated to the people. For example, in 1997, Colorado rebated $142 million in tax revenues to taxpayers, while Missouri gave back $318 million in rebate tax credits. The evidence suggests that states with tax and expenditure limitations have done a better job of restraining state government growth than states without such disciplining measures. In 2002, the average per capita savings on taxes would have been $278 if every state had implemented a

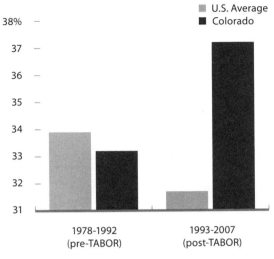

FIGURE 3
PER CAPITA INCOME GROWTH BEFORE AND AFTER TABOR

Source: National Taxpayers Union

population plus inflation tax cap prior to the post-9/11 expansion. Support for TABOR has been strong in Colorado. In 2008, a proposal to gut TABOR was placed on the ballot, but was defeated by a 55 to 45 percent margin.[51]

Another 11 states, including Arizona, California and Nevada, have adopted measures requiring that any tax increase by the legislature must pass by a supermajority vote in both houses.[52] Most require a two-thirds vote, but others require three-fourths or three-fifths. Those measures have been highly effective at deterring routine tax increases during non-emergencies.[53]

Supermajority requirements are most effective when they are applied to *all* tax increases and fees – whether income taxes, business taxes, sales taxes or excise taxes. (See ALEC's model language on supermajority requirements in Appendix C.) We believe supermajority requirements are effective deterrents to runaway taxing authority by the legislature, and recommend that every state adopt one of these constitutional restrictions on taxes.

ENDNOTES

1 Development Counsellors International. "A Continuing Survey of Corporate Executives with Site Selection Responsibilities." July 28, 2008.

2 Author's calculations, based on various published state budget reports.

3 Seib, Gerald F. "U.S. grows more like South; Northeast stands apart." *The Wall Street Journal.* October 1996.

4 Barone, Michael. "The Almanac of American Politics 2001." See also, Michael Barone, TownHall.com. Monday, June 11, 2007, *Red Nation, Blue Nation.*

5 Woolsey, Matt. "America's Richest Counties." Forbes. January 22, 2008. http://www.forbes.com/2008/01/22/counties-rich-income-forbeslife-cx_mw_0122realestate_slide_9.html?thisSpeed=30000.

6 Interview with Author.

7 Interview with Author.

8 Census Bureau, 2008.

9 Census Bureau, 2008; Author's calculations.

10 Census Bureau, 2008.

11 Census Bureau, 2008.

12 "2008 Statistical Abstract of the United States." Census Bureau.

13 National Right to Work Foundation. October 2008.

14 Census Bureau, 2008.

15 Moore, Stephen and Stansel, Dean. "The Myth of America's Underfunded Cities." Cato Institue, *Policy Analysis.* 1993.

16 Bureau of Labor Statistics.

17 Gittell, Ross and Rudokas, Jason. "New England Has the Highest Increase in Income Disparity in the Nation." *Carsey Institute.* Spring 2007.

18 *Ibid.*

19 Census Bureau, 2008.

20 "A Biography of Rudolph W. Giuliani." New York City Government. http://www.nyc.gov/html/records/rwg/html/.

21 Moore, Stephen. "Republicans Who Love Taxes." Cato Institute. February 23, 1993.

22 "Taxpayer Group Calls on Corzine to Denounce Assembly Democrat Tax Increase." Americans for Tax Reform. June 29, 2005; Hladky, Gregory B. "Tax Increase Certain." *New Haven Register.* February 12, 2007; Dubay, Curtis. "Significant Tax Increase for Pennsylvania." Tax Foundation. February 2007.

23 Cranshaw, Dave. "Aging population places focus on health care jobs." *Providence Business News.* November 19, 2005.

24 Interview with Author.

25 House of Representatives, Office of the Clerk.

26 http://money.cnn.com/magazines/fortune/fortune500/2008/index.html.

27 McMahon, E.J. "The Star Delusion." *New York Post.* June 13, 2006.

28 Mathur, Aparna and Hasset, Kevin. "Predicting Tax Reform." American Enterprise Institute. Working Paper. August 1, 2007.

29 Hayek, F.A. *The Constitution of Liberty.* University of Chicago Press, 1960, pp 306-323.

30 Vedder, Richard. "Taxes and Economic Growth." Taxpayers Network. September 2001.

31 Malanga, Steven. "The Mob that Whacked Jersey: How Rapacious Government Withered the Garden State." *City Journal,* Spring 2006.

32 See our page on New Jersey in Chapter Four.

33 "The Global Flat Tax Revolution: Lessons for Policy Makers." Center for Freedom and Prosperity. February 2008.

34 The correlation is -0.54.

35 Moore, Stephen and Tanner, Michael. "The Cost of Welfare." Cato Institute, Policy Analysis. 1995.

36 Vedder, Richard. "Taxes and Economic Growth." Taxpayers Network. September 2001.

37 Laffer, Arthur B. "Proposition 13: the Tax Terminator." June 27, 2003. Laffer Associates.

38 Becsi, Zsolt. "Do State and Local Taxes Affect Relative State Growth?" Federal Reserve Bank of Atlanta. *Economic Review.* March/April 1996, p. 34.

39 The American College of Trust and Estate Counsel. State Death Tax Study. Revised April 21, 2008.

40 Moore, Stephen. "Bullish on Bush: How George Bush's Ownership Society Will Make America Stronger." Madison Books. 2004.

41 Malanga, Steven. "The Conspiracy Against the Taxpayers: Why Public Servants Live Better than the Public." *City Journal.* Autumn 2005.

42 *Ibid.*

43 McQuillan, Lawrence J. and Abramyan, Hovannes. "The Tort Tax." *The Wall Street Journal.* March 27, 2007.

44 Manhattan Institue. Trial Lawyers Inc., New York, NY. 2003.

45 David, Jesse. "The Secondary Impacts of Asbestos Liabilities." (Prepared by NERA Economic Consulting for the U.S. Chamber of Commerce). January 23, 2003. www.legalreformnow.com/resources/012303secondar.pdf.

46 McQuillan, Lawrence and Glober, Andrew. "How to Fix California's Broken Workers' Compensation System." Pacific Research Institute. December 17, 2003. http://www.pacificresearch.org/pub/sab/entre/Workers_Comp.pdf.

47 "Union Members in 2007." Bureau of Labor Statistics. Department of Labor. January 25, 2008.

48 *Ibid.*

49 To learn more about the benefits of right-to-work in Iowa, see: Hough, Michael. "A Tale of Two States." *Inside ALEC.* October 2007. http://www.alec.org/am/pdf/apf/taleoftwocities.pdf.

50 New, Michael J. "Reforming TABOR in Colorado." Cato Institute. May 2, 2004.

51 Sepp, Pete and Rasmussen, Kristina. "Election 2008 Results: How Taxpayers Fared at the Ballot Box." National Taxpayers Union. November 11, 2008.

52 National Association of State Budget Officers. "Budget Processes in the States." Summer 2008.

53 Moore, Stephen. "Voters Say No to New Taxes..." *National Review Online.* March 5, 2004. http://www.nationalreview.com/moore/moore200403051114.asp.

San Antonio, Texas

Chapter Two

Texas vs. California

Texas vs. California

At the time of this book's publication, California was in the middle of its longest budget impasse ever. Gov. Schwarzenegger had warned the federal government that his state may need an emergency loan just to make ends meet. During this record-long – and yet oh so typical – budget crisis, the usual suspects in Sacramento and the media excoriated the governor as a modern-day Ebenezer Scrooge. To hear the popular press explain it, fiscal conservatives wanted to balance the budget on the backs of the poor, rather than having the rich pay their "fair share." In fact, it was the governor who proposed a one-cent sales tax increase as a counter to the 12 percent highest marginal income tax rate proposed by the legislature's Democrats. Ah, if only this were true.

In reality, despite his campaign pledge to "cut up the credit cards," the muscular governor lacked the political strength to resist a huge spending binge during his tenure. The budget that just passed amidst much gnashing of teeth, was a $144 billion grab-bag that actually contains the most General Fund spending in state history. And the cold-hearted austerity measures touted by the governor's office as a "rainy day fund with teeth," contain all sorts of loopholes that can be exploited by future legislatures to suit their spending desires.

Some of us have been arguing, literally for decades, that the citizens of California control their own destiny. People deserve the governments they get. It's true, there's not much California can do about periodic earthquakes.

However, they *do* have the power to stop their periodic *budgetary* earthquakes, if only they had the discipline. California's fiscal system creates the boom-bust cycle in tax revenue that causes the familiar pattern of spending hikes during the fat years, which inevitably lead to crises every time the economy slows down.

Specifically, the problem is that California has the most "progressive" (ah, what a deceptive term!) income tax code in the country. Tax progressivity exaggerates the normal ups-and-downs of the overall economy, and explains why income tax receipts in California are among the most volatile of all the 50 states. When times are good, California citizens earn more, pushing many of them into a higher tax bracket, thereby giving the state a larger fraction of a bigger pie. But then the opposite holds true during recession: People earn less income in general, thereby shrinking of the tax base, as many fall into lower tax brackets and pay a smaller fraction of smaller paychecks. This one-two punch explains why hard times seem to hit California harder than other states.

Of course, what seems obvious to us appears as right-wing science fiction to many California legislators and pundits. They claim that serious reform of the tax code is unrealistic, that a large state has many duties to fulfill, and that it is irresponsible to call for a return to a 19th century view of the role of government.

But here's where the present chapter comes in. The insiders in Sacramento don't need to look to the original Thirteen Colonies to see small government in action. In fact, we direct their attention only three states to the east. Not only does Texas lack a highly progressive income tax – it doesn't have one at all! We hasten to add that the last time we checked, Texas still had literate kids, navigable roads and functioning hospitals, which one would think impossible given the hysterical rhetoric coming from defenders of California's punitive tax system. In fact, the Texas success story illustrates everything we have been recommending for California all these years. How do they do that?

The Economic Scorecard:
Texas vs. California

In life, once every now and then, we come across something that is simple and says it all. In the 1950s, for example, when asked about life in Canada, the person who was asked the question answered that 90 percent of all Canadians live within 100 miles of the U.S.-Canadian border, while only 10 percent of all Americans live within 100 miles of the same border. That said it all.

When comparing California with Texas, U-Haul says it all. To rent a 26-foot truck one-way from San Francisco to Austin, the charge is $3,236, and yet the one-way charge for that same truck from Austin to San Francisco is just $399. Clearly what is happening is that far more people want to move from San Francisco to Austin than vice versa, so U-Haul has to pay its own employees to drive the empty trucks back from Texas. The great thing about this example is that it's a market price set in the real world – you don't need to rely on a fancy economic model to see our point. If two haughty-taughty food critics were arguing about restaurants A and B, the average Joe could ignore their jargon and just look at which place had a line out the door. When it comes to California and Texas, people are backed up, waiting to move out of the former and into the latter. We rest our case.

Economics isn't a zero-sum game. If one state does well economically, generally speak-

ing, that is a boon to the citizens of the other 49 states as well. Even so, we can compare the economic performance of different states to assess how well – or how poorly – their government policies promote a strong economy.

When it comes to interstate economic competition, there is no "finish line." It is a never-ending struggle requiring states to consistently maintain an advantageous economic environment *vis-à-vis* other states. States that establish and maintain the most pro-growth economic environments will be leaders in the inter-state economic competition. This is especially true with respect to key economic rivals. A key economic rivalry is the one between Texas and California – the two economic heavyweights of the United States.

Both Texas and California have the allure of geography, and the economies of both states have outperformed national trends. But, current policies matter for future economic performance. Texas' superior policies over the past several years are making the Lone Star State more resilient to the current economic downturn and will provide powerful tailwinds for the Texas economy going forward. The opposite is true for California.

The results of a head-to-head competition between the two economic heavyweights are not even close. Economically, Texas is just too much for California to handle. At the state level, there are six broad categories in which the states compete: taxes on labor income, taxes on capital income, taxes on consumption, overall tax environment, government spending policies and government regulatory policies. On net, Texas's economic environment is more competitive in all of these categories (see Table 10).

Current state economic policies have important implications for future economic performance. Texas's win over California is an encouraging sign for Texas's future and an ominous sign for California's. Texas's future prosperity looks bright: stronger income, wealth and employment growth will occur in the Lone Star

TABLE 10
TEXAS VS. CALIFORNIA

COMPETITIVE EVENT	CALIFORNIA	TEXAS	WINNER
Taxes on Labor			
Top Marginal Personal Income Tax Rate	10.30%	0.00%	Texas
Marginal Personal Income Tax (average income earner)	9.30%	0.00%	
Taxes on Capital			
Property Tax Burden (per $1,000 of personal income)	$26.63	$41.06	Texas
Estate/Inheritance Tax Levied	NO	NO	
Top Marginal Rate: Income, Dividends and Capital Gains	10.3%	0.0%	
Top Marginal Corporate Tax Rate	8.84%	5% [1]	
Taxes on Consumption			
State Sales Tax Rate	7.25%	6.25%	Texas
Sales Tax Burden (per $1,000 of personal income)	$23.72	$23.31	
Overall Tax Environment			
Overall Tax Burden	$118.33	$99.49	Texas
Personal Income Tax Progressivity	$34.88	$0.00	
Recently Legislated Tax Changes (per $1,000 of personal income)	+$0.88	-$3.92	
Number of Tax Expenditure Limits	2	1	
Regulatory Environment			
State Liability System Rank	44th	41st	Texas
State Minimum Wage	$8.00	$6.55	
Average Workers' Compensation Cost	$2.72	$2.61	
Right-to-Work State	NO	YES	
Government Spending Policies			
Total Expenditures per Capita	$10,099.89	$6,845.26	Texas
Average Growth in State Government Expenditures	7.04%	5.96%	

Sources: CCH Tax Research Network, Laffer Associates, Bureau of Economic Analysis, U.S. Census Bureau, Texas Public Policy Foundation

State relative to California, as well as the country as a whole. The opposite is true for California: weaker economic performance and less relative growth will ensue. The relative success of Texas gives California policy-makers a realistic goal to shoot for. If they can do it in Texas, they can do it in California, too.

Texas vs. California: Economic Growth Prospects for the 21st Century
States fiercely compete with one another – they compete for jobs, they compete for businesses and they compete for people. The results of this economic competition have real implica-

tions for future state economic performance. As in other arenas of life, when it comes to state economies, strong competition is a good thing because it keeps everyone striving for excellence. States with strong competitive environments have flourishing economies, while states with weak competitive environments have struggling economies. A dismal competitive environment in Michigan, for instance, led to the Michigan Recession, while the rest of the country prospered.[2]

Arizona provides another historical example. Prior to Fife Symington's election as governor (in a runoff in 1991), Arizona was the textbook case on how to screw up a state. Govs. Babbitt (1978-1987), Mecham (1987-1988) and Mofford (1988-1991) were unmitigated disasters. Their playbooks raised taxes, and then when that didn't work, raised them some more. (Sounds familiar, eh?) The results were just what you would expect. Not only did Arizona bungle its fiscal situation badly, but it also became the buffoon of states – and there is some stiff competition in that category. The Martin Luther King Day fracas was truly embarrassing. Then came Gov. Mecham's impeachment, followed by the Keating crisis and the prominence of Arizona's senatorial contingent in the bad press of that time – two of the Keating Five were Arizona senators. Then came the sting on Arizona's legislature and the wholesale corruption the sting uncovered. Arizona was the worst of all the states, and asset values reflected the Arizona environment. You couldn't have gotten more depressed asset values if you had employed Mephistopheles himself. We believe asset values are a very good indication of expert opinion on the prospects of a region because investors are paying for ownership over a future flow of returns. Investors did not like what they saw in Arizona. Although economics is a neutral science, we can't help but point out that the same crew that was up to its neck in S&L corruption also helped themselves to more of the taxpayers' hard-earned money.[3]

Many factors impact a state's competitive environment. A number of these factors – such as climate, natural resources or geographical location – do not change. State economic policies (i.e. tax, expenditure and regulatory policies) vary across states and across time within a state and have significant implications for a state's economic prospects. For this reason, state economic policies are crucial economic competitiveness metrics. As we wrote earlier, California can't do much about its earthquakes, and Texas can't do much about hurricanes, but each state can control its economic future. As we have shown and will continue to explain, Texas has been doing a much better job on this front.

The result of a head-to-head competition between Texas and California is an economic blowout. The economic environment in Texas has significant advantages over California. The implications of this competitive advantage are clear: Texas's economic prospects are bright and the Texas economy will significantly outperform California's. Put another way: In a heavyweight competition between Texas and California, Texas wins!

State Economic Policies Really Do Matter!

We have been preaching the low-tax, business-friendly religion for decades now, and it never ceases to amaze us how many seemingly intelligent, articulate people refuse to admit that state economic policies really do matter. During the current budget crisis in California, apologists for its tax-and-spend ways would dismiss supply-side "myths," and instead blame California's woes on "the economy" – as if state policies don't affect the economy. Some analysts look at migratory data (which we'll examine in a bit) and say, "It's not high taxes driving people out – it's the lack of jobs."

Talk about begging the question! But because this opposing view is so prevalent, some background information on the importance of the competitive events is appropriate. Whether it is excessive taxation, excessive regulations or excessive expenditures, the result is the same – poor economic policies lead to poor economic outcomes.

Excessive taxation, regulations and expenditures are detrimental to labor and capital, poor and rich, men and women, and old and young. Poor economic policies are equal opportunity tormentors. In the short run, poor economic policies lead to higher taxes on labor or capital and lower after-tax earnings. In the longer run, mobile factors "vote with their feet" and leave the state, leaving immobile factors (such as low wage workers and land and property) to suffer the tax and regulatory burdens. Businesses suffer lower after-tax earnings, and residents suffer decreased employment growth. The incentives to work, save and produce are all diminished.

Government expenditures also directly impact the overall economic growth environment. In order to spend money, the government must first take it from the private sector, either through taxes or borrowing – there is no Tooth Fairy it can draft into service. Some people describe the process as robbing Peter to pay Paul, but it's actually worse because the troll needs his toll as well. In other words, for the government to give $1,000 to Paul, it needs to take, say, $1,300 from Peter, because Philip the IRS agent needs to get his $300 salary. To make matters worse still, we have to recognize that the higher the tax rate, the greater the "deadweight loss," meaning the fewer trades that occur, even though people in the private sector would mutually benefit from them. So to give Paul that $1,000, and Philip, the tax man, his $300 salary, we need to rob Peter of $1,300, which leads him to turn down an offer to work overtime for Phineas. (At this point we'll stop, since we're running out of names that start with "P.")

The above arguments don't establish the case for anarchy – some things must be paid for by the government. Our point is that the costs of government expenditures are typically understated. Depending upon how these revenues are spent, the contribution of the government expenditures to the economy may be less than the value of the money to the economy prior to its removal from the private sector. When this is the case, government expenditures create additional negative impacts on economic growth and development beyond the tax impacts already considered.

One of the present writers has produced decades of research demonstrating that states that impose high and/or increasing taxes, burdensome regulations and poor expenditure policies, experience relative income and population declines, rising relative unemployment and declines in housing values. Alternatively, states that impose a pro-growth economic policy consisting of low taxes, appropriate regulations and disciplined expenditure policies, experience accelerated income and population growth, declining unemployment and rising housing values.

Examining the economic growth performance in the states with the highest tax burdens compared to the economic growth performance in the states with the lowest tax burdens illustrates these trends. Not surprisingly, the economic performance of the low-tax states beats the economic performance of the high-tax states. For example, back in Table 8, we compare the performance of those states with the highest and lowest corporate income tax rates. Not surprisingly, we find that the states which penalize corporate profits have slower growth in income and population.

Further substantiating the relationship between personal income taxes and economic growth, we compared state tax rates to state personal income growth in Table 7. While other factors impact state personal income growth, there is a negative and significant relationship between a state's top marginal personal income tax rate and the economic growth rate in the state – the higher the top marginal personal income tax rate, the lower the expected economic growth rate.

Incidentally, the comparable unemployment rates (4.2 percent vs. 4.4 percent) per se, are no strike against our thesis. For one thing, the low-tax states had much higher population growth than the high-tax states, so they had more work to do to keep their unemployment rates down. Economic theory suggests that as long as wage rates can adjust, in the long-run, everybody can find a job who wants one. The difference is that people can get *better-paying* jobs in the low-tax states, as Tables 7 and 8 clearly show.

The pattern of low-tax states economically outperforming high-tax states is consistent with the theory of incentives, which provides the basis for establishing an optimal tax policy. Changes to marginal tax rates are critical for growth because they change incentives to demand, and supply work effort and capital.

Firms base their decisions to employ workers, in part, on the workers' total cost to the firm. Holding all else equal, the greater the cost to the firm of employing each additional worker, the fewer workers the firm will employ. Conversely, the lower the marginal cost per worker, the more workers the firm will hire. For the firm, the decision to employ is based upon gross wages paid, a concept which encompasses all costs borne by the firm.

Workers, on the other hand, care little about the cost to the firm of employing them. The worker really only cares about his *net* pay in exchange for the expected amount of effort, after all the deductions and taxes are taken out. The greater net wages received, the more willing a worker is to work. If wages received fall, workers find work effort less attractive and they will do less of it. The difference between what it costs a firm to employ a worker, and what that worker receives net, is the "tax wedge."

Government economic policies matter because these policies impact the incentives to work, save and invest for workers, employers and investors. States with greater incentives

to work, save and invest have higher economic growth rates.

With respect to the competition between Texas and California, the future economic prospects of these two powerhouse states are crucially dependent on the respective impact that each state's policies have on the incentives to work, save and produce. The competitive events analyzed below are designed to capture these impacts.

Introducing the Competitors

Texas and California have a similar history. The U.S.-Mexican War began with Texas's entry into the United States – it ended with California's. The lure of climate, opportunity and resources helped both Texas and California grow into the two largest states in the country. Thanks to this extraordinary growth, the economies of Texas and California now dwarf the size of most countries. As of 2006, the California and Texas economies were the 7th and 10th largest economies in the world, respectively.[4] And yet, the recent performance of both of these states has varied.

Overall Economic Growth

Texas's overall economy has grown more than California's since 1998 – even including the impacts of the Internet revolution on California's economy during the late 1990s (see Figure 4). On average, Texas's real economy has grown 4.3 percent a year since 1998. In contrast, California's real economy has grown at a slower rate of 3.6 percent, and the nation as a whole has grown at an even slower, but still impressive, rate of 2.9 percent. Since the end of the tech boom, the economic environment has skewed even further in Texas's favor. Since the end of the 9/11 recession, real economic growth accelerated in Texas (4.9 percent), while California's economic growth rate was slightly less strong at 3.3 percent. Income growth tells a similar story, albeit slightly more favorable to Texas (see Figure 5).

FIGURE 4
CUMULATIVE GDP GROWTH:
TEXAS AND CALIFORNIA, 1998-2007
scaled to 1.0 as of 1998

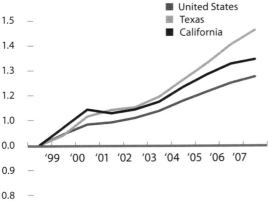

FIGURE 5
CUMULATIVE PERSONAL INCOME GROWTH:
TEXAS AND CALIFORNIA, 1998-2007
scaled to 1.0 as of 1998

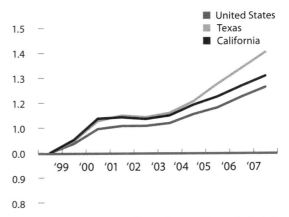

Source: Bureau of Economic Analysis

Source: Bureau of Economic Analysis

Real personal income in Texas grew 4.24 percent a year on average between 1998 and 2007. This exceeded average personal income growth in California over this time period (3.51 percent) and for the nation as a whole (2.99 percent). Since 2002, Texas's real personal income growth premium has expanded further as personal income growth in Texas has continued expanding 4.2 percent a year while real personal income growth has slowed in California (2.87 percent) and for the nation as a whole (2.66 percent).

From a broad macroeconomic perspective, the Texas economy has been expanding at an accelerated rate compared to California and the nation overall.

Employment

The employment trends of the competitors have been more erratic. Employment growth in both Texas and California have outpaced employment growth in the nation as a whole. Employment growth in Texas is currently outpacing employment growth in California, though this was not the case from 1997 through 2003.

Table 11 and Figure 6 each illustrate that

California's employment growth of 3.3 percent during the tech boom years was especially strong. Texas's employment growth rate of 3.1 percent was also exceptional, but did not keep pace with California's. Employment growth turned to declines from 2001 to 2003 in both Texas and California, as it did for the country as a whole. Since the "jobless recovery" has ended, Texas's employment record has been stellar – growing more than twice as fast as California and nearly twice as fast as employment growth for the country as a whole.

Population Trends

Every day, people vote with their feet by moving, and over the past eight years, more people have voted for Texas than California. The total U.S. population is estimated to have grown one percent a year between 2000 and 2007. California's population grew at approximately the national average for a total population increase of 2.7 million people. Texas's average annual growth was nearly twice the national average (1.9 percent or a total population increase of 3.1 million people).

Total population increases include what the

TABLE 11
**AVERAGE ANNUAL EMPLOYMENT GROWTH
IN SELECT PERIODS: TEXAS AND CALIFORNIA**

	U.S.	Texas	California
1998-2000	2.4%	3.1%	3.3%
2001-2003	-0.7%	-0.8%	-0.7%
2004-2007	1.5%	2.9%	1.4%

Source: Bureau of Labor Statistics

FIGURE 6
**CUMULATIVE EMPLOYMENT GROWTH:
TEXAS AND CALIFORNIA, 1998-2007**
scaled to 1.0 as of 1998

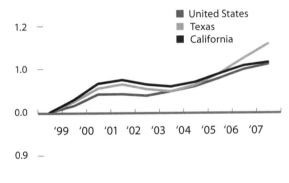

Source: Bureau of Labor Statistics

U.S. Census calls "natural increases," or total births and deaths. Such measures do not reflect people *choosing* to enter or leave a state. The U.S. Census tracks a more accurate measure of Americans voting for states with their feet called "net internal migration," which tracks the choices U.S. residents make with respect to the state in which they want to live. Net internal migration is measured as the number of residents moving to a state (from another U.S. state), minus the number of residents leaving the state (for another U.S. state). By this measure, California looks sickly, while Texas looks stellar. On net, over one-half million U.S. residents chose to move to Texas from some other state between 2000 and 2007 – the third highest total behind Flor-

ida and Arizona. California, on the other hand, lost over 1.2 million residents within the same time period. The net internal migration figure removes the noise from California's influx of foreign immigrants, and allows us to see what people do once they're in the Golden State.

Texas's total package is attractive enough to retain, on net, all of its current U.S. residents, and attract one-half million more. California's total package is not attractive enough to retain, on net, all of its current U.S. residents. Of course, we realize that relocating one's life is a personal decision, but economics matters too. It's true that an aspiring actress may move to Hollywood, regardless of marginal tax rates, or that a swooning boy may move to Texas to marry his Southern sweetheart, even though he is completely oblivious to job prospects. Even though individuals make decisions for all sorts of reasons, in the aggregate, economic policies will affect the totals.

In January 2006, Arthur Laffer made the decision to leave California and go to a zero income tax state (Tennessee) where he had never been before. At the age of 65, he and his family packed up their belongings and left the Golden State for good. And why? Because of taxes, and the transformation of Gov. Schwarzenegger from a proponent of pro-growth, supply-side policies, into a pandering, pro-union, big spending appeaser of anti-growth interests. Don't get us wrong, we have worked closely with the famous actor, and have enjoyed a lot of good times. But in terms of the governor's awful policies, Laffer decided enough was enough. And how does Laffer feel about his decision now? *Great.* Everything he knew about Tennessee before he left California turned out to be true, and the preponderance of things he was unsure of came out far better than he had expected.

The data presented above show that Texas's economy has been stellar. Perhaps more importantly, the economic policy environment is very pro-growth, indicating that Texas will experience future job and income growth. The same cannot be said of California. The economic environment in California has taken a turn for the worse. Out of control spending, rising regulatory burdens and rising taxes, all point toward diminished economic opportunities in California now and in the future. Such outcomes are the consequences of losing the state economic competition, and the rewards of winning.

And Now the Main Event

The competition between Texas and California is measured in three broad categories:

- Tax Policy
- Regulatory Policy
- Expenditure Policy

Government policies, especially tax policies, have large and varied impacts on the competitive economic environment of a state. To account for these broad impacts, it is useful to track the impact of government tax policies on the economy's production process.

For instance, someone has to exert effort to create all of the goods and services in our economy. Economists generally classify this effort as the "labor input" of production. The other inputs of production are classified as capital or the tools and machines people use (which comes from savings and investments), and technology or the know-how/skills needed to create the things we need and want. Government policies matter because the taxes levied by governments, or the expenditures made by governments, or the regulations imposed by governments impact the inputs of production. These impacts either discourage or encourage the use of labor, capital and technology.

Due to the importance of labor and capital in the economic process, it is useful to further divide the tax-policy competition into its impact on labor and capital, the tax burden on consumption and the overall tax burden in the state.

Competition I: The Tax Burden on Labor

People do not work to pay taxes. People work to earn the highest wages possible, after taxes. High (or rising) taxes on labor reduce workers' after-tax wages, thereby reducing their incentive to work. Because workers can receive a higher (or rising) after-tax wage for the same gross wage if they moved to a state with a lower (or falling) tax burden, the economic climates of other states are critical. People have an incentive to leave a state with high (or rising) taxes on labor income and relocate to a state where the taxes on labor income are lower (or falling). As people respond to these incentives, income growth, employment growth and overall economic growth suffer in the state with high or rising taxes.

California levies a progressive income tax system – as people's income increases, the tax rate on the higher income increases. It is this marginal tax rate that is relevant from an economic perspective. Because the marginal tax rate varies depending upon the income of the worker in California, we track two marginal income tax rates: the marginal tax rate faced by the highest income earners and the marginal tax rate faced by the average (or median) worker.

FIGURE 7
**MARGINAL INCOME TAX RATES:
TEXAS AND CALIFORNIA**

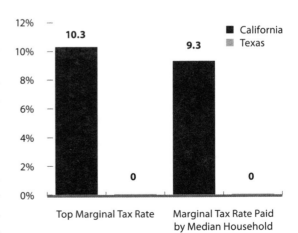

Source: CCH Tax Research Network

California imposes the highest top marginal state income tax rate in the country – 10.3 percent. The median household income in California in 2006 was $55,319.[5] The average or median family faces a 9.3 percent marginal state income tax rate in California.

Texas does not impose a state income tax. By definition, the marginal income tax rate for both the highest income earners and the average worker is zero percent. Figure 7 summarizes the comparisons between Texas and California.

These comparative tax rates clearly illustrate Texas's economic attractiveness and California's economic unattractiveness. If there are two workers earning $55,319 a year – one in California and one in Texas – then the Texas worker's after-tax income would be $1,952 higher than the California worker's after-tax income.[6] Texas's tax savings provides workers with a 3.5 percent raise compared to their California counterparts. This is a huge difference, despite the pooh-poohing of our critics. With respect to the income taxes imposed on labor competition, Texas is the winner.

COMPETITION I WINNER: TEXAS

Competition II: The Tax Burden on Capital

Capital taxes are more complicated than taxes on labor income. State governments do not treat all forms of capital equally. Oftentimes, states (and the federal government) double or even triple tax capital income. All factories, equipment, land, etc., used to produce goods and services are considered capital from an economic perspective.[7] Purchases of capital require an investment on the part of businesses or individuals. Businesses do not invest as a matter of social conscience. They invest to earn the highest possible rate of return on their investments. Businesses and other investors will only purchase capital if the expected return on capital exceeds all costs – including all tax costs.

Taxing the return on capital is synonymous with taxing saving and investment. High taxes on savings and investment lowers the after-tax rate of return from saving and investing, diminishing the incentives to invest. Lower investment translates into a smaller and less productive capital stock. Income, employment and economic growth are all subsequently reduced.

Returns on saving and investment are taxed in many ways. First, corporations earn profits, which are the returns to the investors or the owners of the "capital." These profits are subject to corporate income taxes, or in the case of some firms, personal income taxes. If the profits are then distributed to investors as a taxable dividend, the income is taxed again through dividend taxes. Should the owner of the company – or any income generating asset – decide to sell his ownership rights to the capital, any increase in the value of the stream of payments from the capital (capital gains) are taxed. Similarly, the interest income from savings or bond investments faces income taxes. Finally, states will tax the value of some assets in addition to the income stream generated from those assets – another instance of states taxing the same income multiple times – by taxing property and imposing estate and gift taxes. Table 12 summarizes the tax burden on capital imposed on California versus Texas.

Neither California nor Texas imposes an estate tax – a very encouraging sign for both states. With respect to property taxation, thanks to Proposition 13, California is more competitive than Texas. The tax burden on property in Texas is $41.06 per $1,000 of personal income, while it is only $26.63 per $1,000 of personal income in California. With respect to all other forms of capital taxation, Texas is more competitive than California. Additionally, Texas passed tax legislation in the spring of 2006, later revised in 2007, aimed at reducing this property tax burden. The tax change cut the school property tax by 33 percent, from $1.50 to $1 out of every $100. They also amended the state business tax, adopting a controversial one percent gross receipts, or margins tax.[8] The five percent rate in Tables 12 and 13 represents the effective tax rate on business income if the gross receipts tax were adjusted to resemble a more normal corporate income tax rate structure. Also, both of these changes took effect after the latest period for which property tax revenue data was available. We would therefore expect the Texas property tax burden to fall noticeably in the near future.

California's property tax burden advantage is, however, overwhelmed by its excessive tax burden on income, dividends, capital gains and corporate income. Our statistics overwhelmingly illustrate California's significant competitive disadvantages.

As discussed above, the marginal tax rate a business or individual faces determines the incentives to engage in productive economic activity. In order to see the impacts from these taxes on incentives to acquire capital (i.e., save and invest) we incorporate the impact of federal taxes and simply follow the money.

Imagine two representative companies facing the highest marginal income tax brackets earning an additional $1,000 in profits. One firm is located in California, the other in Texas. Each representative company faces a federal income tax liability. Depending upon the company's structure, the tax liability could be either the top marginal corporate income tax rate or top marginal personal income tax rate. In this example, the representative companies pay a weighted share of the corporate and personal income tax rates. The weights representing the share of total net income subject to the corporate income tax and the share of total net income subject to the personal income tax are calculated based on the share of total net corporate income subject to corporate taxes as reported by the Internal Revenue Service (IRS) Statistics of Income data.[9]

With respect to federal income tax rates, the division is irrelevant, as the top corporate and personal income tax rates are both 35 percent. The distinction for California and Texas

TABLE 12
TAXATION OF CAPITAL

Taxes on Capital	California	Texas
Property Tax Burden (per $1,000 of personal income)	$26.63	$41.06
Estate/Inheritance Tax Levied	NO	NO
Top Marginal Rate: Income, Dividends, and Cap. Gains	10.3%	0.0%
Top Marginal Corporate Tax Rate	8.84%	5.0%

Source: U.S. Census Bureau, CCH Tax Research Network

TABLE 13
TAXATION OF CORPORATE INCOME

	California	Texas
Additional Net Income	**$1,000.00**	**$1,000.00**
Federal Income Tax Liability		
Corporate Income Tax (weighted)	13.7%	13.7%
Personal Income Tax (weighted)	21.3%	21.3%
State Income Tax Liability		
Corporate Income Tax (weighted)	3.5%	5.0%
Personal Income Tax (weighted)	6.3%	0.0%
Additional Net Income After Taxes	**$586.76**	**$637.17**

Source: U.S. Census Bureau, CCH Tax Research Network

income tax rates is relevant. In California, the top corporate income tax rate is 8.84 percent, while the top personal income tax rate is 10.3 percent. In Texas, there is no corporate income tax rate, but there is a one percent gross receipts tax. To put the gross receipts tax on a comparable basis to California's net income tax, we transform the gross receipts tax rate into an equivalent net income tax rate.[10] Based on this transformation, Texas's one percent margins tax is the "equivalent" of a five percent net in-

TABLE 14
CORPORATE INCOME SUBJECT TO DIVIDEND TAXES

	California	Texas
Additional Net Income After Taxes	$586.76	$637.17
Earnings Paid Out	$496.80	$539.48
Earnings Paid Out Subject to Dividends Tax	$156.83	$170.30
Individual Dividend Tax		
Federal	15.0%	15.0%
State	10.3%	0.0%
Total After-tax Income (incl. retained earnings)	$547.09	$611.62

Source: Bureau of Economic Analysis

TABLE 15
TAXATION OF INTEREST AND CAPITAL GAINS INCOME

	California	Texas
Individual Interest Income	$1,000.00	$1,000.00
Federal Interest Income Taxes	35.0%	35.0%
State Interest Income Taxes	10.3%	0.0%
Individual Interest Income (after-tax)	$583.05	$650.00
Capital Gains Income	$1,000.00	$1,000.00
Federal Capital Gains Taxes (long-term)	15.0%	15.0%
Federal Capital Gains Taxes (short term)	35.0%	35.0%
State Capital Gains Taxes	10.3%	0.0%
Capital Gains Income (after-tax)*	$748.88	$834.87

*Based on estimates of long-term vs. short-term capital gains from the IRS.

Source: Internal Revenue Service

come tax. We use the five percent figure as the appropriate corporate income tax rate for our calculations (see Table 12).

The final line of Table 13 calculates the addi-

tional after-tax net income to each one of these companies if they were located in Texas versus California, and takes into account the deductibility of state income taxes. As Table 13 clearly shows, just by locating in Texas, companies can earn an extra $50.41 per $1,000 of net income, or an *8.6 percent higher* after-tax return.

Texas's competitive advantage grows even more because the income tax burden imposed on this income is not finished. The owners of a corporation (individuals) that pay dividends face another round of taxation on this income. Using national payout-ratios based on the Bureau of Economic Analysis National Income and Product Account (NIPA) tables and the ratio of companies that are dividend-paying, we can estimate the percentage of net income subject to dividends taxes. These figures are summarized in Table 14.

This table also illustrates that in total, if both a company and the individual owning the company are located in Texas rather than California, then both the company and its stockholders can earn an extra $64.53 per $1,000 of net income, or an *11.8 percent higher* after-tax return.

There are still more taxes on capital. California and the federal government also tax interest income and capital gains income – Texas does not. This provides another after-tax rate return advantage to the owners of capital from locating in Texas, compared to California. Using a similar methodology, we track $1,000 of interest and capital gains income if it were earned by an individual living in Texas, compared to that same income if it were earned by an individual living in California. The results are summarized in Table 15.

This table also illustrates that the after-tax return to both interest income and capital gains income is significantly higher in Texas compared to California. The after-tax interest and capital gains income for a $1,000 investment is *11.5 percent higher* in Texas than in California for the exact same investment.

The significant after-tax return premium in Texas compared to California with respect to corporate income, interest income and capital gains income gives Texas a significant competitive advantage *vis-à-vis* California in attracting businesses and investors. California's advantages with respect to property tax burdens, which equates to an advantage of 1.4 percent of personal income, does not compensate for the significant disadvantages with respect to the remaining capital taxes in these two states.

The clear winner of Competition II: Texas has the more competitive capital tax environment.
COMPETITION II WINNER: TEXAS

Competition III:
The Tax Burden on Consumption

Texas has to fund state operations. Here, the reader might suppose that *surely* California must impose a smaller tax on consumption than Texas, given California's loss in the tax on labor and tax on capital competitions. Yet such a hypothesis is incorrect. Texas's and California's tax burdens on consumption are actually very similar. Additionally, because Texas does not impose a state income tax, its residents are allowed to deduct state sales taxes from their federal income tax, thereby reducing their effective sales tax liability.

California's general state and universally applied local sales tax rate of 7.25 percent is higher than Texas' sales tax rate of 6.25 percent (see Figure 8). California's sales tax rate is also higher than Texas's when comparing the highest sales tax rates applied in the state (the state sales tax rate plus the highest local tax rate). Under this comparison, California's combined state and highest local sales tax rate is 9.25 percent, compared to 8.25 percent in Texas.

With respect to the actual rate applied, Texas has a distinct advantage compared to California. But, sales tax bases vary tremendously from state to state. Are groceries taxable? What about medicines? Taxing services is an even more complex issue. The result is that a one

percent sales tax in one state is not necessarily comparable to a one percent sales tax in another state. The tax base matters.

A comprehensive review of each state's sales tax base, if conducted with the right amount of diligence, would address these questions, but it would be a tremendous undertaking. There is a shortcut – examine both California's and Texas' sales tax revenues in comparison to the state's total personal income. By definition, total sales tax revenues are a function of the sales tax rate and the sales tax base. Personal income measures the amount of money available to consumers in the state to pay the sales tax. Consequently, we can obtain a sense of the sales tax burden by examining the sales tax revenues as a percentage of personal income. We need to be careful, however, because our shortcut isn't perfect. For example, if a state enacted a 500 percent sales tax just on Snickers bars, we're guessing the legislature wouldn't pull in very much revenue at all from the measure. Most people would switch to Three Musketeers or Paydays for their candy bar craving, and die-hard Snickers fans could stock up at gas stations across the state line. So in this contrived example, the observed low level of revenue from the Snickers tax wouldn't therefore prove that candy bars were lightly taxed in the

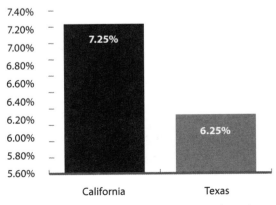

FIGURE 8
STATE SALES TAX RATES

Source: The Sales Tax Clearinghouse

state. Despite these possible pitfalls, our chosen measure of tax burden – defined as total sales tax revenues divided by personal income – is good enough for our purposes.

Using our chosen measure, California's sales tax burden ($23.72 per $1,000 of personal income) is slightly more than Texas' sales tax burden ($23.31 per $1,000 of personal income; see Figure 9). However, the difference between the two is minimal – a little less than fifty cents per $1,000 of personal income, which works out to less than 4/100 of one percent, or four basis points. The ranking of California and Texas compared to the other states further supports the similar, yet slightly more advantageous sales tax burden in Texas. With 1 representing the lowest sales tax burden and 50 representing the highest, California ranks 31st and Texas ranks 27th.

Because Texas has a lower sales tax rate and California has a marginally higher sales tax burden, the tax on consumption competition can be most accurately considered a Texas victory.

COMPETITION III WINNER: TEXAS

Competition IV: The Overall Tax Burden
Our final tax competition examines the overall tax environments between California and Texas. The overall tax environment competition measures the "other" aspects of tax policy that affect overall incentives in each state, but are not covered in the previous three competitions. These include:

- The total tax burden in the state, measured by total tax revenues divided by personal income;

- Personal income progressivity of the state, measured by the change in the tax liability between the top and average tax rates per $1,000 of personal income;

- The net impact of recently legislated tax changes per $1,000 of personal income; and

- The number of tax or expenditure (TEL) limits effective in the state.

The overall tax burden provides a measure for the size of government in California compared to the size of government in Texas. Over-taxed states, per se, restrain economic growth. State tax systems are so complex, however, that it can be difficult to discern which

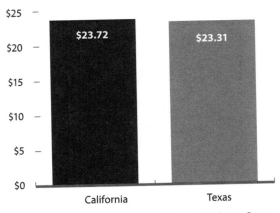

FIGURE 9
STATE SALES TAX BURDEN

Source: U.S. Census Bureau

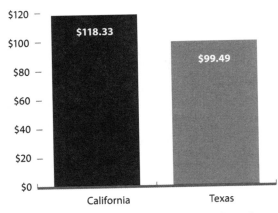

FIGURE 10
OVERALL TAX BURDEN

Source: U.S. Census Bureau

states are more heavily taxed than others. (Recall our example of the hyper-tax on Snickers bars.) This is not the case with California which is over-taxed in comparison to Texas. California's relative over-taxation is clearly visible by looking at total tax revenues in each state as a share of total state personal income. California's current tax burden of $118.33 per $1,000 of personal income is nearly 20 percent higher than Texas's current tax burden of $99.49 per $1,000 of personal income. Such a large discrepancy gives Texas a distinct competitive advantage over California that boils down to one simple reason: More of every dollar earned by a Texan ends up in his pocket, compared to every dollar earned by a Californian.

Progressive state tax systems are one of the most problematic aspects of state tax policies. Despite our best efforts to end recessions, the United States still experiences a business cycle – the economy expands quickly, stagnates and then contracts. By definition of the business cycle, when the economy is expanding, incomes are expanding at a faster than normal rate.

As the economy slows, so does the growth in income. When stagnant income turns to outright decline, personal income will oftentimes decline right along with the economy. These effects are magnified at the upper-income levels where swings in capital gains and corporate profits can have a pronounced impact on personal incomes.

A progressive state tax system amplifies the business cycle's impact on state budget revenues. During the expansion phase of the business cycle, state tax revenues increase because the economy is growing and more people are moving into higher marginal income tax brackets. An even greater revenue surge flows into the state's coffers compared to the surge in economic growth. Human nature being what it is, all too often state governments spend too much (if not all) of this excess revenue surge.

Due to the dynamics of the business cycle, the revenue surge is only temporary. As the inevitable slowdown takes hold and personal income growth stagnates, state tax revenues decrease at an even faster pace while more people move into lower marginal income tax brackets. Because much of the revenue surge has been spent – perhaps even committing the state to higher-than-efficient spending – state budget crises emerge. Oftentimes these budget crises beget calls for state tax increases at precisely the wrong time economically. California is an excellent example of the budgetary problems that arise due to progressive state tax systems.

Figure 11 shows the massive over and underestimates of general fund revenues during the past 20 years. To partially explain these gigantic goofs, Figure 12 shows the large dependence of California revenue on exercised stock options and realized capital gains.

California's cautionary tales warn of the budget instabilities that can arise due to steeply progressive tax systems. The composition of a state's tax burden is as important as its overall

FIGURE 11
CALIFORNIA GENERAL FUND REVENUE (AND TRANSFERS): FORECAST VS. ACTUAL

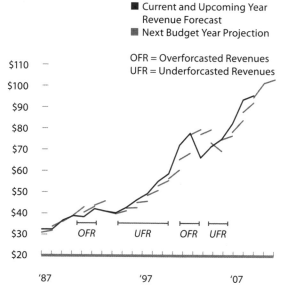

Source: Actual Data from http://www.dof.ca.gov, projections from CA Governor's Budget Summaries, 1987-present

burden. Broad, flat rate and consumption taxes compare favorably to taxes on capital creation and high marginal personal and corporate income tax rates. With respect to tax progressivity, Texas is significantly more competitive than California. Where California's tax system is the most "progressive" (i.e. graduated) in the country, Texas's is one of the best (see Figure 13).

Another key measure of the overall tax environment is the *direction* of the tax burden. Disregarding the level of taxes (whether the tax burden is rising or falling) is also important. States with rising (or falling) tax burdens are lowering (or increasing) the returns to workers, savers and investors. Consequently, previous decisions regarding working, saving and investing will be re-adjusted in light of the current tax implications of these decisions. Employment, income growth and population flows will all be positively or negatively impacted, depending upon whether the tax burden is falling or rising.

Once again, the tax environment in Texas beats the tax environment in California.

Whereas, the overall tax burden in California has been rising, tax burdens have been falling in Texas (see Figure 14).

The final key measure is the number of effective tax expenditure limits in the state. One successful strategy employed by some states to prevent squandering budget surpluses during times of economic expansion is a state tax or expenditure limitation (TEL). In general, tax and expenditure limits use some predetermined rate of growth to limit the government's ability to raise taxes or increase spending. Creating effective tax limits reduces the ability of state legislators to implement anti-growth policies. Conversely, the ability to create a sound tax environment and a more competitive economic environment is enhanced when a state has effective tax and expenditure limits in place.

California truly is a state of exaggerated policy swings, moving from Karl Marx to Adam Smith and back again, in what in fiscal time is but a blink of an eye. (See the following chapter for a complete description of California's history). The legacy of swinging to Adam Smith has

FIGURE 12
CALIFORNIA REVENUE FROM STOCK OPTIONS AND CAPITAL GAINS AS PERCENTAGE OF GENERAL FUND REVENUE
actual through FY 06, estimates through FY 08

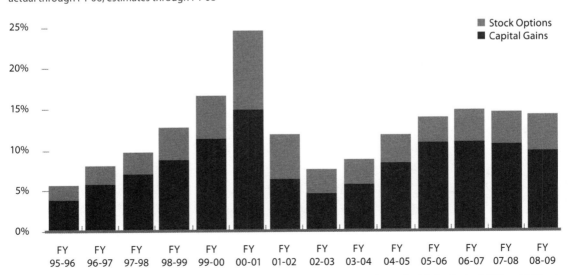

Source: Legislative Analyst's Office of California

FIGURE 13
PERSONAL INCOME TAX PROGRESSIVITY

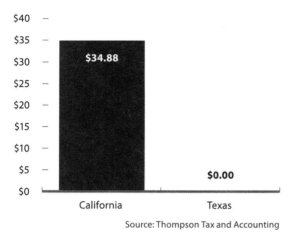

Source: Thompson Tax and Accounting

FIGURE 14
RECENTLY LEGISLATED TAX CHANGES
per $1,000 of personal income for 2007 and 2008

Source: Tax Analysts

left California with two expenditure limits – a very promising sign. Texas, on the other hand, has one tax and expenditure limit.

Judging by the purpose of TELs, Texas has clear advantages compared to California. TELs are designed to limit excessive growth in government, while increasing overall budget stability. Historically, the growth in overall state spending has been significantly more volatile in California than Texas. For instance, between 1996 and 2005, the standard deviation in state spending in California was 4.5 percent, compared to 2.4 percent in Texas. Sound budget practices have also led to an estimated $10.7 billion surplus for Texas in the current fiscal year.[11] In the spirit of a sound TEL, Texas should use the surplus to reduce the corporate tax rate that was just created as part of the property tax reduction package.

Texas's overall tax environment has economic advantages over California's. Texas imposes a smaller burden that is declining and is not progressive. California imposes a large, rising and progressive tax burden. The implications are clear: Texas should experience relatively stronger economic growth with more stable budget revenues. California should ex-

perience relatively weaker economic growth with more volatile budget revenues. Texas is the clear winner of competition four.
COMPETITION IV WINNER: TEXAS

Competition V:
The Regulatory Policy Competition
Regulatory burdens can also create positive or negative economic incentives. Burdensome regulations that excessively increase business costs reduce overall economic incentives. In this competition, we examine five regulatory issues that have important impacts on a state's overall economic competitiveness:

- State Liability System
- Average Workers' Compensation Cost
- State Minimum Wage
- Right-to-Work Status

California has the 44th least competitive state liability tort system out of all 50 states.[12] Texas ranks a slightly more competitive 41st (where the state ranked number one had the most efficient state liability system). California's below-average rank indicates that the tort liability system adds more than average

FIGURE 15
STATE WORKER'S COMPENSATION COSTS
per $100 of payroll

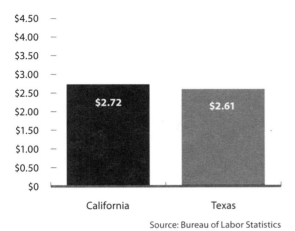

Source: Bureau of Labor Statistics

FIGURE 16
STATE MINIMUM WAGES

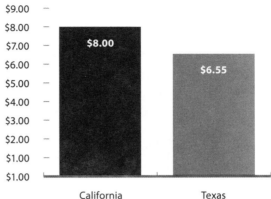

Source: U.S. Department of Labor

costs to businesses that operate in the state compared to businesses that operate in other states, including Texas.

Workers' compensation costs impose additional costs on employers. When employers consider hiring additional workers, it is the total cost of increasing employment that is relevant, which includes all salaries, benefits, taxes and regulatory costs. Workers' compensation increases the cost of employing additional workers. Consequently, these regulations increase overall unemployment and decrease a state's potential economic growth.

Workers' compensation costs add $2.72 per $100 of payroll in California. These additional costs are a major discouragement to employment growth in the Golden State. Texas's workers' compensations costs are $2.61 per $100 of payroll (see Figure 15).

California mandates that businesses in the state pay a minimum wage of $8.00 per hour, which exceeds the federal minimum wage standard. Texas, on the other hand, mandates that businesses in the state only need to meet the federal minimum wage standard, currently $6.55 per hour, which is scheduled to rise to $7.25 per hour in July 2009 (see Figure 16).

Minimum wage laws can have only one of two effects. The minimum wage can be below the wage that would be paid to any employee, so it is irrelevant. On the other hand, minimum wage laws can raise the wage costs for employers, leading to greater unemployment. By imposing a minimum wage in excess of the federal minimum wage, California is unnecessarily increasing employer costs. In so doing, business flexibility is reduced and overall employment in the state is reduced. These effects do not exist in Texas, providing Texas's regulatory environment with another comparative advantage *vis-à-vis* California's.

Despite the shrinking influence of unions on the American economy in general, their last bastion is the public sector, and they are still thriving in California in particular. According to the League of Women Voters, as of 2005 about 54 percent of California's government employees belonged to a union.[13] In both the private and public spheres, the Bureau of Labor Statistics reports that in 2007, 17.8 percent of California employees were either members of unions or were represented by them. In contrast, the figure for Texas was only 5.7 percent.[14]

States are divided into two distinct categories with respect to their union organizing laws. They are either right-to-work, which means workers have the right not to join a union, or non-right-to-work, which means that workers are forced to join a union and pay dues if they work in a unionized industry.[15] The evidence points overwhelmingly to the fact that right-to-work states have much greater growth of employment than non-right-to-work states. Texas is a right-to-work state; California is not.

Combining these divergent regulations, it is once again clear that Texas's economic environment is more competitive than California's. Texas has a more efficient tort litigation environment, lower worker's compensation costs, a lower minimum wage, and freedom from union coercion. Once again, Texas is the clear winner.
COMPETITION V WINNER: TEXAS

Competition VI: The Spending Competition
The final competition measures the amount of fiscal discipline exhibited in both California and Texas. We measure fiscal discipline in two broad categories. The first category measures the current size of the state governments by the total expenditures per capita. The second category measures the growth in government spending by the average growth in total expenditures per capita.

Government spending can negatively impact the state economy through two channels. First, in order for the government to have revenues to spend, it must take this money away from the private sector. As governments become larger, the value of the dollar taken away from the private sector is greater. As a consequence, government spending lowers the total potential output in the state. Second, larger government spending today oftentimes begets even greater government spending and activity tomorrow. In other words, the threat of higher tax and regulatory burdens grows as the size of the government grows.

With respect to our competition, California's total expenditures, when adjusted for the size of its population, are significantly higher than total expenditures in Texas. Currently, expenditures per capita in Texas are 32 percent lower than the expenditures per capita in California. This large discrepancy in the size and scope of government in Texas, compared to California, provides Texas with a significant economic comparative advantage (see Figure 17).

It's not simply the size of California's expenditures that are a comparative disadvantage for the Golden State. Based on data from the U.S. Census, state expenditures between 2001 and 2007 grew more than 7 percent a year on average in California, while they grew at about 6 percent a year in Texas.[16] The California state government's expenditures are much higher per capita than those in Texas and can be expected to continue to widen in the future. This is easy to conclude given the large expenditure increases that have been associated with traditional California budgets. Higher future taxes, increased fiscal crises, and slower economic growth will all follow as a result of the rising government expenditures in California. The reverse is true for Texas.

With respect to competition six, once again, Texas is the clear winner. As Figure 18 above illustrates, California's government expenditures are not only bigger, they have grown faster than spending in Texas. This is particularly notable, as Texas has a relatively larger number of public employees than California, with more than 560 public employees per 10,000 people in Texas. In contrast, there are approximately only 500 public employees per 10,000 people in California. The implications from these trends are clear: Texas's economic competitiveness will be improving, while California's will be weakening. However, Texas should be careful not to mistake this head-to-head match-up as a permanent victory. Significant growth at all levels of government in Texas has frustrated Texas taxpayers. Texas must set out to be more competitive, both compared to California and other states, as well as to the rest of the

FIGURE 17
TOTAL EXPENDITURES PER CAPITA

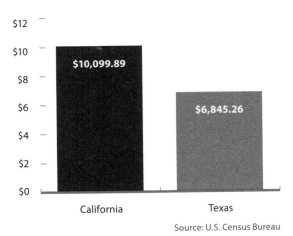

Source: U.S. Census Bureau

FIGURE 18
AVERAGE CHANGE IN TOTAL STATE SPENDING: 2001-2007

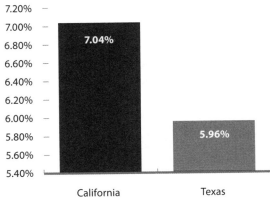

Source: U.S. Census Bureau

world. As noted above, Texas could restrain the growth of the budget immediately by reducing the number of public employees, with hopes of moving from 27th nationally, to California's 9th (with the state ranking 1st having the fewest public employees per 10,000 of population).
COMPETITION VI WINNER: TEXAS

Living with the Results

Matched up in a head-to-head competition, Texas's economic environment beats California's – in fact, it is a knockout. Texas and California are case studies illustrating the cause-and-effect relationship between state tax policies and economic performance. We expect these stark differences to manifest themselves in continued superior economic performance in Texas vis-à-vis California.

Our competition between California and Texas demonstrates how economic theory actually works in the real world. Pro-growth tax, and economic and regulatory policy leads to rising employment, income, home values, population and tax revenues, while high levels of taxes and spending have the opposite effect.

The U.S. Census Bureau has recently released its latest information on estimated population changes of metropolitan areas.[17] These

numbers identify Texas as the big winner in 2007, again. Out of a total of over 360 metropolitan areas, four of the top 10 metropolitan areas with the largest population increases were in Texas. Viewing the Census's results in tandem with the results from our competition between Texas and California illustrates George Gilder's famous maxim: "High tax rates don't redistribute income; they redistribute people."

The stark differences in the fiscal, economic and regulatory policies in Texas compared to California explain the differing outlooks. California continues to increase regulations, raise taxes and spend profligately. These anti-growth policies will continue to sap the economic vitality of California. Texas, on the other hand, has a pro-growth economic environment with a competitive tax system, sound regulations and spending discipline that will help Texas maintain its superior economic performance well into the future.

More than the economic head-to-head comparisons, however, is the fact that *Texas is doing just fine with no personal income tax*. To repeat the point made previously, one would think – considering the recent budget fiasco in California – that a modern state needs a steeply progressive tax code just to survive. The case of Texas is a clear counterexample, showing that these fears are simply a myth. In the long-run, there is no trade-off between healthy government finances and a competitive business environment. After all, punitive tax rates don't bring in much money when businesses relocate to other states.

ENDNOTES

1   In Texas, there is no corporate income tax rate, but there is a one percent gross receipts tax (GRT). To put the gross receipts tax on a comparable basis to California's net income tax, we transform the gross receipts tax rate into an equivalent net income tax rate. Based on this transformation, Texas' one percent GRT is the "equivalent" of a five percent net income tax.

2   State Economic Growth Widespread in: Advance 2006 and Revised 2003-2005 GDP-by-State Estimates. *Bureau of Economic Analysis.* June 7, 2007. BEA 07-24.

3   For more on Arizona, see "Arizona Letter." A.B. Laffer and Associates. March 20, 1992.

4   Sources: IMF World Economic Outlook Database, October 2007, http://www.imf.org; and, U.S. Bureau of Economic Analysis, Regional National Income and Product Accounts (NIPA), http://www.bea.org.

5   U.S. Census, http://www.census.gov/.

6   This calculation assumes a joint household in the 9.3 percent marginal tax bracket for California state income taxes and the 15 percent marginal tax bracket for federal taxes and incorporates the deductibility of state income taxes from federal income taxes.

7   Human capital, oftentimes the most important input into production, is impacted by the tax burden on labor, not the tax burden on capital as it is defined here.

8   Atkins, Chris and Williams, Jonathan. "Tax Foundation Explains Flaws in Texas Tax Reform Commission's Tax Reform Recommendations." *Tax Analysts, State Tax Today.* May 11, 2006.

9   Petska Tom, Michael Parisi, Kelly Luttrell, Lucy Davitian, and Matt Scoffic. "An Analysis of Business Organizational Structure and Activity from Tax Data". IRS SOI. (2005).

10   Specifically, the GRT rate is multiplied by the ratio of GDP to total capital income and profits.

11   Robison, Clay "Oil prices help Texas rake in $10.7 billion surplus: Sales tax revenue also aids projected overflow Perry hopes to share with you." *Houston Chronicle.* May 7, 2008.

12   McQuillan, Lawrence J. and Abramyan, Hovannes. U.S. Tort Liability Index: 2008 Report. Pacific Research Institute.

13   See http://ca.lwv.org/action/prop0511/prop75.html.

14   See Table 5, "Union affiliation of employed wage and salary workers by state," at: http://www.bls.gov/news.release/union2.t05.htm.

15   National Right to Work Foundation, 2006.

16   The most recent expenditure data available from the U.S. Census State Government Finances database is 2006, see: http://www.census.gov/govs/www/state.html. For inter-state comparisons, the U.S. Census data provides a more accurate assessment, as the differing state accounting methods are put on a comparative basis.

17   See http://www.census.gov/population/www/estimates/CBSA-est2007-pop-chg.html.

Los Angeles, California

Chapter Three

The Ghosts of California

The Ghosts of California

In the previous chapter, we illustrated the superior past performance, and likely future performance, of Texas versus California, in terms of population, income and job growth. We argued this disparity wasn't due to dumb luck, or even to unidentifiable factors outside of human control. On the contrary, the empirical outcomes display just what economic theory leads us to expect: When you tax something, you get less of it. That's why the government jacks up taxes on cigarettes to discourage teen smoking and fines drivers who are caught speeding. By the very same logic, when California politicians impose the largest marginal income tax rate in the nation on the most productive members of the community, they shouldn't be shocked to see high-skilled laborers and innovative entrepreneurs flocking to other states.

The prior chapter demonstrated that you can run a fully-functioning modern state without excessive taxation. Yet, despite all of the evidence we marshaled in the previous chapter, we can just *hear* our critics complaining, "California is different! If we adopted your advice and copied Texas, our state would fall apart!"

In this chapter we tackle the objection head-on. In chapter two, we compared *current* trends in California and Texas. Now we compare California of today with *California of the past*. Indeed, the history of California – centered on the tax revolt crystallized in Proposition 13 – shows a laboratory experiment in which the state went from fiscal malaise to fiscal health

– then back to malaise again. By showing the current class of legislators the ghost of California past, we hope they can begin picturing the ghosts of California's future as identified by much lower taxes and much higher economic growth.

The Historical Context of Proposition 13: The Tax Revolt Heard 'Round the World

Because it will play such a pivotal role in our story, some background on Proposition (Prop.) 13 is in order.

It was more than 30 years ago – June 6, 1978 – that Arthur Laffer won the one-dollar bill framed on his office wall and America was jolted by this political equivalent of a sonic boom. Political analysts often argue when the modern-day conservative movement in America was officially launched. Some say it was Barry Goldwater's campaign in 1964. Others cite the election of Ronald Reagan in November 1980. We believe the strongest case can be made that the conservative, anti-big government tide began in 1978, when almost 60 percent of voters declared thumbs up to the brainchild of Howard Jarvis and Paul Gann.

Specifically, Prop. 13 reduced property tax rates on homes, businesses and farms by more than 50 percent, to a rate not to exceed one percent of the property's market value. For properties where sales had not occurred more recently than 1976, the 1976 assessed value plus a presumed appreciation of no more than two percent per year was used for tax purposes.

Property tax increases on any given property, therefore, were limited to two percent a year, as long as the property was not sold. In addition, Prop. 13 required all tax increases, whether they be property tax increases or increases in any other taxes, to be approved by a two-thirds vote of the electorate or legislature. In 1979, the legislature passed an addendum to Prop. 13, permanently exempting business inventories from property tax, effective July 1, 1980.

This last point on the inventory exemption may seem minor, but let us share a little history you won't find in most economics textbooks. Every December 31 prior to 1980, you could find miles and miles of trucks lined up along the state's border, waiting to enter California at 12:01 a.m. on January 1, in order to avoid the prior year's inventory tax. Yikes! Even Rube Goldberg would be embarrassed. How can some of these doubting Thomases in academia continue to deny that tax policies significantly alter business behavior?

This was arguably the greatest tax revolt since the Boston Tea Party. As in so many other ways, here too, California was a trend-setter: The spirit of Prop. 13 was rapidly exported to the rest of the country. Within five years of Prop. 13's passage, nearly half the states strapped a similar straitjacket on politicians' tax-raising capabilities by cutting income, property taxes, or both. In many ways, Prop. 13 presaged the improbable presidential election of Ronald Reagan, who sailed to the White House on the crest of a national anti-tax wave by promising supply-side 30 percent income tax cuts for all. Once again, the old maxim was proven true: As goes California, so goes the nation.

Two patriots led this tax revolt – Paul Gann and Howard Jarvis – men described by the *Los Angeles Times* as "the chief spokesmen for this expanding group of angry and disgruntled taxpayers across the state who believe they are paying too much for the cost of government." And that was the essence of the Prop. 13 revolt. After a decade-long voracious expansion in the

size of the Great Society welfare state, coupled with years of double-digit inflation and escalating tax burdens through bracket creep, while erasing family purchasing power, Americans no longer believed government was giving them anywhere near their money's worth. In the 1970s, family tax burdens rose at almost twice the pace of real family income. In California, uncapped property tax assessments were driving thousands of residents out of their homes – particularly fixed income seniors who had little capacity to pay the double-digit rates of increase in the taxes on their homes.

One of the authors, Arthur Laffer, was extensively involved with Prop. 13, having worked closely with each of its authors. In fact, he co-authored no fewer than three other propositions with Gann and Jarvis and succeeded Jarvis as director of the California Taxpayers Association.

Almost everyone of consequence in both political parties, and almost every organized interest group in the state condemned the measure as reckless. Even Ronald Reagan was originally skeptical. Joel Fox, the longtime director of the Howard Jarvis Taxpayers Association, writes in his book, *The Legend of Proposition 13*: "Surprising to many, was that big business stood opposed. Businesses not only lent their names to the 'NO on 13' campaign, they helped finance it." The opponents warned voters of the doom that awaited the state if Prop. 13 passed: San Francisco's schools and libraries would be closed on June 6, 2,500 Los Angeles policemen would be laid off, the prison gates would be opened up for lack of funds and the UCLA Business School predicted a loss of 450,000 jobs in the state.

Fortunately, few voters listened to the hysteria. Taxes were so suffocatingly high in California that even firefighters in Los Angeles voted two to one in favor of Prop. 13.

Once they got started, California voters put further restraints on the gluttonous politicians. In 1978, all personal income tax brackets, standard deductions and personal credit amounts were indexed to the California consumer price index, less three percent. The legislature removed the three percent threshold for 1980 and 1981. Voters then made full indexation permanent when they passed Prop. 7 in June 1982. Voters also overwhelmingly passed Prop. 6, which repealed inheritance and gift taxes.

Political aversion to heavy taxes went hand in hand with a desire to tighten the reins on spending. In November 1979, Prop. 4 placed a constitutional limit on state and local government spending. This limit, commonly referred to as the Gann limit, allowed spending to increase each year based on 1) the statewide population growth and 2) inflation as measured by the lesser of the Consumer Price Index (CPI) for the United States or California per capita personal income. Appropriations for unrestricted subventions to school districts and community college districts were exempted from the Gann spending limit, as were debt service and funding for court and federal mandates.

The two tax expenditure limits listed for California cover the gamut. The hugely effective Prop. 13, authored by Howard Jarvis and Paul Gann in 1978, has been a stalwart of tax limitations. Property taxes in 1978 were legislated not to exceed one percent of the property's value – ever – and if the property didn't change hands, the total property taxes couldn't grow more than two percent in any one year. In addition to this truly effective tax limitation, Prop. 13 also required any tax increase to have at least a two-thirds majority of the vote. Not bad!

In contrast, Prop. 4, a spending limit authored by Paul Gann, passed a few years later but was eviscerated by Prop. 98, having done almost no good. While still on the books, Prop. 4 is now as meaningless as the 10th Amendment at the federal level. Beyond the truly rare and fascinating economics experiment – the focus of the present chapter – the California experience of the late 1970s through early 2000s could provide fodder for several political science dissertations.

So ... Did it Work?!

As we noted above, this bold proposal terrified many people, including conservative Republicans. At the same time, many readers may be surprised to learn that Democrat Gov. Jerry Brown was instrumental in passing Prop. 13 and the rest of the pro-growth initiatives. Amid the dire forecasts of financial catastrophe, Gov. Brown saw to it that the state assessor sent out tax notices the week before the election, indicating a five-fold increase in property taxes. This clever move allowed Brown to say he had a much larger surplus than people had originally thought. The point, of course, was to disarm the critics who said Prop. 13 was fiscally irresponsible.

In 1976, Arthur Laffer was quite recognizable to the television-viewing public, since he had been the presence voicing opposition to the Cesar Chavez movement. When Prop. 13 passed, Gov. Brown and his chief of staff, Gray Davis, invited Laffer (an outspoken proponent of the measure) to Sacramento, where they held discussions over the course of three days. On the way to a joint press conference, Gov. Brown remarked, "Professor Laffer, I hope you don't take this opportunity to dump all over me." His

FIGURE 19
STATE & LOCAL TAX BURDEN CALIFORNIA VS. U.S.
per $1,000 of personal income; FY 1963-FY 1990

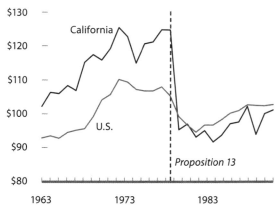

Source: U.S. Census Bureau, State and Local Government Finances

awkwardness was only exceeded by his good governance. Gov. Brown made sure Prop. 13 would be implemented correctly.

While drumming up support for Prop. 13, Laffer wrote a pamphlet for the United Organization of Taxpayers in March 1978 – 10 weeks before the vote. He predicted the static revenue forecasts overstated the losses to the state treasury from Prop. 13, because of supply-side effects:

> Property tax revenues will fall by less than [the static forecasted] $7 billion because property values will rise and new construction activity will expand. Both of these effects will expand the tax base, and thus lead to less property tax revenue loss. In the out-years, property tax receipts will fall by far less than $7 billion annually. Take, for example, a $100,000 home, paying taxes of 3.5 percent of market value. Taxes would be $3,500 per year without Jarvis. If Jarvis passes, the tax rate would fall to one percent of market, but tax receipts would be greater than $1,000. Using a discount rate of 10 percent, the approximate receipts would initially be $1,250, reflecting a rise in the market value of the house to $125,000.

> In short order, the higher values of homes would encourage more new construction and an enlarged property base. As this process progressed, total property values would rise by far more than the 25 percent of the example.

> Tax revenues elsewhere would expand absolutely. Social welfare mandated spending would fall. With property taxes lower, businesses will expand their activities within the State. This expansion will create new jobs, more investment, and higher real wages. Sales, incomes, and other forms of activity will expand. Sales taxes, income taxes, etc., all will rise. In addition, state outlays for

> social welfare will fall (unemployment compensation, rent subsidies, medical, etc.).

> Tax revenues in future years will be reduced by less or, quite conceivably, even expanded as a result of Jarvis-Gann. When combined with the healthier economic base and, as a direct consequence, less social welfare expenditures, the state should shortly be back in a surplus condition.

We are happy to report that history vindicated Laffer's supply-side analysis. This is clearly captured in Figure 20, which shows that the tremendous tax cut for Californians led to a substantial economic recovery relative to the rest of the nation.

The fiscal outcome also played out just as Laffer predicted: Prop. 13 passed on June 6, 1978, one month prior to the end of FY 1978. State and local property tax revenues fell $5.0 billion, from $11.0 billion in FY 1978 to $6.0 billion in FY 1979, far short of the static revenue loss forecasts of $7.0 billion. In addition,

FIGURE 20
EXCESS STATE & LOCAL TAX BURDEN VS. EXCESS UNEMPLOYMENT
per $1,000 of personal income; FY 1963-FY 1990

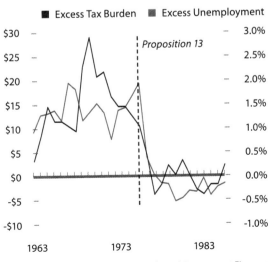

Source: U.S. Census Bureau, State and Local Government Finances

this drop was largely offset by higher revenues in every other major tax category. Total state and local revenues fell by only $1.1 billion that first year.

Looking at the bigger picture, the combined state and local tax burden per $1,000 of personal income fell from $124.57 in FY 1978 to $94.93 in FY 1982, a 24 percent reduction. Yet in spite of the precipitous fall in the state's average tax rate, state and local revenues did not fall proportionately. In fact, total tax revenue grew by 19 percent from $27.4 billion in FY 1978 to $32.5 billion in FY 1982. The tax base expanded by more than enough to offset the

reduction in tax rates. Even after adjusting for inflation, which can distort economic data during this high inflationary period, tax revenues fell much less than the reduction in the state and local tax burden.

Economic expansion and higher property values led to healthy property tax growth over the following years, and by FY 1985, property tax collections were back to their FY 1978 $11.0 billion level. The disruptive shortage of funds so widely anticipated never materialized. During the interim, while property taxes were catching back up, Gov. Brown made sure that local governments – who rely heavily on property

TABLE 16
CALIFORNIA LOCAL GOVERNMENT REVENUES[1]
millions of dollars

	1976	1977	1978	1979	1980	1981	1982	1983
Total General Revenue	$22,915	$25,029	$28,820	$27,914	$31,461	$36,067	$37,877	$45,252
Federal transfers	1,414	1,655	2,275	2,116	2,356	2,699	2,131	2,063
State transfers	8,237	8,819	9,848	13,354	14,874	16,920	16,928	17,230
Local own source revs	13,264	14,555	16,157	12,444	14,231	16,449	18,818	20,112
Property tax revenues	8,561	9,586	10,476	5,428	5,800	6,498	7,616	7,990
Non-property tax revs	4,703	4,969	5,681	7,016	8,431	9,951	11,202	12,122

Source: U.S. Census Bureau

TABLE 17
CALIFORNIA LOCAL GOVERNMENT SPENDING[2]
millions of dollars

	1977	1978	1979	1980	1981	1982	1983
Total General Direct Expenditures	$22,590	$25,218	$25,880	$29,346	$32,754	$35,221	$37,290
Education	9,443	10,478	10,307	11,526	12,668	13,302	13,686
Highways	821	942	1,021	1,150	1,275	1,300	1,400
Public welfare	2,545	2,775	2,736	3,163	3,736	4,135	4,169
Health and hospital	1,636	1,886	2,202	2,571	2,816	3,292	3,669
Police and fire	1,869	2,066	2,153	2,399	2,766	3,109	3,325
Other	6,276	7,071	7,461	8,537	9,493	10,083	11,041

Source: U.S. Census Bureau

taxes – were "made whole" by a state subvention of revenues. We realize how impossible it all sounds to those unfamiliar with supply-side economics, but Table 16 speaks for itself. The drop in property tax revenues from 1978 to 1979 is stark indeed, and was what all the critics had warned about. But what the critics failed to realize – which Laffer confidently explained *before it happened* – was that the boost in overall economic activity would cause large increases in other tax categories. It was the wisdom of Gov. Brown to reallocate those windfalls, in order not to make local governments bear the brunt of the huge – and well-deserved – program of tax relief for the citizens.

Turning our attention to spending, total state and local direct general expenditures were not slashed between FY 1978 and FY 1979 as skeptics had predicted. In fact, expenditures increased 1.6 percent from $36.9 billion to $37.5 billion over this period. Even better, spending on police and fire services increased 3.7 percent in FY 1979. We specifically mentioned fire trucks because in the midst of the battle surrounding Prop. 13, Harvard Professor John Kenneth Galbraith sent Laffer a toy fire engine, which was his contribution to make up for all of the real fire engines that would (allegedly) no longer be purchased, as a consequence of Laffer's "irresponsible" economics. To wit, much later when all the data were in, Laffer responded to Galbraith and the other doomsayers, "Neener, neener, neener." As Table 17 reveals, the tax reduction which had invigorated the state's economy so profoundly did not impose any significant reduction in government services.

For Californians, the legacy of Prop. 13 has been to save the average homeowner in California tens of thousands of dollars in property tax payments over the past 30 years. This is money that would have fueled an even more rapid escalation in California's state and local public bureaucracies if those dollars had been sent to Sacramento and city hall. Californians

intuitively understand this. That is why every major poll has confirmed that a large majority of residents in California say they would still vote for Prop. 13 again if it were on the ballot today – 30 years later.

Taxpayers nationwide also owe a debt of gratitude to Howard Jarvis and Paul Gann. They helped reverse the economically disabling era of unrestrained over-taxation, overspending and overregulation of government at all levels in America that dragged the nation into a malaise at the end of the 1970s. Just as importantly, they taught us all an enduring civics lesson we should never forget: In America, you really can fight city hall. Unfortunately, Californians would forget this lesson just more than a decade later.

What Went Wrong?
Pete Wilson's One-Two Punch
The great tax revolt of the late 1970s gradually faded away during the 1980s, as memories of the pre-Prop. 13 troubled economy vanished. State spending and taxes crept up. California once again had become the proverbial frog who was slowly being boiled to death. Then, Gov. Pete Wilson did his best to enact the mirror image of the Prop. 13 era reforms.[3] Unfortunately, the results were also the mirror image of the prosperity flowing from the Jarvis-Gann initiative.

First, the legislature was very clever in obeying the letter, but certainly not the spirit, of Prop. 4. Recall that the Gann limit addressed the appropriation of tax revenues. Ah, here was a loophole the politicians drove a Mack truck through! From FY 1980 to FY 1989, state and local tax revenues – which provided the basis for Gann's spending straitjacket – grew by 45 percent in real terms. But non-tax revenues – fees, charges, fines, etc. – grew by 100 percent in real terms over the same period. As a percentage of overall revenues, the Gann-applicable tax portion shrunk from 63 percent in FY 1981, down to 57 percent by FY 1990.[4] As we wrote earlier, this isn't just economics. This is interesting from a purely political viewpoint, too. We can just see a term paper now: "To Raise Taxes or Hike Fees? Incentives Matter."

The beginning of the end actually occurred under Gov. Deukmejian, with the passage of Prop. 98 and Prop. 111. The audacious Prop. 98 required that K-12 schools and community colleges receive 41 percent of all general revenue funds. This minimum share of the budget must go to schools regardless of the state's fiscal circumstances or the impact on other programs. When Prop. 98 first passed, times were good and it didn't appear onerous. But when revenues stagnated, other state services disproportionately felt the brunt so schools could get their automatic allotment.

In June of 1990, Prop. 111 passed, further eroding the Gann spending limit. Instead of using the lesser of inflation as measured by the CPI or California's per capita personal income, only per capita personal income would be used to revise the limit. Spending by local governments would also have the local option of per capita personal income or an alternate growth factor which would account for the change in the assessed valuation of local commercial construction. In addition, Prop. 111 exempted from the spending limit appropriations for "qualified capital outlay projects." Thus, highway spending was removed from the Gann spending limit without lowering the limit. Virtually any and every spending category was given free rein. For all practical purposes, this meant the Gann limit was no longer operational.

California, year in, year out, has used the education industry as a focal point of the state's politics. California's state universities have always viewed themselves as the best of the best and have used their reputation to extract ever increasing funds from the state government.

But the real political powerhouse in California's education industry is the California Teachers Association, a union with megabucks and a perpetual craving for tax revenue. As Table 18 shows, California's teachers are the highest paid in the United States. Yet California's K-12 students consistently rank among the group of the very lowest achievers in the nation. In the 2005 special election called by then reform-minded Gov. Schwarzenegger, the California Teachers union almost single-handedly engineered the defeat of 1) anti-gerrymandering redistricting reform, 2) a meaningful state spending limit, 3) the rights of union members to withhold dues used for political purposes they don't support and 4) teacher tenure after five years instead of only two years on the job. And in 2007, based on comprehensive testing results carried out by the Department of Education, California's K-12 students were only able to test higher than the students in one other state – Mississippi (see Table 19).

On the tax side, Prop. 111 increased the state tax on gasoline and diesel fuel five cents per gallon, followed by one cent increases on the first day of each of the next four years. It also increased the truck weight tax by 40 percent and raised ethanol and methanol taxes. The increase in fuel taxes was estimated to generate $687 million during FY 1991 and $970 million during FY 1992.

Yet the tax hikers were just getting warmed up. On July 1, 1991 – the first day of the 1992 fiscal year – the '92 budget agreement took effect. The top rates on the personal income tax, the corporate tax and capital gains tax were raised from 9.3 to 11 percent, while certain credits and deductions were suspended. The Alternative Minimum Tax (AMT) on personal income was increased from seven percent to 8.5 percent. The per-gallon excise tax on beer was increased from four cents to 20 cents, while the tax on distilled spirits increased from $2.00 to $3.30 per gallon, and rose from 1 to 20 cents for wine. Two weeks later, the state sales tax went up to 6 percent from 4.75 percent.

To understand the magnitude of these hikes, consider that on a static revenue basis, total state tax collections were projected to rise some $8.6 billion from FY 1991 to FY 1992;

$2.2 billion of the projected increase was due to natural growth, while the remaining $6.4 billion from the tax increase (based on a static analysis). This represented a 15 percent increase over total tax revenues collected in FY 1990, making it the largest state tax increase in U.S. history. In terms of percentages, Prop. 111 and subsequent tax increases were nearly four times larger than the record-breaking tax increases being proposed at that time by President Clinton for the U.S. economy.

Gov. Wilson imposed such massive tax increases ostensibly to balance the budget. This approach is totally unjustified in terms of economics – you don't want to kick the economy when it's already down. After all, how is it good

TABLE 18
AVERAGE TEACHER SALARY BY STATE : 2007

Rank	State	Salary	Rank	State	Salary
1	California	59,825	27	North Carolina	43,922
2	Connecticut	59,304	28	Virginia*	43,823
3	District of Columbia*	59,000	29	Florida	43,302
4	Illinois	58,686	30	Wyoming	43,255
5	New Jersey	58,156	31	South Carolina	43,011
6	New York	57,354	32	Arkansas	42,768
7	Massachusetts	56,369	33	Kentucky	42,592
8	Michigan	54,739	34	Tennessee	42,537
9	Rhode Island*	54,730	35	Texas	41,744
10	Maryland	54,333	36	New Mexico	41,637
11	Delaware	54,264	37	Kansas	41,467
12	Pennsylvania*	54,027	38	Idaho*	41,150
13	Alaska*	53,553	39	Iowa	41,083
14	Ohio*	50,314	40	Maine	40,737
15	Oregon	50,044	41	Mississippi	40,576
16	Hawaii	49,292	42	Missouri	40,462
17	Minnesota*	48,489	43	Nebraska	40,382
18	Georgia	48,300	44	Alabama	40,347
19	Indiana	47,255	45	Louisiana	40,029
20	Vermont*	46,622	46	Utah	40,007
21	Wisconsin*	46,390	47	Montana	39,832
22	Washington	46,326	48	Oklahoma	38,772
23	New Hampshire	45,263	49	West Virginia	38,284
24	Arizona*	44,672	50	North Dakota	37,764
25	Colorado	44,439	51	South Dakota	34,709
26	Nevada	44,426	**U.S.**		**49,026***

* NEA estimate where no data is available from state Department of Education.
Source: National Education Association; Figures are average salaries of public school teachers from 2005-2006.

TABLE 19
OVERALL STUDENT NAEP TEST SCORES BY STATE
based on most recent 4th and 8th grade performance in math, reading, science and writing

Rank	State	4th Grade Test Scores			8th Grade Test Scores				Overall
		Math	Reading	Science	Math	Reading	Science	Writing	
1	Massachusetts	252	236	160	298	273	161	167	1547
2	Vermont	246	228	160	291	273	162	162	1522
3	New Jersey	249	231	154	289	270	153	175	1521
4	New Hampshire	249	229	161	288	270	162	160	1519
5	North Dakota	245	226	160	292	268	163	154	1509
6	Montana	244	227	160	287	271	162	157	1506
7	Minnesota	247	225	156	292	268	158	156	1503
8	Maine	242	226	160	286	270	158	161	1502
9	Virginia	244	227	161	288	267	155	157	1499
10	Connecticut	243	227	155	282	267	152	172	1497
11	Wyoming	244	225	157	287	266	159	158	1496
12	South Dakota	241	223	158	288	270	161	155	1496
13	Ohio	245	226	157	285	268	155	156	1491
14	Wisconsin	244	223	158	286	264	158	158	1491
15	Kansas	248	225	151	290	267	150	156	1487
16	Colorado	240	224	155	286	266	155	161	1487
17	Pennsylvania	244	226	151	286	268	150	159	1485
18	Washington	243	224	153	285	265	154	158	1481
19	Idaho	241	223	155	284	265	158	154	1480
20	Delaware	242	225	152	283	265	152	158	1477
21	Iowa	243	225	151	285	267	150	155	1476
22	Indiana	245	222	152	285	264	150	155	1473
23	Missouri	239	221	158	281	263	154	153	1469
24	Nebraska	238	223	151	284	267	150	155	1468
25	New York	243	224	151	280	264	150	154	1466

Source: National Assessment of Education Progress (NAEP)

governance to balance the government's budget at the expense of every household's budget? In any event, the actual revenues from the massive hikes fell short of their projections. Not only did they fall far short of projections, *actual tax receipts fell* in spite of a (static) $6.4 billion tax increase on a budget in the $35 billion range. And who says there's no Laffer Curve?[5] Go figure!

Wilson's successor, Gray Davis, actually was more a victim of circumstance than a bad governor. Although he had pushed for tax hikes that (fortunately) were blocked because of Prop. 13's supermajority requirement, it was not Gray Davis's fault that some 25 percent of his general fund revenues in 2001 came from *exercised* stock options and *realized* capital gains (refer back to Figure 12). When the stock market crashed and

Rank	State	4th Grade Test Scores			8th Grade Test Scores				Overall
		Math	Reading	Science	Math	Reading	Science	Writing	
26	Utah	239	221	155	281	262	154	152	1465
27	Maryland	240	225	149	286	265	145	155	1464
28	Kentucky	235	222	158	279	262	153	151	1461
29	Oregon	236	215	151	284	266	153	155	1460
30	Illinois	237	219	148	280	263	148	160	1455
31	Texas	242	220	150	286	261	143	151	1453
32	Michigan	238	220	152	277	260	155	151	1453
33	Florida	242	224	150	277	260	141	158	1452
34	Alaska	237	214	151	283	259	150	155	1449
35	North Carolina	242	218	149	284	259	144	153	1448
36	Oklahoma	237	217	150	275	260	147	153	1438
37	Rhode Island	236	219	146	275	258	146	154	1434
38	Georgia	235	219	148	275	259	144	153	1433
39	Tennessee	233	216	150	274	259	145	156	1433
40	South Carolina	237	214	148	282	257	145	148	1431
41	Arkansas	238	217	147	274	258	144	151	1429
42	West Virginia	236	215	151	270	255	147	146	1421
43	Arizona	232	210	139	276	255	140	148	1400
44	Alabama	229	216	142	266	252	138	148	1391
45	Louisiana	230	207	143	272	253	138	147	1390
46	Hawaii	234	213	142	269	251	136	144	1390
47	Nevada	232	211	140	271	252	138	143	1387
48	New Mexico	228	212	141	268	251	138	143	1380
49	California	230	209	137	270	251	136	148	1380
50	Mississippi	228	208	133	265	250	132	142	1358

took his budget surplus with it, the catastrophe was outside of his control. Even so, in fairness, we must remember that it was others who created the explosive tax code that Davis inherited. No matter what exogenous circumstances he inherited, however, Davis could have exercised more fiscal responsibility in the face of such a financial crisis.

By the end of Davis's tenure, out of control state spending and general fiscal frivolity, along with recurring energy problems, had laid the groundwork for California's worst debt position in state history. As of December 31, 2003, the amount of California's outstanding general obligation (GO) debt was $31.7 billion, with another $22.2 billion slated for 2004.[6] California's debt rating was BBB at the end of 2003, the lowest debt rating of any state and tied for the lowest credit rating any state had ever been assigned.[7]

This brings us up to the Schwarzenegger period. Despite heavy rhetoric, debt levels remain high and a GO debt downgrade appears to be looming. The yield spread between California's outstanding debt and a AAA GO debt municipal benchmark is a measure of the premium investors must receive to hold California debt versus the lowest risk municipal debt (see Figure 21). California's Standard and Poor's debt rating is also shown. California's spread over the AAA benchmark at the time of Davis' departure was as high as it had ever been, and the spread appears headed back to that level.

State Economic Policies Matter

As with our comparison of Texas vs. California in the previous chapter, here too we find that a state's economic policies really do matter. Now that we understand the historical background and their associated tax-and-spend policies, we can look at the results of this grand experiment. Just as economic theory predicts, we find that the California economy prospered during the period of fiscal discipline, and then fell into repeated stagnation and budget crises once the

legislators returned to their profligate ways.

Tax-and-Spend Democrats?

Fiscally conservative Republicans may be surprised by the following charts. Contrary to popular belief, Democrats (at least in California) are not the only ones to spend like drunken sailors.

This cavalier attitude toward public spending has left the California state government, as well as many of its municipalities, a little worse for the wear, to say the least. In the beginning of December 2008, Gov. Schwarzenegger was forced to declare a fiscal emergency, allowing him to call a Prop. 58 special legislative session to address the crisis. The current fiscal year budget shortfall is projected to reach $11.2 billion, while over the next 18 months, analysts project it could reach an almost insurmountable $40 billion. In fact, budget conditions have gotten so bad, that in early December, the Los Angeles City Council voted to halt further funding for a planned $42 million exhibit at the Los Angeles Zoo – $12 million of which has already been spent. This year, the city is look-

FIGURE 21
CALIFORNIA'S GENERAL OBLIGATION (GO) DEBT RATING AND YIELD SPREAD BETWEEN STATE GO DEBT AND AAA GO BENCHMARK

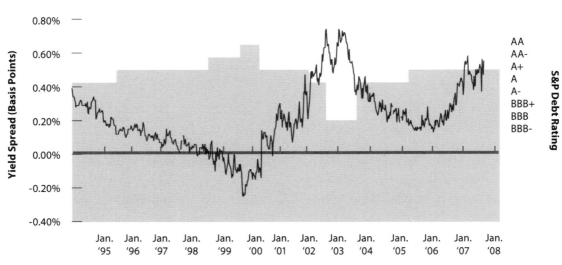

Source: Standard and Poors

FIGURE 22
CALIFORNIA GENERAL FUND EXPENDITURES
in $billions; FY 1990/91-FY 2007/08; FY 2008/09 estimated

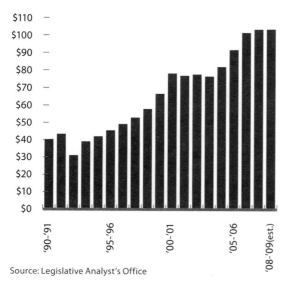

Source: Legislative Analyst's Office

FIGURE 23
GENERAL FUND DEBT SERVICE RATIOS:
FY 1958/59-FY 2008/09

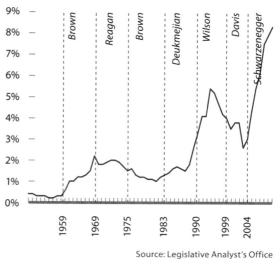

Source: Legislative Analyst's Office

ing at a shortfall of about $110 million out of its $7 billion budget and a potential $300 million shortfall in the next fiscal year. The City Council is widely expected to cut funding for a variety of public services including crossing guards and public libraries. They are also discussing privatization options for the zoo as well as plans that would involve freeing the zoo's last elephant, 21-year-old Billy, who was supposed to reside in the now suspended new exhibit.[8]

And how does the current governor plan to close such budget gaps? Recent proposals to come out of Schwarzenegger's office have involved a $4.4 billion tax hike, which includes a three year, 1.5 percent increase in the state sales tax, mineral extraction taxes on local oil companies, and the acceleration of about $1 billion in infrastructure spending.[9] Has he learned nothing from his last five years in office?

But perhaps the most extreme example of fiscal irresponsibility in the State of California belongs to the city of Vallejo. The city, which lies approximately 35 miles northeast

of San Francisco and contains a population of 120,000, is experiencing a budget crisis so large, they were forced to declare bankruptcy this past spring. In fact, the city estimates its budget deficit stood somewhere around $17 million for FY 2008. In the past, municipalities have filed for Chapter 9 due to poor investment decisions or perhaps some unlucky legal rulings, but this is not the case for Vallejo. Their dilemma is primarily the result of declining revenues and an overburdened public payroll. According to Dean Gloster, a Vallejo city union lawyer, "Vallejo was sort of the canary in the coal mine ... even better-run cities are going to be facing similar issues as health care costs rise and the baby boomer generation reaches retirement age."[10]

The main problem lies in the city's large employee salaries and benefit packages, which comprise 75 percent of the general fund budget. Base pay for firefighters is more than $80,000 per year. Furthermore, public employees can retire at age 50 with a pension equal to 90 percent of salary. The city is now fighting to legally void collective-bargaining agreements that are responsible for overly high employee pay. Inflated public sector wages and benefits are creating budgetary pressure in local governments across the country. In a recent survey of the nation's cities, the National League of Cities found that bloated public payrolls are plaguing our country's city budgets. Almost 95 percent of finance officers said employee-related costs, including wages, have increased over the previous year, 86 percent said health benefit costs have increased, and 79 percent said pensions have risen over the previous year.[11]

Sacramento Pols:

Only You Can Prevent Unemployment

We have been in this game for a while, and we've heard all sorts of excuses to explain why high taxes and stifling regulations aren't *really* responsible for job losses and stagnant economic growth. Apologists for big government will usually blame everything on "the recession" or some other exogenous feature. But there's an obvious way to correct for this: We can look at

standard measures of economic health, such as growth and unemployment rates, and compare California's numbers against the U.S. average. This allows us to isolate the effect of state-level policies, to determine if a high-unemployment year, for example, should be attributed to a nationwide calamity, or to something that California politicians could control.

Using this approach, Figures 24 and 25 illustrate that economic theory works. When California's legislature was shackled by Prop. 13 and other measures, it fared well compared to the rest of the United States. But when the politicians broke free from the chains its voters had placed on them in the late 1970s, all hell broke loose too, economically speaking. California's unemployment shot up well above the U.S. average, and its growth fell well below it.

A Crucial Part of the Story:

Population Flows

California is a state whose economy is driven by population growth. In his 2006 State of the State address, the governor laid out the proposi-

FIGURE 24
UNEMPLOYMENT & EXCESS UNEMPLOYMENT RATES: CALIFORNIA VS. UNITED STATES
monthly through September 2008

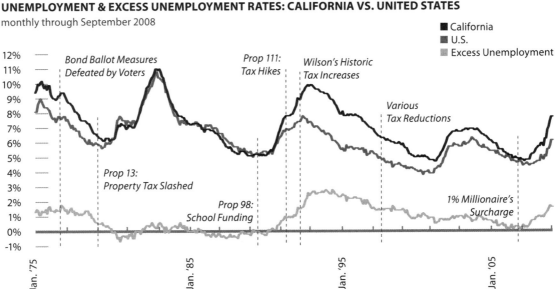

Source: Legislative Analyst's Office

tion that, "California's population is expected to increase by as much as 30 percent over the next 20 years." In fact, it is this population forecast that is the basis for the huge increase in infrastructure that had been proposed by the governor. Population growth is the end-all-and-be-all of California's economy. But in this regard, there are ominous harbingers of things to come.

First and foremost, even if California maintained its relative attractiveness *vis-à-vis* the rest of the country – which it most definitely has NOT – it is a wild stretch to believe that California's population could grow by 30 percent in the next two decades. It is true that over the past decade, California's population has grown 12.5 percent (through 2007). But California is now a much larger share of the overall country, and the rest of the country is relatively smaller. The same, or even higher, growth rates as those that occurred during the past decade correspond to a much larger absolute population movement than anything that has ever occurred both from the standpoint of the receiving state and the dispensing states.

On the basis of the latest population data, California's population growth rates are heading south. According to Census Bureau estimates of population growth from July 2000 to July 2001, California was the 9th fastest growing state in the nation. Six years later, through July 2007, California's annual growth rank slipped to 25th. In Figure 25, we have plotted population growth rates for California and the United States, and then the difference between the two.

The state's changing growth rate reflects changes to the growth rates of the components that make up changes to total population – a fact not unfamiliar to those who have studied California's past. State population growth has three components: 1) natural increase (births minus deaths of state residents), 2) net foreign immigration (net immigration into and out of California from foreign countries) and 3) net domestic migration (net migration into and out of California from the rest of the United States.

As one might expect, California's "natural increase" is relatively constant over time, sub-

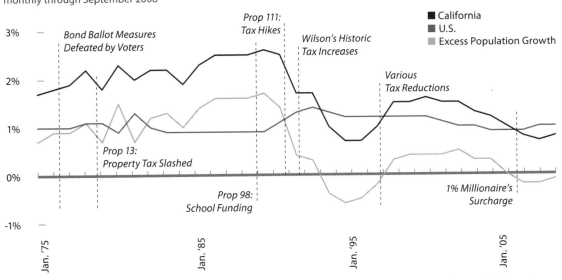

FIGURE 25
POPULATION GROWTH & EXCESS POPULATION GROWTH RATES: CALIFORNIA VS. UNITED STATES
monthly through September 2008

Source: U.S. Census Bureau

FIGURE 26
**NET CALIFORNIA DOMESTIC MIGRATION
AS PERCENTAGE OF EACH YEAR'S TOTAL POPULATION**
data began in 1981, annual through FY 2007

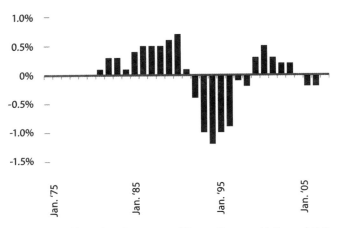

Source: California State Department of Finance, Demographic Research Unit

ject to the slow whims of decades-long demographic trends. Similarly, foreigners looking for a better life in California are not particularly swayed by the economic fortunes of the times, and represent a constant new inflow. It is quite clear net domestic migration is the true driver of changes in the rate of population growth in California (see Figure 26).

Just look at that domestic migration chart and see if you aren't shocked. Our past research has demonstrated that California's excess population growth (or lack thereof) closely mirrors the relative performance of the state's economy. At the peak of California's struggles in FY 1994, a net 362,000 Californians – or more than one percent of the state's total population – picked up and moved elsewhere. According to the U.S. Census Bureau, this figure was even larger – 434,000 Californians.[12]

Today, in addition to California's annual population growth continuing to come in below the U.S. average, an increasing number of Californians are choosing to leave the state. The California Demographic Research Unit estimates that in FY 2007, this net outflow was 89,000 people. The U.S. Census Bureau deter-

mined the outflow to be even larger – 263,000. (While it's unfortunate that between these two organizations a more exact figure cannot be reached, the underlying trend in either series is virtually the same.)

As if those charts aren't enough, we can also give some anecdotal evidence to buttress our theme. There were some 44,000 millionaires in California in 2000, and they contributed $15 billion to the state treasury in that year. That is an unbelievable statistic when you think about it. It means that the richest 0.15 percent of Californians contributed roughly 20 percent of the state's income tax revenues! According to data provided to the audit committee by the State Board of Equalization, about 80 percent of the state's revenue losses between 2001 and 2003 were a result of disappearing millionaires. The number of reported millionaires in California astonishingly dropped from 44,000 in 2000 to 29,000 in 2002. These tax émigrés represented a loss of roughly $6 billion in annual tax revenue collections.[13]

Some of the loss of millionaires in this decade wasn't a result of people leaving, but people losing money in the dot-com bust that thrust many Californians into a horrific riches to rags spiral. In the late 1990s, stock options from high-tech ventures reached their peak, creating a huge spike in temporary millionaires and centimillionaires. It is estimated revenues from stock options and capital gains generated a $5 to $10 billion one-time revenue windfall in the late 1990s. But we also know from the Census Bureau data that high wealth individuals have been leaving the state en masse. Figure 27 shows where these displaced Californians have been going.

We can illustrate our story by relying on the annual official press release from United Van Lines. As you might expect, United Van

FIGURE 27
2007 MIGRATION TRENDS
United Van Lines Shipment Data

■ Inbound States: moving outbound <45%
■ Outbound States: moving outbound >55%
■ Neutral States: moving outbound >45%, <55%

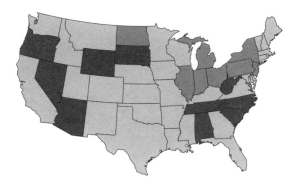

TABLE 20
TOP 10 MIGRATION "WINNERS" AND "LOSERS"

Rank	State	% of Moves Outbound
Winners		
1	North Carolina	38.40%
2	Nevada	40.60%
3	Oregon	41.60%
4	Alabama	42.10%
5	South Carolina	42.20%
6	South Dakota	42.60%
7	Wyoming	42.80%
8	Arizona	44.20%
9	West Virginia	44.30%
10	Tennessee	44.90%
Losers		
50	Michigan	67.80%
49	North Dakota	67.20%
48	New Jersey	61.00%
47	New York	59.40%
46	Illinois	57.60%
45	Ohio	57.00%
44	Pennsylvania	56.60%
43	Indiana	56.40%
42	Wisconsin	54.60%
41	Maryland	54.10%

Note: Alaska and Hawaii not part of the study.
Source: "2007 Migration Study," United Van Lines

Lines keeps close track of where its customers are moving and shipping their belongings in terms of inbound and outbound moves for each state. Fortunately for us, they make these data available on a very timely basis. In Figure 27, we have shaded light blue those states where outbound shipments accounted for 55 percent or more of all shipments in 2007, and we have shaded dark blue those states where inbound shipments accounted for 55 percent or more of all shipments in 2007. Those states that are light grey were somewhere between 45 percent and 55 percent. Doesn't this just say it all? As occurred in the early 1990s, California's neighbors once again stand to benefit tremendously from California's troubles.

These displays and anecdotes all tell the same story. California is moving into a zone where people are voting against the government of California with their feet. Why? The reason is as simple as the basic proposition of economics: taxes, taxes and more taxes.

Progressive Taxes will
Drive You Progressively Broke
If we had to sum up the booms and busts of California's volatile history, one word would

suffice: *taxes*. When the state and local tax burden was low, California prospered by just about any measure you like. And the opposite holds true as well, the present situation being yet more proof of that principle. Although macroeconomists lament they have no truly controlled experiments to study the effects of different fiscal policies, the case of California comes pretty close to fitting the bill.

Our basic story runs as follows: Politicians in Sacramento inevitably paint themselves into a corner. The tax code is steeply progressive. California has the highest marginal income and capital gains tax rates in the nation, and the richest 10 percent of earners pay almost 75 percent of the income tax. This setup showers riches on the state during periods of prosperity, which are of course immediately spent. Then, when the downturn comes, state revenues are hit disproportionately because of the loss of high income earners. Yet since budgets are much easier to expand than contract, the revenue shortfalls lead to massive deficits. To close the gap, the "solution" all too often is to hike taxes even more, which serves to further discourage employment and output – and hence the tax base. Because of the dynamic effects (as illustrated by the Laffer Curve), the tax hikes don't raise as much revenue as predicted, and thus the budget deficits persist. At the same time, welfare rolls and other support programs expand because of rising unemployment. The downward spiral is arrested when the public is finally fed up and demands drastic tax relief. Yet, old habits die hard; the vicious cycle resumes once again in a few years when the public has forgotten the lesson. But at each new cycle, the tax and spending problems ratchet up further and further. California may just be testing how far this vicious cycle can go.

In our opinion, relying on the vigilance of the voters to "guard the guardians" is naïve. A more promising approach is to completely revamp California's tax code, replacing it with a flat tax. By reducing the highest marginal tax rates, such a reform would immediately energize the state's most productive individuals, as well as attract more talent from outside its borders. Beyond the boost to average incomes and growth, the switch to a flat tax would also reduce the volatility in California's tax revenue stream.

In Figure 12, we showed the shocking dependence of California revenue on exercised stock options and realized capital gains.

Our quick lesson leads to the obvious conclusion: If Gov. Schwarzenegger wants to balance his budget and revitalize the California economy, he cannot increase tax rates – ideally he would replace the whole mess with a flat tax. Reducing tax burdens and rationalizing tax policy has worked wonders before and will work wonders again.

All of this circles back to the policy mess in Sacramento, especially to its steeply progressive income tax that encourages budget boom and bust. The Golden State applies a top marginal income tax rate of 10.3 percent, the highest on earnings of any state (excluding some local levies, such as New York City), according to the Tax Foundation. A rising share of those who pay the 10.3 percent rate are now hit by the federal Alternative Minimum Tax, so about one-third of California's income tax is no longer deductible from federal tax liability. This is one more reason for taxpayers to flee the state.

Conclusion

In a very real sense, California went from Karl Marx to Adam Smith, and back to Marx again. The effects are just what economic theory predicts. Whether you look at California versus low-tax states like Texas, or California versus its earlier, low-tax incarnation, the results are the same. The economy grows, and the legislature has fewer budget crises with tax and spending restraint. When asked how well California would ever survive without an income tax, property tax or a sales tax, you now have the answer: "Very well, thank you."

ENDNOTES

1   Adapted from Table 2 of "The Great California Tax Experiment," A.B. Laffer and Associates. May 28, 1993. p. 5.

2   Reproduced from Table 1 in "The Great California Tax Experiment." p. 4.

3   On a personal level, Pete Wilson is one of the nicest, well-meaning people we know. In fact, prior to his becoming governor, Arthur Laffer personally did several appearances at fundraisers for him. Little did he know.

4   See "The Great California Tax Experiment." p. 6.

5   Some have cautioned that the supply-side effects we are discussing would be muted if all states raised (or lowered) their tax rates accordingly. In the extreme, there's no reason to move out of California if every other state is run by socialists too. We concede the point. However, our advice is not a beggar-thy-neighbor policy. If all states simultaneously implemented huge marginal tax rate reductions, their citizens would benefit greatly, and we don't think the state politicians would regret their actions either. It's analogous to getting vaccinated – if you're the only person to do it, it's really worth your while, but even if most others are doing it, it's still a good idea.

6   Taken from Schedule 11 of the "FY2004-05 Governor's Budget Summary."

7   Also rated BBB were Alaska in the 1960s and Massachusetts in the early 1990s. Source: "The State of California's Bonds." Bernstein Municipal Bond Research. November 2003.

8   Sanders, Peter. "City Budget Crunch Hits the Zoo Los Angeles Weighs Setting Billy the Elephant Free as Funds Become Extinct." *Wall Street Journal*. December 4, 2008.

9   Lin, Judy. "Schwarzenegger: $4.4b in tax hikes to end deficit." *Associated Press*. November 6, 2008.

10 Sostek, Anya. "Vallejo's Fiscal Freefall." November 2008.

11 Pagano, Michael A. and Hoene, Christopher W. "City Fiscal Conditions in 2008." National League of Cities. September 2008.

12 The California Demographic Research Unit of the California Department of Finance estimates components of population change using four main components: drivers license "surrenders," IRS tax filings, Medicare recipient addresses, and student loan information. The U.S. Census Bureau uses primarily just IRS tax filings. Estimates of domestic migration from these two sources, while significantly different in absolute terms, demonstrate very similar trends over time. In our research, except when comparing states, we have usually used the Demographic Research Unit data.

13 See Laffer, Arthur and Moore, Stephen. "California, Who Are You? Part II." Laffer Associates, January 18, 2008.

Come on IN
for lower taxes, business and housing costs

IndianaSmar____e.com

INDIANA

Chapter Four

State Rankings

Alabama

26 Economic Performance Rank: 2009

16 Economic Outlook Rank: 2009

Economic Performance Rank (1=best 50=worst)
A historical measure based on a state's performance (equally weighted average) in the three important performance variables shown below. These variables are highly influenced by state policy.

Economic Outlook Rank (1=best 50=worst)
A forecast based on a state's standing (equally weighted average) in the 15 important state policy variables shown below. Data reflect state + local rates and revenues and any effect of federal deductibility.

Personal Income Per Capita
Cumulative Growth 1997-2007   **54.6%   Rank: 20**

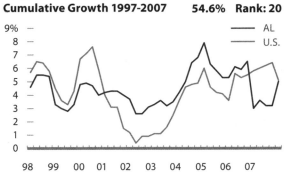

Historical Ranking Comparison
2008 ECONOMIC OUTLOOK RANK 15

Variable	Data	Rank
Top Marginal Personal Income Tax Rate	4.25%	12
Top Marginal Corporate Income Tax Rate	4.23%	5
Personal Income Tax Progressivity (change in tax liability per $1,000 of income)	-$1.51	1
Property Tax Burden (per $1,000 of personal income)	$14.00	1
Sales Tax Burden (per $1,000 of personal income)	$22.67	25
Remaining Tax Burden (per $1,000 of personal income)	$23.23	36
Estate/Inheritance Tax Levied?	No	1
Recently Legislated Tax Changes (2007 & 2008, per $1,000 of personal income)	-$0.21	24
Debt Service as a Share of Tax Revenue	6.9%	17
Public Employees Per 10,000 of Population (full-time equivalent)	614.5	40
State Liability System Survey (tort litigation treatment, judicial impartiality, etc.)	47.5	47
State Minimum Wage (federal floor is $6.55)	$6.55	1
Average Workers' Compensation Costs (per $100 of payroll)	$2.90	42
Right-to-Work State? (option to join or support a union)	Yes	1
Number of Tax or Expenditure Limits (0= least/worst, 3=most/best)	0	29

Absolute Domestic Migration
Cumulative 1998-2007   **65,574   Rank: 16**

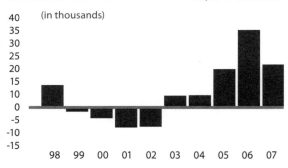

Non-Farm Payroll Employment
Cumulative Growth 1997-2007   **7.5%   Rank: 39**

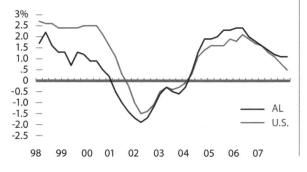

Alaska

25 Economic Performance
Rank: 2009

38 Economic Outlook
Rank: 2009

Economic Performance Rank (1=best 50=worst)

A historical measure based on a state's performance (equally weighted average) in the three important performance variables shown below. These variables are highly influenced by state policy.

Economic Outlook Rank (1=best 50=worst)

A forecast based on a state's standing (equally weighted average) in the 15 important state policy variables shown below. Data reflect state + local rates and revenues and any effect of federal deductibility.

Personal Income Per Capita
Cumulative Growth 1997-2007   **49.5%**   **Rank: 33**

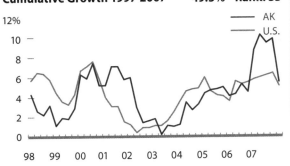

Historical Ranking Comparison
2008 ECONOMIC OUTLOOK RANK   **37**

Variable	Data	Rank
Top Marginal Personal Income Tax Rate	0.00%	1
Top Marginal Corporate Income Tax Rate	9.40%	43
Personal Income Tax Progressivity (change in tax liability per $1,000 of income)	$0.00	2
Property Tax Burden (per $1,000 of personal income)	$38.72	38
Sales Tax Burden (per $1,000 of personal income)	$5.73	5
Remaining Tax Burden (per $1,000 of personal income)	$16.41	15
Estate/Inheritance Tax Levied?	No	1
Recently Legislated Tax Changes (2007 & 2008, per $1,000 of personal income)	$60.51	50
Debt Service as a Share of Tax Revenue	11.6%	49
Public Employees Per 10,000 of Population (full-time equivalent)	761.8	49
State Liability System Survey (tort litigation treatment, judicial impartiality, etc.)	62.6	20
State Minimum Wage (federal floor is $6.55)	$7.15	32
Average Workers' Compensation Costs (per $100 of payroll)	$3.97	50
Right-to-Work State? (option to join or support a union)	No	50
Number of Tax or Expenditure Limits (0= least/worst, 3=most/best)	1	13

Absolute Domestic Migration
Cumulative 1998-2007   **-13,308**   **Rank: 31**

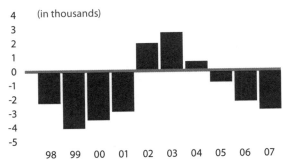

Non-Farm Payroll Employment
Cumulative Growth 1997-2007   **18.1%**   **Rank: 10**

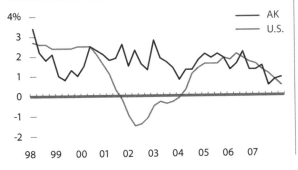

Arizona

8 Economic Performance
Rank: 2009

3 Economic Outlook
Rank: 2009

Economic Performance Rank (1=best 50=worst)
A historical measure based on a state's performance (equally weighted average) in the three important performance variables shown below. These variables are highly influenced by state policy.

Economic Outlook Rank (1=best 50=worst)
A forecast based on a state's standing (equally weighted average) in the 15 important state policy variables shown below. Data reflect state + local rates and revenues and any effect of federal deductibility.

Personal Income Per Capita Cumulative Growth 1997-2007   47.9% **Rank: 36**

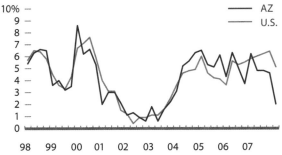

Absolute Domestic Migration Cumulative 1998-2007   817,169 **Rank: 2**

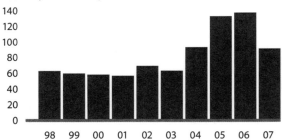

Non-Farm Payroll Employment Cumulative Growth 1997-2007   34.4% **Rank: 2**

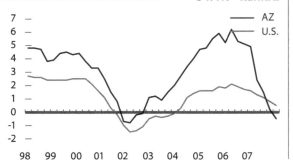

Historical Ranking Comparison
2008 ECONOMIC OUTLOOK RANK 6

Variable	Data	Rank
Top Marginal Personal Income Tax Rate	4.54%	15
Top Marginal Corporate Income Tax Rate	6.97%	23
Personal Income Tax Progressivity (change in tax liability per $1,000 of income)	$10.37	31
Property Tax Burden (per $1,000 of personal income)	$28.83	19
Sales Tax Burden (per $1,000 of personal income)	$31.97	44
Remaining Tax Burden (per $1,000 of personal income)	$13.81	5
Estate/Inheritance Tax Levied?	No	1
Recently Legislated Tax Changes (2007 & 2008, per $1,000 of personal income)	-$1.34	11
Debt Service as a Share of Tax Revenue	7.8%	30
Public Employees Per 10,000 of Population (full-time equivalent)	473.8	2
State Liability System Survey (tort litigation treatment, judicial impartiality, etc.)	65.3	15
State Minimum Wage (federal floor is $6.55)	$6.90	29
Average Workers' Compensation Costs (per $100 of payroll)	$1.67	7
Right-to-Work State? (option to join or support a union)	Yes	1
Number of Tax or Expenditure Limits (0= least/worst, 3=most/best)	2	4

Arkansas

15 Economic Performance Rank: 2009

12 Economic Outlook Rank: 2009

Economic Performance Rank (1=best 50=worst)
A historical measure based on a state's performance (equally weighted average) in the three important performance variables shown below. These variables are highly influenced by state policy.

Economic Outlook Rank (1=best 50=worst)
A forecast based on a state's standing (equally weighted average) in the 15 important state policy variables shown below. Data reflect state + local rates and revenues and any effect of federal deductibility.

Personal Income Per Capita
Cumulative Growth 1997-2007   55.8%   **Rank: 15**

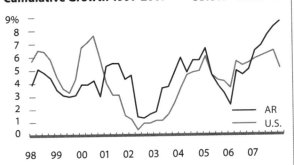

Absolute Domestic Migration
Cumulative 1998-2007   70,395   **Rank: 15**

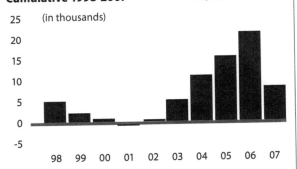

Non-Farm Payroll Employment
Cumulative Growth 1997-2007   9.0%   **Rank: 33**

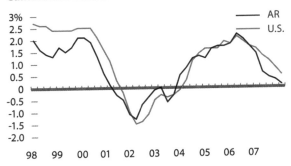

Historical Ranking Comparison
2008 ECONOMIC OUTLOOK RANK 11

Variable	Data	Rank
Top Marginal Personal Income Tax Rate	7.00%	33
Top Marginal Corporate Income Tax Rate	6.50%	19
Personal Income Tax Progressivity (change in tax liability per $1,000 of income)	$13.23	40
Property Tax Burden (per $1,000 of personal income)	$17.08	4
Sales Tax Burden (per $1,000 of personal income)	$35.47	46
Remaining Tax Burden (per $1,000 of personal income)	$17.59	21
Estate/Inheritance Tax Levied?	No	1
Recently Legislated Tax Changes (2007 & 2008, per $1,000 of personal income)	-$0.69	15
Debt Service as a Share of Tax Revenue	5.5%	3
Public Employees Per 10,000 of Population (full-time equivalent)	587.0	34
State Liability System Survey (tort litigation treatment, judicial impartiality, etc.)	58.0	34
State Minimum Wage (federal floor is $6.55)	$6.55	1
Average Workers' Compensation Costs (per $100 of payroll)	$1.61	5
Right-to-Work State? (option to join or support a union)	Yes	1
Number of Tax or Expenditure Limits (0= least/worst, 3=most/best)	1	13

California

27 Economic Performance Rank: 2009

43 Economic Outlook Rank: 2009

Economic Performance Rank (1=best 50=worst)
A historical measure based on a state's performance (equally weighted average) in the three important performance variables shown below. These variables are highly influenced by state policy.

Economic Outlook Rank (1=best 50=worst)
A forecast based on a state's standing (equally weighted average) in the 15 important state policy variables shown below. Data reflect state + local rates and revenues and any effect of federal deductibility.

**Personal Income Per Capita
Cumulative Growth 1997-2007** 56.0% **Rank: 12**

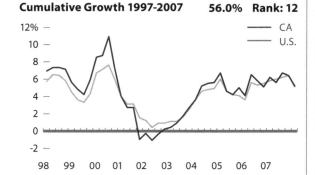

**Absolute Domestic Migration
Cumulative 1998-2007** -1,438,480 **Rank: 49**

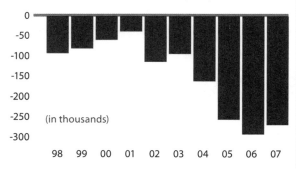

**Non-Farm Payroll Employment
Cumulative Growth 1997-2007** 15.5% **Rank: 15**

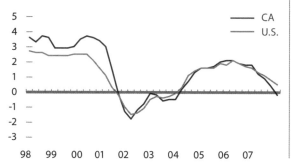

Historical Ranking Comparison
2008 ECONOMIC OUTLOOK RANK 42

Variable	Data	Rank
Top Marginal Personal Income Tax Rate	10.30%	49
Top Marginal Corporate Income Tax Rate	8.84%	37
Personal Income Tax Progressivity (change in tax liability per $1,000 of income)	$34.88	50
Property Tax Burden (per $1,000 of personal income)	$26.63	14
Sales Tax Burden (per $1,000 of personal income)	$23.72	31
Remaining Tax Burden (per $1,000 of personal income)	$16.99	18
Estate/Inheritance Tax Levied?	No	1
Recently Legislated Tax Changes (2007 & 2008, per $1,000 of personal income)	$0.88	40
Debt Service as a Share of Tax Revenue	8.3%	35
Public Employees Per 10,000 of Population (full-time equivalent)	500.6	7
State Liability System Survey (tort litigation treatment, judicial impartiality, etc.)	51.8	44
State Minimum Wage (federal floor is $6.55)	$8.00	48
Average Workers' Compensation Costs (per $100 of payroll)	$2.72	37
Right-to-Work State? (option to join or support a union)	No	50
Number of Tax or Expenditure Limits (0= least/worst, 3=most/best)	2	4

Colorado

10
Economic Performance
Rank: 2009

2
Economic Outlook
Rank: 2009

Economic Performance Rank (1=best 50=worst)
A historical measure based on a state's performance (equally weighted average) in the three important performance variables shown below. These variables are highly influenced by state policy.

Economic Outlook Rank (1=best 50=worst)
A forecast based on a state's standing (equally weighted average) in the 15 important state policy variables shown below. Data reflect state + local rates and revenues and any effect of federal deductibility.

Personal Income Per Capita
Cumulative Growth 1997-2007   **52.1%   Rank: 27**

Absolute Domestic Migration
Cumulative 1998-2007   **248,322   Rank: 9**

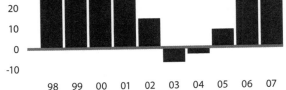

Non-Farm Payroll Employment
Cumulative Growth 1997-2007   **17.7%   Rank: 11**

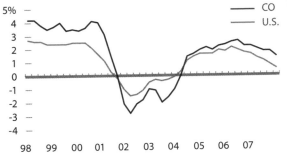

Historical Ranking Comparison
2008 ECONOMIC OUTLOOK RANK

Variable	Data	Rank
Top Marginal Personal Income Tax Rate	4.63%	16
Top Marginal Corporate Income Tax Rate	4.63%	7
Personal Income Tax Progressivity (change in tax liability per $1,000 of income)	$0.00	2
Property Tax Burden (per $1,000 of personal income)	$28.97	20
Sales Tax Burden (per $1,000 of personal income)	$22.13	24
Remaining Tax Burden (per $1,000 of personal income)	$11.80	2
Estate/Inheritance Tax Levied?	No	1
Recently Legislated Tax Changes (2007 & 2008, per $1,000 of personal income)	-$0.28	23
Debt Service as a Share of Tax Revenue	11.3%	48
Public Employees Per 10,000 of Population (full-time equivalent)	539.4	20
State Liability System Survey (tort litigation treatment, judicial impartiality, etc.)	67.5	9
State Minimum Wage (federal floor is $6.55)	$7.02	31
Average Workers' Compensation Costs (per $100 of payroll)	$1.76	9
Right-to-Work State? (option to join or support a union)	No	50
Number of Tax or Expenditure Limits (0= least/worst, 3=most/best)	3	1

Connecticut

37 Economic Performance Rank: 2009

32 Economic Outlook Rank: 2009

Economic Performance Rank (1=best 50=worst)
A historical measure based on a state's performance (equally weighted average) in the three important performance variables shown below. These variables are highly influenced by state policy.

Economic Outlook Rank (1=best 50=worst)
A forecast based on a state's standing (equally weighted average) in the 15 important state policy variables shown below. Data reflect state + local rates and revenues and any effect of federal deductibility.

**Personal Income Per Capita
Cumulative Growth 1997-2007   58.2%   Rank: 10**

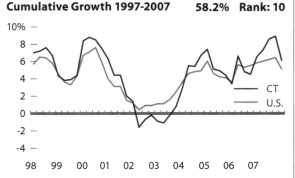

**Absolute Domestic Migration
Cumulative 1998-2007   -113,892   Rank: 41**

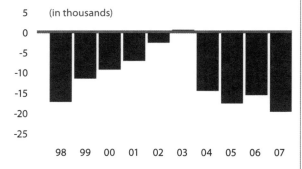

**Non-Farm Payroll Employment
Cumulative Growth 1997-2007   5.6%   Rank: 43**

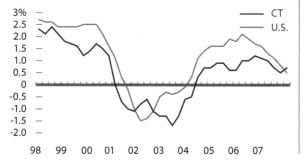

Historical Ranking Comparison
2008 ECONOMIC OUTLOOK RANK   40

Variable	Data	Rank
Top Marginal Personal Income Tax Rate	5.00%	17
Top Marginal Corporate Income Tax Rate	7.50%	26
Personal Income Tax Progressivity (change in tax liability per $1,000 of income)	$11.17	34
Property Tax Burden (per $1,000 of personal income)	$43.46	43
Sales Tax Burden (per $1,000 of personal income)	$17.38	12
Remaining Tax Burden (per $1,000 of personal income)	$15.76	8
Estate/Inheritance Tax Levied?	Yes	50
Recently Legislated Tax Changes (2007 & 2008, per $1,000 of personal income)	$0.28	34
Debt Service as a Share of Tax Revenue	7.1%	20
Public Employees Per 10,000 of Population (full-time equivalent)	532.1	15
State Liability System Survey (tort litigation treatment, judicial impartiality, etc.)	63.2	19
State Minimum Wage (federal floor is $6.55)	$7.65	44
Average Workers' Compensation Costs (per $100 of payroll)	$2.46	31
Right-to-Work State? (option to join or support a union)	No	50
Number of Tax or Expenditure Limits (0= least/worst, 3=most/best)	1	13

Delaware

28 Economic Performance Rank: 2009

31 Economic Outlook Rank: 2009

Economic Performance Rank (1=best 50=worst)
A historical measure based on a state's performance (equally weighted average) in the three important performance variables shown below. These variables are highly influenced by state policy.

Economic Outlook Rank (1=best 50=worst)
A forecast based on a state's standing (equally weighted average) in the 15 important state policy variables shown below. Data reflect state + local rates and revenues and any effect of federal deductibility.

Personal Income Per Capita
Cumulative Growth 1997-2007   48.8%   Rank: 34

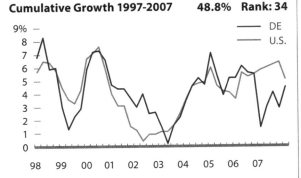

Absolute Domestic Migration
Cumulative 1998-2007   51,010   Rank: 19

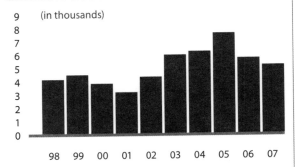

Non-Farm Payroll Employment
Cumulative Growth 1997-2007   12.7%   Rank: 24

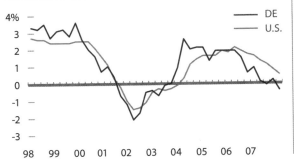

Historical Ranking Comparison
2008 ECONOMIC OUTLOOK RANK **31**

Variable	Data	Rank
Top Marginal Personal Income Tax Rate	7.20%	37
Top Marginal Corporate Income Tax Rate	8.70%	36
Personal Income Tax Progressivity (change in tax liability per $1,000 of income)	$11.34	35
Property Tax Burden (per $1,000 of personal income)	$16.47	3
Sales Tax Burden (per $1,000 of personal income)	$0.00	1
Remaining Tax Burden (per $1,000 of personal income)	$33.74	49
Estate/Inheritance Tax Levied?	No	1
Recently Legislated Tax Changes (2007 & 2008, per $1,000 of personal income)	$1.24	45
Debt Service as a Share of Tax Revenue	6.9%	16
Public Employees Per 10,000 of Population (full-time equivalent)	593.1	36
State Liability System Survey (tort litigation treatment, judicial impartiality, etc.)	71.5	1
State Minimum Wage (federal floor is $6.55)	$7.15	32
Average Workers' Compensation Costs (per $100 of payroll)	$2.96	43
Right-to-Work State? (option to join or support a union)	No	50
Number of Tax or Expenditure Limits (0= least/worst, 3=most/best)	2	4

Florida

2
Economic Performance
Rank: 2009

11
Economic Outlook
Rank: 2009

Economic Performance Rank (1=best 50=worst)
A historical measure based on a state's performance (equally weighted average) in the three important performance variables shown below. These variables are highly influenced by state policy.

Economic Outlook Rank (1=best 50=worst)
A forecast based on a state's standing (equally weighted average) in the 15 important state policy variables shown below. Data reflect state + local rates and revenues and any effect of federal deductibility.

Personal Income Per Capita
Cumulative Growth 1997-2007 55.0% **Rank: 19**

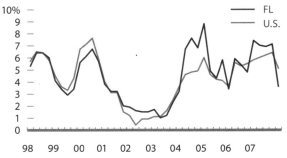

Absolute Domestic Migration
Cumulative 1998-2007 1,579,704 **Rank: 1**

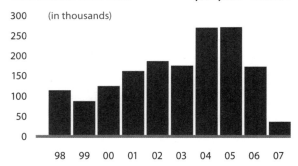

Non-Farm Payroll Employment
Cumulative Growth 1997-2007 25.5% **Rank: 6**

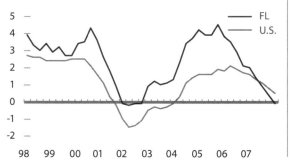

Historical Ranking Comparison
2008 ECONOMIC OUTLOOK RANK **16**

Variable	Data	Rank
Top Marginal Personal Income Tax Rate	0.00%	1
Top Marginal Corporate Income Tax Rate	5.50%	13
Personal Income Tax Progressivity (change in tax liability per $1,000 of income)	$0.00	2
Property Tax Burden (per $1,000 of personal income)	$35.84	34
Sales Tax Burden (per $1,000 of personal income)	$26.92	39
Remaining Tax Burden (per $1,000 of personal income)	$28.45	46
Estate/Inheritance Tax Levied?	No	1
Recently Legislated Tax Changes (2007 & 2008, per $1,000 of personal income)	-$0.35	21
Debt Service as a Share of Tax Revenue	7.5%	24
Public Employees Per 10,000 of Population (full-time equivalent)	488.0	5
State Liability System Survey (tort litigation treatment, judicial impartiality, etc.)	54.9	42
State Minimum Wage (federal floor is $6.55)	$6.79	27
Average Workers' Compensation Costs (per $100 of payroll)	$2.20	23
Right-to-Work State? (option to join or support a union)	Yes	1
Number of Tax or Expenditure Limits (0= least/worst, 3=most/best)	2	4

Georgia

20
Economic Performance
Rank: 2009

8
Economic Outlook
Rank: 2009

Economic Performance Rank (1=best 50=worst)
A historical measure based on a state's performance (equally weighted average) in the three important performance variables shown below. These variables are highly influenced by state policy.

Economic Outlook Rank (1=best 50=worst)
A forecast based on a state's standing (equally weighted average) in the 15 important state policy variables shown below. Data reflect state + local rates and revenues and any effect of federal deductibility.

Personal Income Per Capita
Cumulative Growth 1997-2007   38.5%   Rank: 48

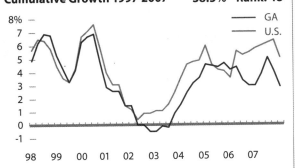

Absolute Domestic Migration
Cumulative 1998-2007   679,420   Rank: 4

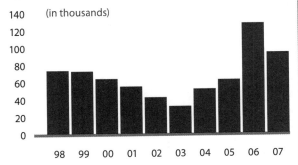

Non-Farm Payroll Employment
Cumulative Growth 1997-2007   14.7%   Rank: 18

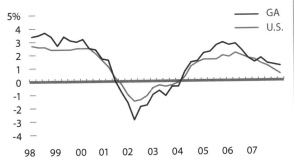

Historical Ranking Comparison
2008 ECONOMIC OUTLOOK RANK   8

Variable	Data	Rank
Top Marginal Personal Income Tax Rate	6.00%	26
Top Marginal Corporate Income Tax Rate	6.00%	15
Personal Income Tax Progressivity (change in tax liability per $1,000 of income)	$6.53	25
Property Tax Burden (per $1,000 of personal income)	$30.52	24
Sales Tax Burden (per $1,000 of personal income)	$23.60	29
Remaining Tax Burden (per $1,000 of personal income)	$11.95	3
Estate/Inheritance Tax Levied?	No	1
Recently Legislated Tax Changes (2007 & 2008, per $1,000 of personal income)	-$0.37	20
Debt Service as a Share of Tax Revenue	5.8%	6
Public Employees Per 10,000 of Population (full-time equivalent)	544.4	22
State Liability System Survey (tort litigation treatment, judicial impartiality, etc.)	61.4	28
State Minimum Wage (federal floor is $6.55)	$6.55	1
Average Workers' Compensation Costs (per $100 of payroll)	$2.29	26
Right-to-Work State? (option to join or support a union)	Yes	1
Number of Tax or Expenditure Limits (0= least/worst, 3=most/best)	0	29

Hawaii

21 Economic Performance
Rank: 2009

41 Economic Outlook
Rank: 2009

Economic Performance Rank (1=best 50=worst)
A historical measure based on a state's performance (equally weighted average) in the three important performance variables shown below. These variables are highly influenced by state policy.

Economic Outlook Rank (1=best 50=worst)
A forecast based on a state's standing (equally weighted average) in the 15 important state policy variables shown below. Data reflect state + local rates and revenues and any effect of federal deductibility.

Personal Income Per Capita
Cumulative Growth 1997-2007   **54.4%   Rank: 21**

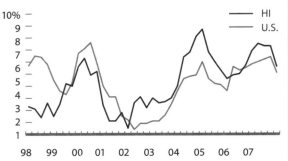

Absolute Domestic Migration
Cumulative 1998-2007   **-64,054   Rank: 38**

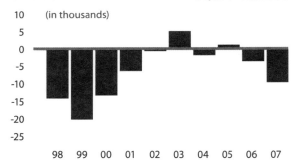

Non-Farm Payroll Employment
Cumulative Growth 1997-2007   **17.3%   Rank: 12**

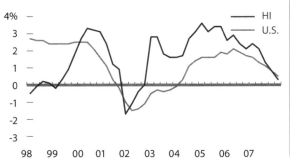

Historical Ranking Comparison
2008 ECONOMIC OUTLOOK RANK **41**

Variable	Data	Rank
Top Marginal Personal Income Tax Rate	8.25%	43
Top Marginal Corporate Income Tax Rate	6.40%	18
Personal Income Tax Progressivity (change in tax liability per $1,000 of income)	$13.22	39
Property Tax Burden (per $1,000 of personal income)	$21.51	8
Sales Tax Burden (per $1,000 of personal income)	$40.15	50
Remaining Tax Burden (per $1,000 of personal income)	$24.53	42
Estate/Inheritance Tax Levied?	No	1
Recently Legislated Tax Changes (2007 & 2008, per $1,000 of personal income)	-$1.51	9
Debt Service as a Share of Tax Revenue	9.1%	39
Public Employees Per 10,000 of Population (full-time equivalent)	557.2	27
State Liability System Survey (tort litigation treatment, judicial impartiality, etc.)	51.5	45
State Minimum Wage (federal floor is $6.55)	$7.25	37
Average Workers' Compensation Costs (per $100 of payroll)	$2.08	16
Right-to-Work State? (option to join or support a union)	No	50
Number of Tax or Expenditure Limits (0= least/worst, 3=most/best)	1	13

Idaho

7 Economic Performance
Rank: 2009

14 Economic Outlook
Rank: 2009

Economic Performance Rank (1=best 50=worst)
A historical measure based on a state's performance (equally weighted average) in the three important performance variables shown below. These variables are highly influenced by state policy.

Economic Outlook Rank (1=best 50=worst)
A forecast based on a state's standing (equally weighted average) in the 15 important state policy variables shown below. Data reflect state + local rates and revenues and any effect of federal deductibility.

Personal Income Per Capita
Cumulative Growth 1997-2007   **53.5%   Rank: 22**

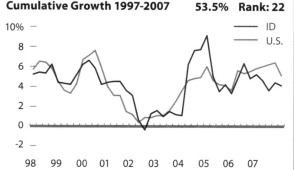

Absolute Domestic Migration
Cumulative 1998-2007   **120,671   Rank: 13**

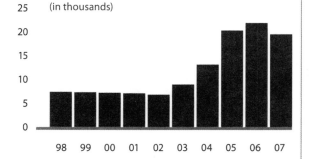

Non-Farm Payroll Employment
Cumulative Growth 1997-2007   **29.7%   Rank: 3**

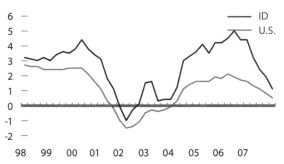

Historical Ranking Comparison
2008 ECONOMIC OUTLOOK RANK   **10**

Variable	Data	Rank
Top Marginal Personal Income Tax Rate	7.80%	39
Top Marginal Corporate Income Tax Rate	7.60%	27
Personal Income Tax Progressivity (change in tax liability per $1,000 of income)	$13.26	42
Property Tax Burden (per $1,000 of personal income)	$29.07	21
Sales Tax Burden (per $1,000 of personal income)	$23.36	28
Remaining Tax Burden (per $1,000 of personal income)	$17.10	19
Estate/Inheritance Tax Levied?	No	1
Recently Legislated Tax Changes (2007 & 2008, per $1,000 of personal income)	-$0.71	14
Debt Service as a Share of Tax Revenue	4.5%	2
Public Employees Per 10,000 of Population (full-time equivalent)	536.4	19
State Liability System Survey (tort litigation treatment, judicial impartiality, etc.)	61.5	26
State Minimum Wage (federal floor is $6.55)	$6.55	1
Average Workers' Compensation Costs (per $100 of payroll)	$2.12	18
Right-to-Work State? (option to join or support a union)	Yes	1
Number of Tax or Expenditure Limits (0= least/worst, 3=most/best)	1	13

Illinois

48 Economic Performance
Rank: 2009

44 Economic Outlook
Rank: 2009

Economic Performance Rank (1=best 50=worst)
A historical measure based on a state's performance (equally weighted average) in the three important performance variables shown below. These variables are highly influenced by state policy.

Economic Outlook Rank (1=best 50=worst)
A forecast based on a state's standing (equally weighted average) in the 15 important state policy variables shown below. Data reflect state + local rates and revenues and any effect of federal deductibility.

Personal Income Per Capita
Cumulative Growth 1997-2007   47.1%   Rank: 39

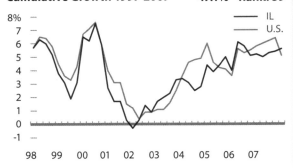

Absolute Domestic Migration
Cumulative 1998-2007   -735,768   Rank: 48

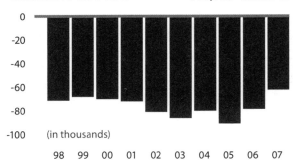

Non-Farm Payroll Employment
Cumulative Growth 1997-2007   3.6%   Rank: 48

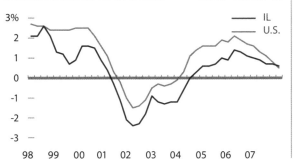

Historical Ranking Comparison
2008 ECONOMIC OUTLOOK RANK   **43**

Variable	Data	Rank
Top Marginal Personal Income Tax Rate	3.00%	10
Top Marginal Corporate Income Tax Rate	7.30%	24
Personal Income Tax Progressivity (change in tax liability per $1,000 of income)	$0.80	15
Property Tax Burden (per $1,000 of personal income)	$40.99	39
Sales Tax Burden (per $1,000 of personal income)	$16.11	11
Remaining Tax Burden (per $1,000 of personal income)	$25.06	43
Estate/Inheritance Tax Levied?	Yes	50
Recently Legislated Tax Changes (2007 & 2008, per $1,000 of personal income)	$0.74	38
Debt Service as a Share of Tax Revenue	9.4%	42
Public Employees Per 10,000 of Population (full-time equivalent)	500.8	8
State Liability System Survey (tort litigation treatment, judicial impartiality, etc.)	51.3	46
State Minimum Wage (federal floor is $6.55)	$7.75	46
Average Workers' Compensation Costs (per $100 of payroll)	$2.79	40
Right-to-Work State? (option to join or support a union)	No	50
Number of Tax or Expenditure Limits (0= least/worst, 3=most/best)	0	29

Indiana

47 Economic Performance
Rank: 2009

17 Economic Outlook
Rank: 2009

Economic Performance Rank (1=best 50=worst)
A historical measure based on a state's performance (equally weighted average) in the three important performance variables shown below. These variables are highly influenced by state policy.

Economic Outlook Rank (1=best 50=worst)
A forecast based on a state's standing (equally weighted average) in the 15 important state policy variables shown below. Data reflect state + local rates and revenues and any effect of federal deductibility.

Personal Income Per Capita
Cumulative Growth 1997-2007   **40.9%   Rank: 47**

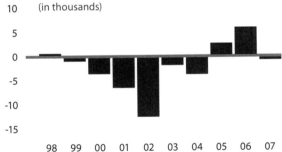

Absolute Domestic Migration
Cumulative 1998-2007   **-20,285   Rank: 32**

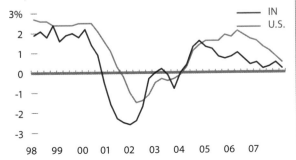

Non-Farm Payroll Employment
Cumulative Growth 1997-2007   **4.6%   Rank: 45**

Historical Ranking Comparison
2008 ECONOMIC OUTLOOK RANK

Variable	Data	Rank
Top Marginal Personal Income Tax Rate	4.30%	13
Top Marginal Corporate Income Tax Rate	8.50%	33
Personal Income Tax Progressivity (change in tax liability per $1,000 of income)	$0.57	14
Property Tax Burden (per $1,000 of personal income)	$32.40	30
Sales Tax Burden (per $1,000 of personal income)	$23.61	30
Remaining Tax Burden (per $1,000 of personal income)	$15.69	7
Estate/Inheritance Tax Levied?	Yes	50
Recently Legislated Tax Changes (2007 & 2008, per $1,000 of personal income)	$0.96	42
Debt Service as a Share of Tax Revenue	6.7%	15
Public Employees Per 10,000 of Population (full-time equivalent)	533.0	16
State Liability System Survey (tort litigation treatment, judicial impartiality, etc.)	69.1	4
State Minimum Wage (federal floor is $6.55)	$6.55	1
Average Workers' Compensation Costs (per $100 of payroll)	$1.23	2
Right-to-Work State? (option to join or support a union)	No	50
Number of Tax or Expenditure Limits (0= least/worst, 3=most/best)	0	29

Iowa

45 Economic Performance Rank: 2009

35 Economic Outlook Rank: 2009

Economic Performance Rank (1=best 50=worst)
A historical measure based on a state's performance (equally weighted average) in the three important performance variables shown below. These variables are highly influenced by state policy.

Economic Outlook Rank (1=best 50=worst)
A forecast based on a state's standing (equally weighted average) in the 15 important state policy variables shown below. Data reflect state + local rates and revenues and any effect of federal deductibility.

Personal Income Per Capita
Cumulative Growth 1997-2007   **47.5%   Rank: 37**

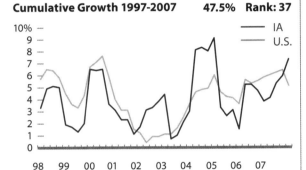

Absolute Domestic Migration
Cumulative 1998-2007   **-63,754   Rank: 37**

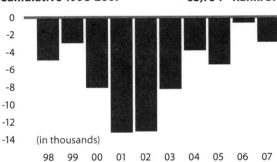

Non-Farm Payroll Employment
Cumulative Growth 1997-2007   **7.8%   Rank: 38**

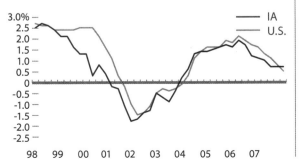

Historical Ranking Comparison
2008 ECONOMIC OUTLOOK RANK 23

Variable	Data	Rank
Top Marginal Personal Income Tax Rate	5.84%	25
Top Marginal Corporate Income Tax Rate	9.90%	46
Personal Income Tax Progressivity (change in tax liability per $1,000 of income)	$12.11	36
Property Tax Burden (per $1,000 of personal income)	$35.63	32
Sales Tax Burden (per $1,000 of personal income)	$20.95	19
Remaining Tax Burden (per $1,000 of personal income)	$18.39	25
Estate/Inheritance Tax Levied?	Yes	50
Recently Legislated Tax Changes (2007 & 2008, per $1,000 of personal income)	$1.10	44
Debt Service as a Share of Tax Revenue	5.6%	4
Public Employees Per 10,000 of Population (full-time equivalent)	609.9	39
State Liability System Survey (tort litigation treatment, judicial impartiality, etc.)	68.0	7
State Minimum Wage (federal floor is $6.55)	$7.25	37
Average Workers' Compensation Costs (per $100 of payroll)	$1.86	11
Right-to-Work State? (option to join or support a union)	Yes	1
Number of Tax or Expenditure Limits (0= least/worst, 3=most/best)	0	29

Kansas

42
Economic Performance
Rank: 2009

24
Economic Outlook
Rank: 2009

Economic Performance Rank (1=best 50=worst)
A historical measure based on a state's performance (equally weighted average) in the three important performance variables shown below. These variables are highly influenced by state policy.

Economic Outlook Rank (1=best 50=worst)
A forecast based on a state's standing (equally weighted average) in the 15 important state policy variables shown below. Data reflect state + local rates and revenues and any effect of federal deductibility.

**Personal Income Per Capita
Cumulative Growth 1997-2007**   51.5%   **Rank: 29**

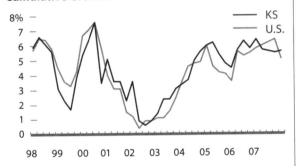

**Absolute Domestic Migration
Cumulative 1998-2007**   -73,660   **Rank: 40**

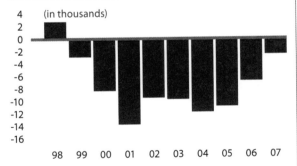

**Non-Farm Payroll Employment
Cumulative Growth 1997-2007**   8.6%   **Rank: 34**

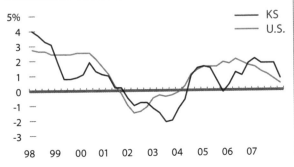

Historical Ranking Comparison
2008 ECONOMIC OUTLOOK RANK 29

Variable	Data	Rank
Top Marginal Personal Income Tax Rate	6.45%	27
Top Marginal Corporate Income Tax Rate	7.35%	25
Personal Income Tax Progressivity (change in tax liability per $1,000 of income)	$10.82	33
Property Tax Burden (per $1,000 of personal income)	$35.78	33
Sales Tax Burden (per $1,000 of personal income)	$26.07	37
Remaining Tax Burden (per $1,000 of personal income)	$14.27	6
Estate/Inheritance Tax Levied?	Yes	50
Recently Legislated Tax Changes (2007 & 2008, per $1,000 of personal income)	-$0.55	16
Debt Service as a Share of Tax Revenue	8.5%	36
Public Employees Per 10,000 of Population (full-time equivalent)	677.1	48
State Liability System Survey (tort litigation treatment, judicial impartiality, etc.)	66.7	10
State Minimum Wage (federal floor is $6.55)	$6.55	1
Average Workers' Compensation Costs (per $100 of payroll)	$1.77	10
Right-to-Work State? (option to join or support a union)	Yes	1
Number of Tax or Expenditure Limits (0= least/worst, 3=most/best)	0	29

Kentucky

31 Economic Performance Rank: 2009

36 Economic Outlook Rank: 2009

Economic Performance Rank (1=best 50=worst)

A historical measure based on a state's performance (equally weighted average) in the three important performance variables shown below. These variables are highly influenced by state policy.

Economic Outlook Rank (1=best 50=worst)

A forecast based on a state's standing (equally weighted average) in the 15 important state policy variables shown below. Data reflect state + local rates and revenues and any effect of federal deductibility.

Personal Income Per Capita
Cumulative Growth 1997-2007   46.8%   Rank: 40

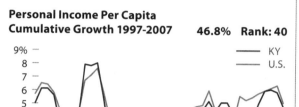

Historical Ranking Comparison
2008 ECONOMIC OUTLOOK RANK   44

Variable	Data	Rank
Top Marginal Personal Income Tax Rate	8.20%	41
Top Marginal Corporate Income Tax Rate	8.20%	31
Personal Income Tax Progressivity (change in tax liability per $1,000 of income)	$5.28	19
Property Tax Burden (per $1,000 of personal income)	$20.09	6
Sales Tax Burden (per $1,000 of personal income)	$19.97	14
Remaining Tax Burden (per $1,000 of personal income)	$23.85	40
Estate/Inheritance Tax Levied?	Yes	50
Recently Legislated Tax Changes (2007 & 2008, per $1,000 of personal income)	-$0.46	18
Debt Service as a Share of Tax Revenue	9.5%	44
Public Employees Per 10,000 of Population (full-time equivalent)	579.6	32
State Liability System Survey (tort litigation treatment, judicial impartiality, etc.)	61.3	29
State Minimum Wage (federal floor is $6.55)	$6.55	1
Average Workers' Compensation Costs (per $100 of payroll)	$2.96	43
Right-to-Work State? (option to join or support a union)	No	50
Number of Tax or Expenditure Limits (0= least/worst, 3=most/best)	1	13

Absolute Domestic Migration
Cumulative 1998-2007   82,336   Rank: 14

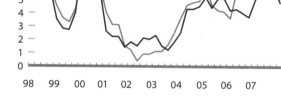

Non-Farm Payroll Employment
Cumulative Growth 1997-2007   9.2%   Rank: 32

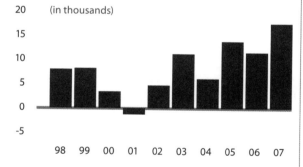

Louisiana

35
Economic Performance
Rank: 2009

18
Economic Outlook
Rank: 2009

Economic Performance Rank (1=best 50=worst)
A historical measure based on a state's performance (equally weighted average) in the three important performance variables shown below. These variables are highly influenced by state policy.

Economic Outlook Rank (1=best 50=worst)
A forecast based on a state's standing (equally weighted average) in the 15 important state policy variables shown below. Data reflect state + local rates and revenues and any effect of federal deductibility.

Personal Income Per Capita
Cumulative Growth 1997-2007   74.4%   **Rank: 3**

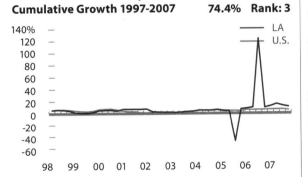

Historical Ranking Comparison
2008 ECONOMIC OUTLOOK RANK

Variable	Data	Rank
Top Marginal Personal Income Tax Rate	3.90%	11
Top Marginal Corporate Income Tax Rate	5.20%	12
Personal Income Tax Progressivity (change in tax liability per $1,000 of income)	$9.15	28
Property Tax Burden (per $1,000 of personal income)	$21.42	7
Sales Tax Burden (per $1,000 of personal income)	$38.22	48
Remaining Tax Burden (per $1,000 of personal income)	$19.04	27
Estate/Inheritance Tax Levied?	No	1
Recently Legislated Tax Changes (2007 & 2008, per $1,000 of personal income)	-$6.10	1
Debt Service as a Share of Tax Revenue	8.2%	32
Public Employees Per 10,000 of Population (full-time equivalent)	615.4	41
State Liability System Survey (tort litigation treatment, judicial impartiality, etc.)	42.9	49
State Minimum Wage (federal floor is $6.55)	$6.55	1
Average Workers' Compensation Costs (per $100 of payroll)	$2.76	39
Right-to-Work State? (option to join or support a union)	Yes	1
Number of Tax or Expenditure Limits (0= least/worst, 3=most/best)	2	4

Absolute Domestic Migration
Cumulative 1998-2007   -390,998   **Rank: 44**

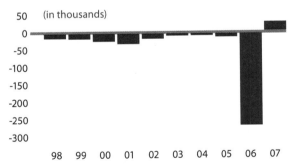

Non-Farm Payroll Employment
Cumulative Growth 1997-2007   3.9%   **Rank: 47**

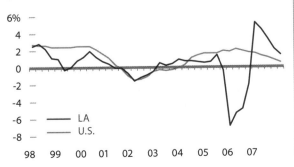

Maine

24 Economic Performance Rank: 2009

47 Economic Outlook Rank: 2009

Economic Performance Rank (1=best 50=worst)

A historical measure based on a state's performance (equally weighted average) in the three important performance variables shown below. These variables are highly influenced by state policy.

Economic Outlook Rank (1=best 50=worst)

A forecast based on a state's standing (equally weighted average) in the 15 important state policy variables shown below. Data reflect state + local rates and revenues and any effect of federal deductibility.

Personal Income Per Capita
Cumulative Growth 1997-2007 **52.1% Rank: 26**

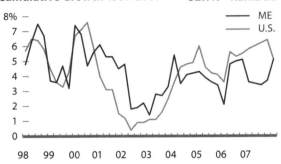

Absolute Domestic Migration
Cumulative 1998-2007 **38,809 Rank: 20**

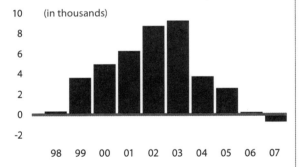

Non-Farm Payroll Employment
Cumulative Growth 1997-2007 **11.5% Rank: 27**

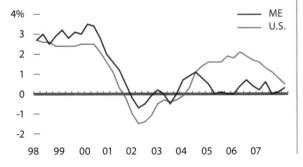

Historical Ranking Comparison
2008 ECONOMIC OUTLOOK RANK **46**

Variable	Data	Rank
Top Marginal Personal Income Tax Rate	8.50%	44
Top Marginal Corporate Income Tax Rate	8.93%	38
Personal Income Tax Progressivity (change in tax liability per $1,000 of income)	$17.82	46
Property Tax Burden (per $1,000 of personal income)	$53.41	48
Sales Tax Burden (per $1,000 of personal income)	$21.63	22
Remaining Tax Burden (per $1,000 of personal income)	$23.36	38
Estate/Inheritance Tax Levied?	Yes	50
Recently Legislated Tax Changes (2007 & 2008, per $1,000 of personal income)	-$0.83	13
Debt Service as a Share of Tax Revenue	5.8%	7
Public Employees Per 10,000 of Population (full-time equivalent)	578.0	31
State Liability System Survey (tort litigation treatment, judicial impartiality, etc.)	69.3	3
State Minimum Wage (federal floor is $6.55)	$7.25	37
Average Workers' Compensation Costs (per $100 of payroll)	$3.04	45
Right-to-Work State? (option to join or support a union)	No	50
Number of Tax or Expenditure Limits (0= least/worst, 3=most/best)	0	29

Maryland

17 Economic Performance Rank: 2009

28 Economic Outlook Rank: 2009

Economic Performance Rank (1=best 50=worst)
A historical measure based on a state's performance (equally weighted average) in the three important performance variables shown below. These variables are highly influenced by state policy.

Economic Outlook Rank (1=best 50=worst)
A forecast based on a state's standing (equally weighted average) in the 15 important state policy variables shown below. Data reflect state + local rates and revenues and any effect of federal deductibility.

**Personal Income Per Capita
Cumulative Growth 1997-2007**   61.1%   **Rank: 9**

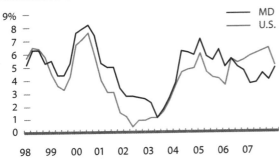

Historical Ranking Comparison
2008 ECONOMIC OUTLOOK RANK 28

Variable	Data	Rank
Top Marginal Personal Income Tax Rate	9.30%	47
Top Marginal Corporate Income Tax Rate	8.30%	32
Personal Income Tax Progressivity (change in tax liability per $1,000 of income)	$5.78	21
Property Tax Burden (per $1,000 of personal income)	$24.83	11
Sales Tax Burden (per $1,000 of personal income)	$10.98	6
Remaining Tax Burden (per $1,000 of personal income)	$23.08	35
Estate/Inheritance Tax Levied?	Yes	50
Recently Legislated Tax Changes (2007 & 2008, per $1,000 of personal income)	$4.29	49
Debt Service as a Share of Tax Revenue	5.7%	5
Public Employees Per 10,000 of Population (full-time equivalent)	534.0	18
State Liability System Survey (tort litigation treatment, judicial impartiality, etc.)	60.6	30
State Minimum Wage (federal floor is $6.55)	$6.55	1
Average Workers' Compensation Costs (per $100 of payroll)	$1.72	8
Right-to-Work State? (option to join or support a union)	No	50
Number of Tax or Expenditure Limits (0= least/worst, 3=most/best)	0	29

**Absolute Domestic Migration
Cumulative 1998-2007**   -65,868   **Rank: 39**

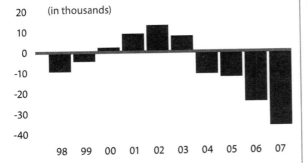

**Non-Farm Payroll Employment
Cumulative Growth 1997-2007**   15.0%   **Rank: 17**

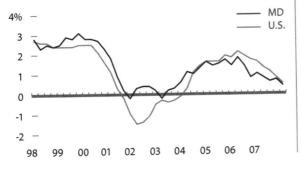

Massachusetts

36 Economic Performance Rank: 2009

26 Economic Outlook Rank: 2009

Economic Performance Rank (1=best 50=worst)
A historical measure based on a state's performance (equally weighted average) in the three important performance variables shown below. These variables are highly influenced by state policy.

Economic Outlook Rank (1=best 50=worst)
A forecast based on a state's standing (equally weighted average) in the 15 important state policy variables shown below. Data reflect state + local rates and revenues and any effect of federal deductibility.

**Personal Income Per Capita
Cumulative Growth 1997-2007**   61.4%   Rank: 7

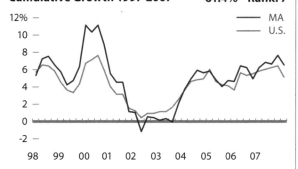

**Absolute Domestic Migration
Cumulative 1998-2007**   -335,391   Rank: 43

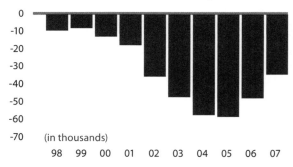

**Non-Farm Payroll Employment
Cumulative Growth 1997-2007**   5.3%   Rank: 44

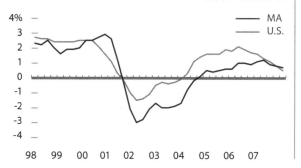

Historical Ranking Comparison
2008 ECONOMIC OUTLOOK RANK   **22**

Variable	Data	Rank
Top Marginal Personal Income Tax Rate	5.30%	20
Top Marginal Corporate Income Tax Rate	9.50%	44
Personal Income Tax Progressivity (change in tax liability per $1,000 of income)	$2.92	17
Property Tax Burden (per $1,000 of personal income)	$37.45	36
Sales Tax Burden (per $1,000 of personal income)	$12.55	8
Remaining Tax Burden (per $1,000 of personal income)	$11.50	1
Estate/Inheritance Tax Levied?	Yes	50
Recently Legislated Tax Changes (2007 & 2008, per $1,000 of personal income)	$0.61	36
Debt Service as a Share of Tax Revenue	13.3%	50
Public Employees Per 10,000 of Population (full-time equivalent)	516.2	12
State Liability System Survey (tort litigation treatment, judicial impartiality, etc.)	63.5	18
State Minimum Wage (federal floor is $6.55)	$8.00	48
Average Workers' Compensation Costs (per $100 of payroll)	$1.39	3
Right-to-Work State? (option to join or support a union)	No	50
Number of Tax or Expenditure Limits (0= least/worst, 3=most/best)	1	13

Michigan

50 Economic Performance Rank: 2009

34 Economic Outlook Rank: 2009

Economic Performance Rank (1=best 50=worst)
A historical measure based on a state's performance (equally weighted average) in the three important performance variables shown below. These variables are highly influenced by state policy.

Economic Outlook Rank (1=best 50=worst)
A forecast based on a state's standing (equally weighted average) in the 15 important state policy variables shown below. Data reflect state + local rates and revenues and any effect of federal deductibility.

Personal Income Per Capita
Cumulative Growth 1997-2007   33.8%   Rank: 50

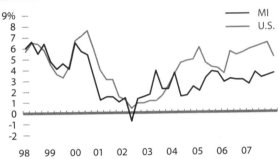

Historical Ranking Comparison 2008 ECONOMIC OUTLOOK RANK	17

Variable	Data	Rank
Top Marginal Personal Income Tax Rate	6.85%	31
Top Marginal Corporate Income Tax Rate	9.01%	41
Personal Income Tax Progressivity (change in tax liability per $1,000 of income)	$1.97	16
Property Tax Burden (per $1,000 of personal income)	$41.11	41
Sales Tax Burden (per $1,000 of personal income)	$23.73	32
Remaining Tax Burden (per $1,000 of personal income)	$17.18	20
Estate/Inheritance Tax Levied?	No	1
Recently Legislated Tax Changes (2007 & 2008, per $1,000 of personal income)	$3.65	48
Debt Service as a Share of Tax Revenue	7.7%	28
Public Employees Per 10,000 of Population (full-time equivalent)	486.9	4
State Liability System Survey (tort litigation treatment, judicial impartiality, etc.)	59.7	33
State Minimum Wage (federal floor is $6.55)	$7.40	42
Average Workers' Compensation Costs (per $100 of payroll)	$2.15	20
Right-to-Work State? (option to join or support a union)	No	50
Number of Tax or Expenditure Limits (0= least/worst, 3=most/best)	2	4

Absolute Domestic Migration
Cumulative 1998-2007   -419,961   Rank: 46

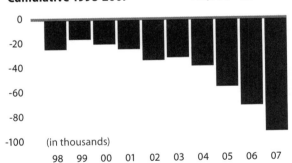

Non-Farm Payroll Employment
Cumulative Growth 1997-2007   -4.0%   Rank: 50

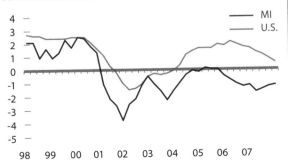

Minnesota

34 Economic Performance Rank: 2009

40 Economic Outlook Rank: 2009

Economic Performance Rank (1=best 50=worst)
A historical measure based on a state's performance (equally weighted average) in the three important performance variables shown below. These variables are highly influenced by state policy.

Economic Outlook Rank (1=best 50=worst)
A forecast based on a state's standing (equally weighted average) in the 15 important state policy variables shown below. Data reflect state + local rates and revenues and any effect of federal deductibility.

Personal Income Per Capita
Cumulative Growth 1997-2007 50.7% **Rank: 31**

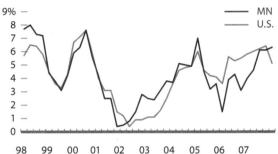

Absolute Domestic Migration
Cumulative 1998-2007 -8,267 **Rank: 30**

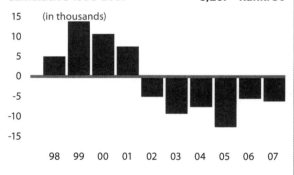

Non-Farm Payroll Employment
Cumulative Growth 1997-2007 10.9% **Rank: 28**

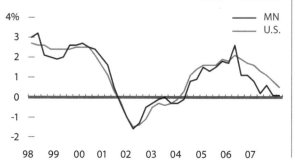

Historical Ranking Comparison
2008 ECONOMIC OUTLOOK RANK 39

Variable	Data	Rank
Top Marginal Personal Income Tax Rate	7.85%	40
Top Marginal Corporate Income Tax Rate	9.80%	45
Personal Income Tax Progressivity (change in tax liability per $1,000 of income)	$9.10	27
Property Tax Burden (per $1,000 of personal income)	$27.34	17
Sales Tax Burden (per $1,000 of personal income)	$20.62	18
Remaining Tax Burden (per $1,000 of personal income)	$23.34	37
Estate/Inheritance Tax Levied?	Yes	50
Recently Legislated Tax Changes (2007 & 2008, per $1,000 of personal income)	$1.08	43
Debt Service as a Share of Tax Revenue	7.6%	25
Public Employees Per 10,000 of Population (full-time equivalent)	539.6	21
State Liability System Survey (tort litigation treatment, judicial impartiality, etc.)	66.5	11
State Minimum Wage (federal floor is $6.55)	$6.55	1
Average Workers' Compensation Costs (per $100 of payroll)	$2.33	27
Right-to-Work State? (option to join or support a union)	No	50
Number of Tax or Expenditure Limits (0= least/worst, 3=most/best)	0	29

Mississippi

39
Economic Performance
Rank: 2009

19
Economic Outlook
Rank: 2009

Economic Performance Rank (1=best 50=worst)
A historical measure based on a state's performance (equally weighted average) in the three important performance variables shown below. These variables are highly influenced by state policy.

Economic Outlook Rank (1=best 50=worst)
A forecast based on a state's standing (equally weighted average) in the 15 important state policy variables shown below. Data reflect state + local rates and revenues and any effect of federal deductibility.

Historical Ranking Comparison
2008 ECONOMIC OUTLOOK RANK 19

Personal Income Per Capita
Cumulative Growth 1997-2007   52.8%   **Rank: 23**

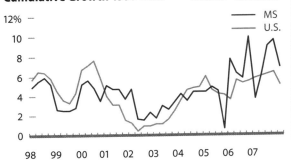

Absolute Domestic Migration
Cumulative 1998-2007   -28,933   **Rank: 33**

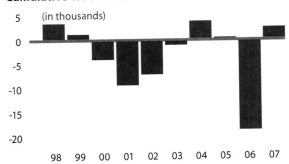

Non-Farm Payroll Employment
Cumulative Growth 1997-2007   4.0%   **Rank: 46**

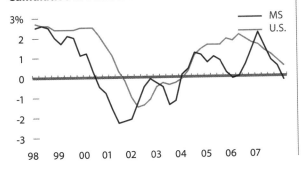

Variable	Data	Rank
Top Marginal Personal Income Tax Rate	5.00%	17
Top Marginal Corporate Income Tax Rate	5.00%	8
Personal Income Tax Progressivity (change in tax liability per $1,000 of income)	$7.53	26
Property Tax Burden (per $1,000 of personal income)	$27.47	18
Sales Tax Burden (per $1,000 of personal income)	$31.66	43
Remaining Tax Burden (per $1,000 of personal income)	$16.38	13
Estate/Inheritance Tax Levied?	No	1
Recently Legislated Tax Changes (2007 & 2008, per $1,000 of personal income)	$0.25	33
Debt Service as a Share of Tax Revenue	6.0%	10
Public Employees Per 10,000 of Population (full-time equivalent)	648.0	45
State Liability System Survey (tort litigation treatment, judicial impartiality, etc.)	43.7	48
State Minimum Wage (federal floor is $6.55)	$6.55	1
Average Workers' Compensation Costs (per $100 of payroll)	$2.33	27
Right-to-Work State? (option to join or support a union)	Yes	1
Number of Tax or Expenditure Limits (0= least/worst, 3=most/best)	1	13

Missouri

44 Economic Performance
Rank: 2009

23 Economic Outlook
Rank: 2009

Economic Performance Rank (1=best 50=worst)
A historical measure based on a state's performance (equally weighted average) in the three important performance variables shown below. These variables are highly influenced by state policy.

Economic Outlook Rank (1=best 50=worst)
A forecast based on a state's standing (equally weighted average) in the 15 important state policy variables shown below. Data reflect state + local rates and revenues and any effect of federal deductibility.

**Personal Income Per Capita
Cumulative Growth 1997-2007**   **43.1%   Rank: 44**

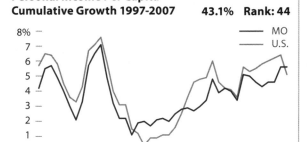

**Absolute Domestic Migration
Cumulative 1998-2007**   **54,459   Rank: 18**

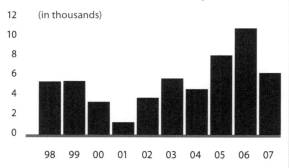

**Non-Farm Payroll Employment
Cumulative Growth 1997-2007**   **6.0%   Rank: 42**

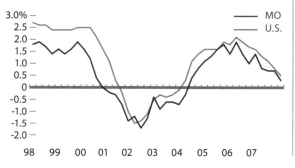

Historical Ranking Comparison
2008 ECONOMIC OUTLOOK RANK **25**

Variable	Data	Rank
Top Marginal Personal Income Tax Rate	7.00%	32
Top Marginal Corporate Income Tax Rate	5.81%	14
Personal Income Tax Progressivity (change in tax liability per $1,000 of income)	$13.24	41
Property Tax Burden (per $1,000 of personal income)	$26.90	15
Sales Tax Burden (per $1,000 of personal income)	$24.52	35
Remaining Tax Burden (per $1,000 of personal income)	$16.55	16
Estate/Inheritance Tax Levied?	No	1
Recently Legislated Tax Changes (2007 & 2008, per $1,000 of personal income)	$0.22	31
Debt Service as a Share of Tax Revenue	8.9%	38
Public Employees Per 10,000 of Population (full-time equivalent)	556.8	26
State Liability System Survey (tort litigation treatment, judicial impartiality, etc.)	60.1	31
State Minimum Wage (federal floor is $6.55)	$6.65	26
Average Workers' Compensation Costs (per $100 of payroll)	$2.20	23
Right-to-Work State? (option to join or support a union)	No	50
Number of Tax or Expenditure Limits (0= least/worst, 3=most/best)	3	1

Montana

4 Economic Performance
Rank: 2009

30 Economic Outlook
Rank: 2009

Economic Performance Rank (1=best 50=worst)
A historical measure based on a state's performance (equally weighted average) in the three important performance variables shown below. These variables are highly influenced by state policy.

Economic Outlook Rank (1=best 50=worst)
A forecast based on a state's standing (equally weighted average) in the 15 important state policy variables shown below. Data reflect state + local rates and revenues and any effect of federal deductibility.

Personal Income Per Capita
Cumulative Growth 1997-2007   66.1%   **Rank: 5**

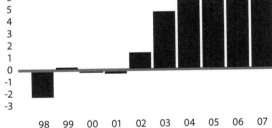

Historical Ranking Comparison
2008 ECONOMIC OUTLOOK RANK 32

Variable	Data	Rank
Top Marginal Personal Income Tax Rate	4.49%	14
Top Marginal Corporate Income Tax Rate	6.75%	21
Personal Income Tax Progressivity (change in tax liability per $1,000 of income)	$5.68	20
Property Tax Burden (per $1,000 of personal income)	$37.26	35
Sales Tax Burden (per $1,000 of personal income)	$0.00	1
Remaining Tax Burden (per $1,000 of personal income)	$26.90	45
Estate/Inheritance Tax Levied?	No	1
Recently Legislated Tax Changes (2007 & 2008, per $1,000 of personal income)	$0.45	35
Debt Service as a Share of Tax Revenue	7.0%	19
Public Employees Per 10,000 of Population (full-time equivalent)	584.1	33
State Liability System Survey (tort litigation treatment, judicial impartiality, etc.)	57.3	38
State Minimum Wage (federal floor is $6.55)	$6.55	1
Average Workers' Compensation Costs (per $100 of payroll)	$3.50	49
Right-to-Work State? (option to join or support a union)	No	50
Number of Tax or Expenditure Limits (0= least/worst, 3=most/best)	1	13

Absolute Domestic Migration
Cumulative 1998-2007   28,382   **Rank: 21**

Non-Farm Payroll Employment
Cumulative Growth 1997-2007   21.2%   **Rank: 7**

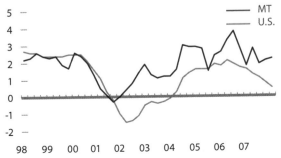

Nebraska

33
Economic Performance
Rank: 2009

29
Economic Outlook
Rank: 2009

Economic Performance Rank (1=best 50=worst)
A historical measure based on a state's performance (equally weighted average) in the three important performance variables shown below. These variables are highly influenced by state policy.

Economic Outlook Rank (1=best 50=worst)
A forecast based on a state's standing (equally weighted average) in the 15 important state policy variables shown below. Data reflect state + local rates and revenues and any effect of federal deductibility.

Historical Ranking Comparison
2008 ECONOMIC OUTLOOK RANK 34

Personal Income Per Capita
Cumulative Growth 1997-2007   **51.6%   Rank: 28**

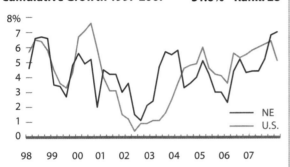

Absolute Domestic Migration
Cumulative 1998-2007   **-51,200   Rank: 36**

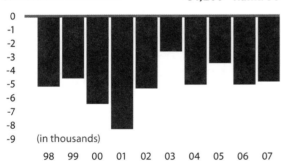

Non-Farm Payroll Employment
Cumulative Growth 1997-2007   **12.4%   Rank: 25**

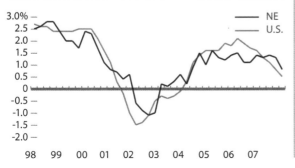

Variable	Data	Rank
Top Marginal Personal Income Tax Rate	6.84%	30
Top Marginal Corporate Income Tax Rate	7.81%	29
Personal Income Tax Progressivity (change in tax liability per $1,000 of income)	$16.42	45
Property Tax Burden (per $1,000 of personal income)	$38.02	37
Sales Tax Burden (per $1,000 of personal income)	$29.40	41
Remaining Tax Burden (per $1,000 of personal income)	$19.63	29
Estate/Inheritance Tax Levied?	Yes	50
Recently Legislated Tax Changes (2007 & 2008, per $1,000 of personal income)	-$2.11	5
Debt Service as a Share of Tax Revenue	5.9%	8
Public Employees Per 10,000 of Population (full-time equivalent)	640.3	44
State Liability System Survey (tort litigation treatment, judicial impartiality, etc.)	71.3	2
State Minimum Wage (federal floor is $6.55)	$6.55	1
Average Workers' Compensation Costs (per $100 of payroll)	$2.15	20
Right-to-Work State? (option to join or support a union)	Yes	1
Number of Tax or Expenditure Limits (0= least/worst, 3=most/best)	0	29

Nevada

9 Economic Performance
Rank: 2009

7 Economic Outlook
Rank: 2009

Economic Performance Rank (1=best 50=worst)
A historical measure based on a state's performance (equally weighted average) in the three important performance variables shown below. These variables are highly influenced by state policy.

Economic Outlook Rank (1=best 50=worst)
A forecast based on a state's standing (equally weighted average) in the 15 important state policy variables shown below. Data reflect state + local rates and revenues and any effect of federal deductibility.

**Personal Income Per Capita
Cumulative Growth 1997-2007   48.4%   Rank: 35**

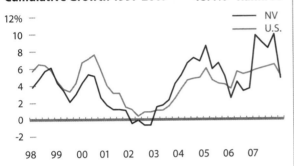

**Absolute Domestic Migration
Cumulative 1998-2007   481,534   Rank: 6**

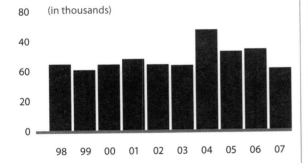

**Non-Farm Payroll Employment
Cumulative Growth 1997-2007   45.0%   Rank: 1**

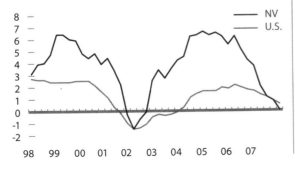

Historical Ranking Comparison
2008 ECONOMIC OUTLOOK RANK

Variable	Data	Rank
Top Marginal Personal Income Tax Rate	0.00%	1
Top Marginal Corporate Income Tax Rate	0.00%	1
Personal Income Tax Progressivity (change in tax liability per $1,000 of income)	$0.00	2
Property Tax Burden (per $1,000 of personal income)	$26.90	16
Sales Tax Burden (per $1,000 of personal income)	$25.58	36
Remaining Tax Burden (per $1,000 of personal income)	$39.55	50
Estate/Inheritance Tax Levied?	No	1
Recently Legislated Tax Changes (2007 & 2008, per $1,000 of personal income)	-$0.52	17
Debt Service as a Share of Tax Revenue	8.3%	34
Public Employees Per 10,000 of Population (full-time equivalent)	429.7	1
State Liability System Survey (tort litigation treatment, judicial impartiality, etc.)	56.9	40
State Minimum Wage (federal floor is $6.55)	$6.85	28
Average Workers' Compensation Costs (per $100 of payroll)	$2.58	33
Right-to-Work State? (option to join or support a union)	Yes	1
Number of Tax or Expenditure Limits (0= least/worst, 3=most/best)	2	4

New Hampshire

19 Economic Performance Rank: 2009

37 Economic Outlook Rank: 2009

Economic Performance Rank (1=best 50=worst)

A historical measure based on a state's performance (equally weighted average) in the three important performance variables shown below. These variables are highly influenced by state policy.

Economic Outlook Rank (1=best 50=worst)

A forecast based on a state's standing (equally weighted average) in the 15 important state policy variables shown below. Data reflect state + local rates and revenues and any effect of federal deductibility.

Personal Income Per Capita
Cumulative Growth 1997-2007   50.1%   **Rank: 32**

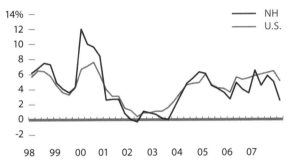

Absolute Domestic Migration
Cumulative 1998-2007   59,286   **Rank: 17**

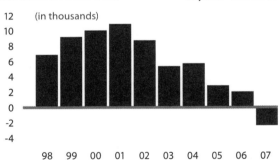

Non-Farm Payroll Employment
Cumulative Growth 1997-2007   13.8%   **Rank: 20**

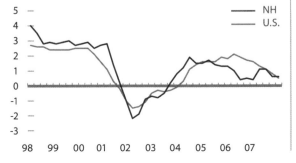

Historical Ranking Comparison
2008 ECONOMIC OUTLOOK RANK **26**

Variable	Data	Rank
Top Marginal Personal Income Tax Rate	0.00%	1
Top Marginal Corporate Income Tax Rate	9.25%	42
Personal Income Tax Progressivity (change in tax liability per $1,000 of income)	$0.00	2
Property Tax Burden (per $1,000 of personal income)	$55.27	50
Sales Tax Burden (per $1,000 of personal income)	$0.00	1
Remaining Tax Burden (per $1,000 of personal income)	$21.27	32
Estate/Inheritance Tax Levied?	No	1
Recently Legislated Tax Changes (2007 & 2008, per $1,000 of personal income)	$0.84	39
Debt Service as a Share of Tax Revenue	10.0%	46
Public Employees Per 10,000 of Population (full-time equivalent)	544.9	23
State Liability System Survey (tort litigation treatment, judicial impartiality, etc.)	64.7	16
State Minimum Wage (federal floor is $6.55)	$7.25	37
Average Workers' Compensation Costs (per $100 of payroll)	$3.06	46
Right-to-Work State? (option to join or support a union)	No	50
Number of Tax or Expenditure Limits (0= least/worst, 3=most/best)	0	29

New Jersey

40
Economic Performance
Rank: 2009

46
Economic Outlook
Rank: 2009

Economic Performance Rank (1=best 50=worst)

A historical measure based on a state's performance (equally weighted average) in the three important performance variables shown below. These variables are highly influenced by state policy.

Economic Outlook Rank (1=best 50=worst)

A forecast based on a state's standing (equally weighted average) in the 15 important state policy variables shown below. Data reflect state + local rates and revenues and any effect of federal deductibility.

Personal Income Per Capita
Cumulative Growth 1997-2007   **52.5%   Rank: 24**

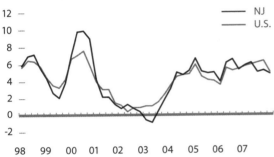

Absolute Domestic Migration
Cumulative 1998-2007   **-468,024   Rank: 47**

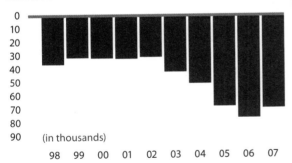

Non-Farm Payroll Employment
Cumulative Growth 1997-2007   **9.4%   Rank: 31**

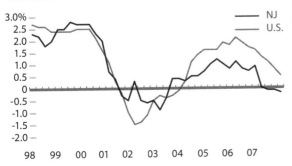

Historical Ranking Comparison
2008 ECONOMIC OUTLOOK RANK 48

Variable	Data	Rank
Top Marginal Personal Income Tax Rate	8.97%	45
Top Marginal Corporate Income Tax Rate	9.00%	39
Personal Income Tax Progressivity (change in tax liability per $1,000 of income)	$24.81	48
Property Tax Burden (per $1,000 of personal income)	$52.50	47
Sales Tax Burden (per $1,000 of personal income)	$15.47	10
Remaining Tax Burden (per $1,000 of personal income)	$16.24	10
Estate/Inheritance Tax Levied?	Yes	50
Recently Legislated Tax Changes (2007 & 2008, per $1,000 of personal income)	-$0.21	24
Debt Service as a Share of Tax Revenue	6.0%	9
Public Employees Per 10,000 of Population (full-time equivalent)	587.5	35
State Liability System Survey (tort litigation treatment, judicial impartiality, etc.)	58.0	34
State Minimum Wage (federal floor is $6.55)	$7.15	32
Average Workers' Compensation Costs (per $100 of payroll)	$2.66	35
Right-to-Work State? (option to join or support a union)	No	50
Number of Tax or Expenditure Limits (0= least/worst, 3=most/best)	0	29

New Mexico

13 Economic Performance
Rank: 2009

25 Economic Outlook
Rank: 2009

Economic Performance Rank (1=best 50=worst)
A historical measure based on a state's performance (equally weighted average) in the three important performance variables shown below. These variables are highly influenced by state policy.

Economic Outlook Rank (1=best 50=worst)
A forecast based on a state's standing (equally weighted average) in the 15 important state policy variables shown below. Data reflect state + local rates and revenues and any effect of federal deductibility.

Personal Income Per Capita
Cumulative Growth 1997-2007   55.8%   Rank: 16

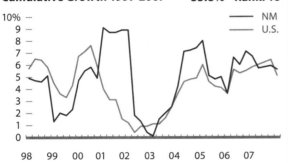

Historical Ranking Comparison
2008 ECONOMIC OUTLOOK RANK   **27**

Variable	Data	Rank
Top Marginal Personal Income Tax Rate	5.30%	20
Top Marginal Corporate Income Tax Rate	7.60%	27
Personal Income Tax Progressivity (change in tax liability per $1,000 of income)	$10.76	32
Property Tax Burden (per $1,000 of personal income)	$17.31	5
Sales Tax Burden (per $1,000 of personal income)	$34.39	45
Remaining Tax Burden (per $1,000 of personal income)	$19.77	30
Estate/Inheritance Tax Levied?	No	1
Recently Legislated Tax Changes (2007 & 2008, per $1,000 of personal income)	-$3.38	3
Debt Service as a Share of Tax Revenue	6.9%	18
Public Employees Per 10,000 of Population (full-time equivalent)	676.8	47
State Liability System Survey (tort litigation treatment, judicial impartiality, etc.)	57.5	37
State Minimum Wage (federal floor is $6.55)	$6.55	1
Average Workers' Compensation Costs (per $100 of payroll)	$2.15	20
Right-to-Work State? (option to join or support a union)	No	50
Number of Tax or Expenditure Limits (0= least/worst, 3=most/best)	0	29

Absolute Domestic Migration
Cumulative 1998-2007   -3,470   Rank: 27

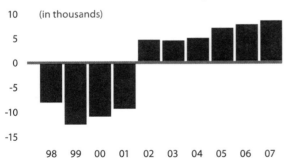

Non-Farm Payroll Employment
Cumulative Growth 1997-2007   19.0%   Rank: 9

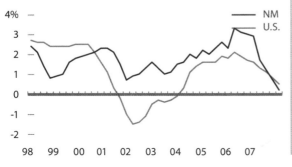

New York

43 Economic Performance Rank: 2009

50 Economic Outlook Rank: 2009

Economic Performance Rank (1=best 50=worst)
A historical measure based on a state's performance (equally weighted average) in the three important performance variables shown below. These variables are highly influenced by state policy.

Economic Outlook Rank (1=best 50=worst)
A forecast based on a state's standing (equally weighted average) in the 15 important state policy variables shown below. Data reflect state + local rates and revenues and any effect of federal deductibility.

Personal Income Per Capita
Cumulative Growth 1997-2007   55.3%   **Rank: 18**

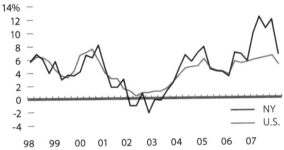

Absolute Domestic Migration
Cumulative 1998-2007   -1,936,127   **Rank: 50**

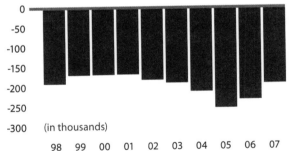

Non-Farm Payroll Employment
Cumulative Growth 1997-2007   8.3%   **Rank: 36**

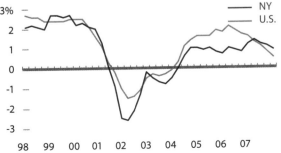

Historical Ranking Comparison
2008 ECONOMIC OUTLOOK RANK **49**

Variable	Data	Rank
Top Marginal Personal Income Tax Rate	10.50%	50
Top Marginal Corporate Income Tax Rate	17.63%	50
Personal Income Tax Progressivity (change in tax liability per $1,000 of income)	$12.71	37
Property Tax Burden (per $1,000 of personal income)	$44.49	44
Sales Tax Burden (per $1,000 of personal income)	$22.88	26
Remaining Tax Burden (per $1,000 of personal income)	$20.90	31
Estate/Inheritance Tax Levied?	Yes	50
Recently Legislated Tax Changes (2007 & 2008, per $1,000 of personal income)	$0.23	32
Debt Service as a Share of Tax Revenue	8.9%	37
Public Employees Per 10,000 of Population (full-time equivalent)	634.3	42
State Liability System Survey (tort litigation treatment, judicial impartiality, etc.)	61.6	25
State Minimum Wage (federal floor is $6.55)	$7.15	32
Average Workers' Compensation Costs (per $100 of payroll)	$2.55	32
Right-to-Work State? (option to join or support a union)	No	50
Number of Tax or Expenditure Limits (0= least/worst, 3=most/best)	0	29

North Carolina

23
Economic Performance
Rank: 2009

21
Economic Outlook
Rank: 2009

Economic Performance Rank (1=best 50=worst)
A historical measure based on a state's performance (equally weighted average) in the three important performance variables shown below. These variables are highly influenced by state policy.

Economic Outlook Rank (1=best 50=worst)
A forecast based on a state's standing (equally weighted average) in the 15 important state policy variables shown below. Data reflect state + local rates and revenues and any effect of federal deductibility.

Personal Income Per Capita Cumulative Growth 1997-2007 — 41.8% Rank: 46

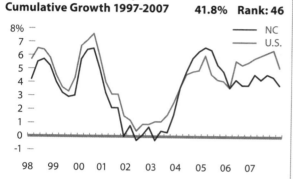

Absolute Domestic Migration Cumulative 1998-2007 — 646,284 Rank: 5

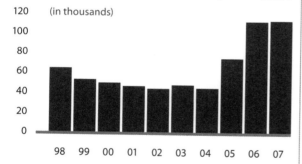

Non-Farm Payroll Employment Cumulative Growth 1997-2007 — 13.7% Rank: 21

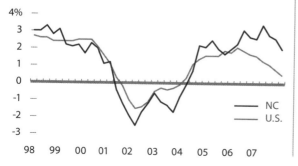

Historical Ranking Comparison
2008 ECONOMIC OUTLOOK RANK — 21

Variable	Data	Rank
Top Marginal Personal Income Tax Rate	7.75%	38
Top Marginal Corporate Income Tax Rate	6.90%	22
Personal Income Tax Progressivity (change in tax liability per $1,000 of income)	$10.35	30
Property Tax Burden (per $1,000 of personal income)	$25.25	12
Sales Tax Burden (per $1,000 of personal income)	$20.59	17
Remaining Tax Burden (per $1,000 of personal income)	$17.89	22
Estate/Inheritance Tax Levied?	Yes	50
Recently Legislated Tax Changes (2007 & 2008, per $1,000 of personal income)	$0.13	29
Debt Service as a Share of Tax Revenue	6.2%	11
Public Employees Per 10,000 of Population (full-time equivalent)	598.2	38
State Liability System Survey (tort litigation treatment, judicial impartiality, etc.)	62.6	20
State Minimum Wage (federal floor is $6.55)	$6.55	1
Average Workers' Compensation Costs (per $100 of payroll)	$2.43	29
Right-to-Work State? (option to join or support a union)	Yes	1
Number of Tax or Expenditure Limits (0= least/worst, 3=most/best)	1	13

North Dakota

14 Economic Performance
Rank: 2009

13 Economic Outlook
Rank: 2009

Economic Performance Rank (1=best 50=worst)

A historical measure based on a state's performance (equally weighted average) in the three important performance variables shown below. These variables are highly influenced by state policy.

Economic Outlook Rank (1=best 50=worst)

A forecast based on a state's standing (equally weighted average) in the 15 important state policy variables shown below. Data reflect state + local rates and revenues and any effect of federal deductibility.

Personal Income Per Capita
Cumulative Growth 1997-2007   **75.3%   Rank: 2**

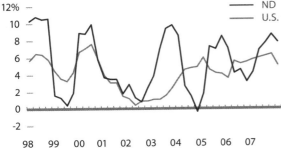

Absolute Domestic Migration
Cumulative 1998-2007   **-38,131   Rank: 35**

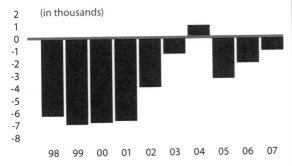

Non-Farm Payroll Employment
Cumulative Growth 1997-2007   **13.9%   Rank: 19**

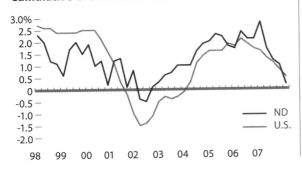

Historical Ranking Comparison
2008 ECONOMIC OUTLOOK RANK **18**

Variable	Data	Rank
Top Marginal Personal Income Tax Rate	5.54%	23
Top Marginal Corporate Income Tax Rate	4.23%	5
Personal Income Tax Progressivity (change in tax liability per $1,000 of income)	$9.77	29
Property Tax Burden (per $1,000 of personal income)	$31.29	27
Sales Tax Burden (per $1,000 of personal income)	$20.99	20
Remaining Tax Burden (per $1,000 of personal income)	$23.41	39
Estate/Inheritance Tax Levied?	No	1
Recently Legislated Tax Changes (2007 & 2008, per $1,000 of personal income)	-$3.24	4
Debt Service as a Share of Tax Revenue	7.8%	29
Public Employees Per 10,000 of Population (full-time equivalent)	650.2	46
State Liability System Survey (tort litigation treatment, judicial impartiality, etc.)	65.6	13
State Minimum Wage (federal floor is $6.55)	$6.55	1
Average Workers' Compensation Costs (per $100 of payroll)	$1.08	1
Right-to-Work State? (option to join or support a union)	Yes	1
Number of Tax or Expenditure Limits (0= least/worst, 3=most/best)	0	29

Ohio

49
Economic Performance
Rank: 2009

45
Economic Outlook
Rank: 2009

Economic Performance Rank (1=best 50=worst)
A historical measure based on a state's performance (equally weighted average) in the three important performance variables shown below. These variables are highly influenced by state policy.

Economic Outlook Rank (1=best 50=worst)
A forecast based on a state's standing (equally weighted average) in the 15 important state policy variables shown below. Data reflect state + local rates and revenues and any effect of federal deductibility.

Personal Income Per Capita
Cumulative Growth 1997-2007   **38.4% Rank: 42**

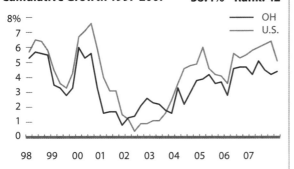

Historical Ranking Comparison
2008 ECONOMIC OUTLOOK RANK **47**

Variable	Data	Rank
Top Marginal Personal Income Tax Rate	8.24%	42
Top Marginal Corporate Income Tax Rate	10.50%	48
Personal Income Tax Progressivity (change in tax liability per $1,000 of income)	$14.43	43
Property Tax Burden (per $1,000 of personal income)	$34.02	31
Sales Tax Burden (per $1,000 of personal income)	$24.49	34
Remaining Tax Burden (per $1,000 of personal income)	$16.21	9
Estate/Inheritance Tax Levied?	Yes	50
Recently Legislated Tax Changes (2007 & 2008, per $1,000 of personal income)	-$1.51	8
Debt Service as a Share of Tax Revenue	7.4%	23
Public Employees Per 10,000 of Population (full-time equivalent)	533.4	17
State Liability System Survey (tort litigation treatment, judicial impartiality, etc.)	60.0	32
State Minimum Wage (federal floor is $6.55)	$7.00	30
Average Workers' Compensation Costs (per $100 of payroll)	$3.32	48
Right-to-Work State? (option to join or support a union)	No	50
Number of Tax or Expenditure Limits (0= least/worst, 3=most/best)	0	29

Absolute Domestic Migration
Cumulative 1998-2007   **-397,899 Rank: 45**

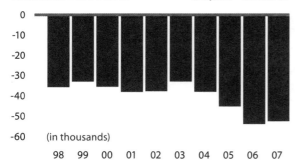

Non-Farm Payroll Employment
Cumulative Growth 1997-2007   **0.6% Rank: 49**

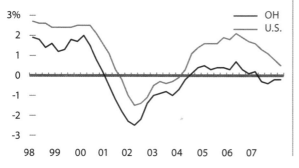

Oklahoma

12 Economic Performance Rank: 2009

15 Economic Outlook Rank: 2009

Economic Performance Rank (1=best 50=worst)
A historical measure based on a state's performance (equally weighted average) in the three important performance variables shown below. These variables are highly influenced by state policy.

Economic Outlook Rank (1=best 50=worst)
A forecast based on a state's standing (equally weighted average) in the 15 important state policy variables shown below. Data reflect state + local rates and revenues and any effect of federal deductibility.

Personal Income Per Capita Cumulative Growth 1997-2007 — 69.3% Rank: 4

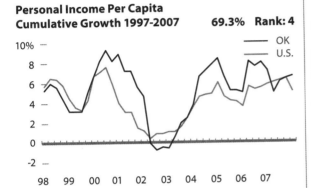

Absolute Domestic Migration Cumulative 1998-2007 — 16,553 Rank: 22

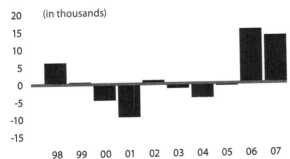

Non-Farm Payroll Employment Cumulative Growth 1997-2007 — 11.9% Rank: 26

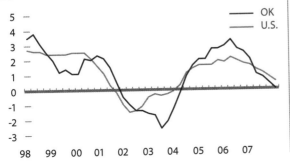

Historical Ranking Comparison
2008 ECONOMIC OUTLOOK RANK 14

Variable	Data	Rank
Top Marginal Personal Income Tax Rate	5.50%	22
Top Marginal Corporate Income Tax Rate	6.00%	15
Personal Income Tax Progressivity (change in tax liability per $1,000 of income)	$5.84	22
Property Tax Burden (per $1,000 of personal income)	$16.09	2
Sales Tax Burden (per $1,000 of personal income)	$23.81	33
Remaining Tax Burden (per $1,000 of personal income)	$18.04	23
Estate/Inheritance Tax Levied?	Yes	50
Recently Legislated Tax Changes (2007 & 2008, per $1,000 of personal income)	-$1.36	10
Debt Service as a Share of Tax Revenue	7.1%	21
Public Employees Per 10,000 of Population (full-time equivalent)	595.7	37
State Liability System Survey (tort litigation treatment, judicial impartiality, etc.)	64.2	17
State Minimum Wage (federal floor is $6.55)	$6.55	1
Average Workers' Compensation Costs (per $100 of payroll)	$2.89	41
Right-to-Work State? (option to join or support a union)	Yes	1
Number of Tax or Expenditure Limits (0= least/worst, 3=most/best)	2	4

Oregon

29
Economic Performance
Rank: 2009

39
Economic Outlook
Rank: 2009

Economic Performance Rank (1=best 50=worst)
A historical measure based on a state's performance (equally weighted average) in the three important performance variables shown below. These variables are highly influenced by state policy.

Economic Outlook Rank (1=best 50=worst)
A forecast based on a state's standing (equally weighted average) in the 15 important state policy variables shown below. Data reflect state + local rates and revenues and any effect of federal deductibility.

Personal Income Per Capita
Cumulative Growth 1997-2007 42.9% **Rank: 45**

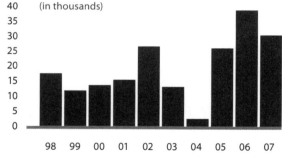

Absolute Domestic Migration
Cumulative 1998-2007 173,408 **Rank: 12**

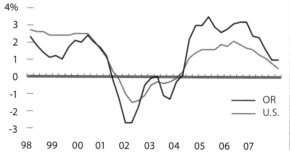

Non-Farm Payroll Employment
Cumulative Growth 1997-2007 12.7% **Rank: 23**

Historical Ranking Comparison
2008 ECONOMIC OUTLOOK RANK 35

Variable	Data	Rank
Top Marginal Personal Income Tax Rate	9.00%	46
Top Marginal Corporate Income Tax Rate	10.25%	47
Personal Income Tax Progressivity (change in tax liability per $1,000 of income)	$13.06	38
Property Tax Burden (per $1,000 of personal income)	$30.94	25
Sales Tax Burden (per $1,000 of personal income)	$0.00	1
Remaining Tax Burden (per $1,000 of personal income)	$21.58	34
Estate/Inheritance Tax Levied?	Yes	50
Recently Legislated Tax Changes (2007 & 2008, per $1,000 of personal income)	$0.74	37
Debt Service as a Share of Tax Revenue	9.1%	40
Public Employees Per 10,000 of Population (full-time equivalent)	507.2	11
State Liability System Survey (tort litigation treatment, judicial impartiality, etc.)	65.4	14
State Minimum Wage (federal floor is $6.55)	$7.95	47
Average Workers' Compensation Costs (per $100 of payroll)	$1.88	13
Right-to-Work State? (option to join or support a union)	No	50
Number of Tax or Expenditure Limits (0= least/worst, 3=most/best)	2	4

Pennsylvania

46
Economic Performance
Rank: 2009

42
Economic Outlook
Rank: 2009

Economic Performance Rank (1=best 50=worst)
A historical measure based on a state's performance (equally weighted average) in the three important performance variables shown below. These variables are highly influenced by state policy.

Economic Outlook Rank (1=best 50=worst)
A forecast based on a state's standing (equally weighted average) in the 15 important state policy variables shown below. Data reflect state + local rates and revenues and any effect of federal deductibility.

Personal Income Per Capita
Cumulative Growth 1997-2007   50.9%   Rank: 30

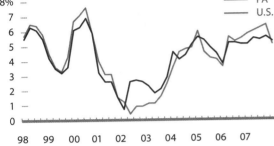

Historical Ranking Comparison
2008 ECONOMIC OUTLOOK RANK   36

Variable	Data	Rank
Top Marginal Personal Income Tax Rate	7.05%	36
Top Marginal Corporate Income Tax Rate	13.97%	49
Personal Income Tax Progressivity (change in tax liability per $1,000 of income)	$0.00	2
Property Tax Burden (per $1,000 of personal income)	$32.13	29
Sales Tax Burden (per $1,000 of personal income)	$17.48	13
Remaining Tax Burden (per $1,000 of personal income)	$24.00	41
Estate/Inheritance Tax Levied?	Yes	50
Recently Legislated Tax Changes (2007 & 2008, per $1,000 of personal income)	-$0.42	19
Debt Service as a Share of Tax Revenue	9.3%	41
Public Employees Per 10,000 of Population (full-time equivalent)	476.1	3
State Liability System Survey (tort litigation treatment, judicial impartiality, etc.)	57.8	36
State Minimum Wage (federal floor is $6.55)	$7.15	32
Average Workers' Compensation Costs (per $100 of payroll)	$2.68	36
Right-to-Work State? (option to join or support a union)	No	50
Number of Tax or Expenditure Limits (0= least/worst, 3=most/best)	0	29

Absolute Domestic Migration
Cumulative 1998-2007   -148,979   Rank: 42

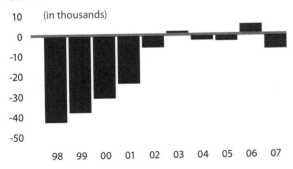

Non-Farm Payroll Employment
Cumulative Growth 1997-2007   7.2%   Rank: 40

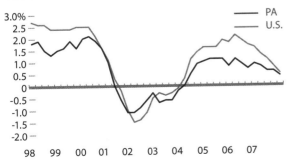

Rhode Island

30
Economic Performance
Rank: 2009

48
Economic Outlook
Rank: 2009

Economic Performance Rank (1=best 50=worst)
A historical measure based on a state's performance (equally weighted average) in the three important performance variables shown below. These variables are highly influenced by state policy.

Economic Outlook Rank (1=best 50=worst)
A forecast based on a state's standing (equally weighted average) in the 15 important state policy variables shown below. Data reflect state + local rates and revenues and any effect of federal deductibility.

Personal Income Per Capita
Cumulative Growth 1997-2007   **55.4%**   **Rank: 17**

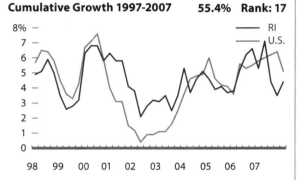

Historical Ranking Comparison
2008 ECONOMIC OUTLOOK RANK 45

Variable	Data	Rank
Top Marginal Personal Income Tax Rate	7.00%	33
Top Marginal Corporate Income Tax Rate	9.00%	39
Personal Income Tax Progressivity (change in tax liability per $1,000 of income)	$25.18	49
Property Tax Burden (per $1,000 of personal income)	$48.62	46
Sales Tax Burden (per $1,000 of personal income)	$20.16	15
Remaining Tax Burden (per $1,000 of personal income)	$18.65	26
Estate/Inheritance Tax Levied?	Yes	50
Recently Legislated Tax Changes (2007 & 2008, per $1,000 of personal income)	$1.77	47
Debt Service as a Share of Tax Revenue	7.6%	26
Public Employees Per 10,000 of Population (full-time equivalent)	504.7	10
State Liability System Survey (tort litigation treatment, judicial impartiality, etc.)	57.1	39
State Minimum Wage (federal floor is $6.55)	$7.40	42
Average Workers' Compensation Costs (per $100 of payroll)	$2.26	25
Right-to-Work State? (option to join or support a union)	No	50
Number of Tax or Expenditure Limits (0= least/worst, 3=most/best)	1	13

Absolute Domestic Migration
Cumulative 1998-2007   **-34,572**   **Rank: 34**

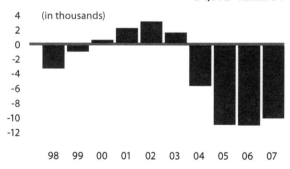

Non-Farm Payroll Employment
Cumulative Growth 1997-2007   **9.6%**   **Rank: 30**

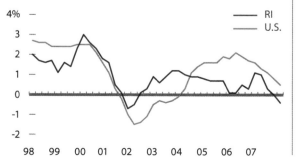

South Carolina

18
Economic Performance
Rank: 2009

20
Economic Outlook
Rank: 2009

Economic Performance Rank (1=best 50=worst)
A historical measure based on a state's performance (equally weighted average) in the three important performance variables shown below. These variables are highly influenced by state policy.

Economic Outlook Rank (1=best 50=worst)
A forecast based on a state's standing (equally weighted average) in the 15 important state policy variables shown below. Data reflect state + local rates and revenues and any effect of federal deductibility.

Personal Income Per Capita
Cumulative Growth 1997-2007   47.3%   Rank: 38

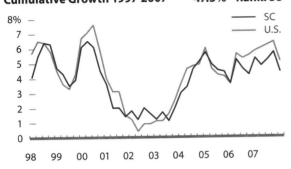

Absolute Domestic Migration
Cumulative 1998-2007   295,074   Rank: 7

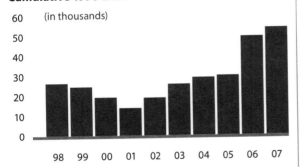

Non-Farm Payroll Employment
Cumulative Growth 1997-2007   13.5%   Rank: 22

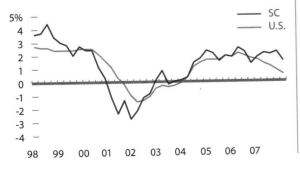

Historical Ranking Comparison
2008 ECONOMIC OUTLOOK RANK   **20**

Variable	Data	Rank
Top Marginal Personal Income Tax Rate	7.00%	33
Top Marginal Corporate Income Tax Rate	5.00%	8
Personal Income Tax Progressivity (change in tax liability per $1,000 of income)	$5.96	23
Property Tax Burden (per $1,000 of personal income)	$31.65	28
Sales Tax Burden (per $1,000 of personal income)	$21.89	23
Remaining Tax Burden (per $1,000 of personal income)	$16.25	11
Estate/Inheritance Tax Levied?	No	1
Recently Legislated Tax Changes (2007 & 2008, per $1,000 of personal income)	-$2.05	6
Debt Service as a Share of Tax Revenue	10.8%	47
Public Employees Per 10,000 of Population (full-time equivalent)	575.5	30
State Liability System Survey (tort litigation treatment, judicial impartiality, etc.)	54.5	43
State Minimum Wage (federal floor is $6.55)	$6.55	1
Average Workers' Compensation Costs (per $100 of payroll)	$2.74	38
Right-to-Work State? (option to join or support a union)	Yes	1
Number of Tax or Expenditure Limits (0= least/worst, 3=most/best)	1	13

South Dakota

11 Economic Performance
Rank: 2009

5 Economic Outlook
Rank: 2009

Economic Performance Rank (1=best 50=worst)

A historical measure based on a state's performance (equally weighted average) in the three important performance variables shown below. These variables are highly influenced by state policy.

Economic Outlook Rank (1=best 50=worst)

A forecast based on a state's standing (equally weighted average) in the 15 important state policy variables shown below. Data reflect state + local rates and revenues and any effect of federal deductibility.

Personal Income Per Capita
Cumulative Growth 1997-2007   63.9%   Rank: 6

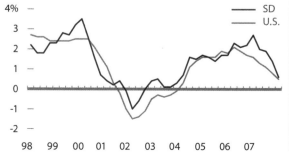

Historical Ranking Comparison
2008 ECONOMIC OUTLOOK RANK   2

Variable	Data	Rank
Top Marginal Personal Income Tax Rate	0.00%	1
Top Marginal Corporate Income Tax Rate	0.00%	1
Personal Income Tax Progressivity (change in tax liability per $1,000 of income)	$0.00	2
Property Tax Burden (per $1,000 of personal income)	$30.45	23
Sales Tax Burden (per $1,000 of personal income)	$30.97	42
Remaining Tax Burden (per $1,000 of personal income)	$19.30	28
Estate/Inheritance Tax Levied?	No	1
Recently Legislated Tax Changes (2007 & 2008, per $1,000 of personal income)	$1.37	46
Debt Service as a Share of Tax Revenue	7.9%	31
Public Employees Per 10,000 of Population (full-time equivalent)	546.4	24
State Liability System Survey (tort litigation treatment, judicial impartiality, etc.)	65.7	12
State Minimum Wage (federal floor is $6.55)	$6.55	1
Average Workers' Compensation Costs (per $100 of payroll)	$2.08	16
Right-to-Work State? (option to join or support a union)	Yes	1
Number of Tax or Expenditure Limits (0= least/worst, 3=most/best)	1	13

Absolute Domestic Migration
Cumulative 1998-2007   -4,554 Rank: 28

Non-Farm Payroll Employment
Cumulative Growth 1997-2007   15.2% Rank: 16

Tennessee

32
Economic Performance
Rank: 2009

9
Economic Outlook
Rank: 2009

Economic Performance Rank (1=best 50=worst)
A historical measure based on a state's performance (equally weighted average) in the three important performance variables shown below. These variables are highly influenced by state policy.

Economic Outlook Rank (1=best 50=worst)
A forecast based on a state's standing (equally weighted average) in the 15 important state policy variables shown below. Data reflect state + local rates and revenues and any effect of federal deductibility.

Personal Income Per Capita
Cumulative Growth 1997-2007   46.5%   Rank: 41

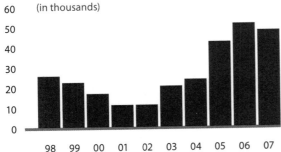

Absolute Domestic Migration
Cumulative 1998-2007   278,698   Rank: 8

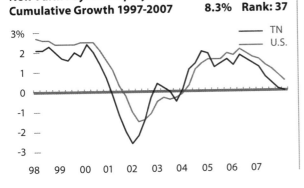

Non-Farm Payroll Employment
Cumulative Growth 1997-2007   8.3%   Rank: 37

Historical Ranking Comparison
2008 ECONOMIC OUTLOOK RANK

Variable	Data	Rank
Top Marginal Personal Income Tax Rate	0.00%	1
Top Marginal Corporate Income Tax Rate	6.50%	19
Personal Income Tax Progressivity (change in tax liability per $1,000 of income)	$0.00	2
Property Tax Burden (per $1,000 of personal income)	$21.75	10
Sales Tax Burden (per $1,000 of personal income)	$36.26	47
Remaining Tax Burden (per $1,000 of personal income)	$16.37	12
Estate/Inheritance Tax Levied?	Yes	50
Recently Legislated Tax Changes (2007 & 2008, per $1,000 of personal income)	$0.94	41
Debt Service as a Share of Tax Revenue	7.1%	22
Public Employees Per 10,000 of Population (full-time equivalent)	525.9	14
State Liability System Survey (tort litigation treatment, judicial impartiality, etc.)	62.3	22
State Minimum Wage (federal floor is $6.55)	$6.55	1
Average Workers' Compensation Costs (per $100 of payroll)	$2.44	30
Right-to-Work State? (option to join or support a union)	Yes	1
Number of Tax or Expenditure Limits (0= least/worst, 3=most/best)	1	13

Texas

1 Economic Performance
Rank: 2009

10 Economic Outlook
Rank: 2009

Economic Performance Rank (1=best 50=worst)
A historical measure based on a state's performance (equally weighted average) in the three important performance variables shown below. These variables are highly influenced by state policy.

Economic Outlook Rank (1=best 50=worst)
A forecast based on a state's standing (equally weighted average) in the 15 important state policy variables shown below. Data reflect state + local rates and revenues and any effect of federal deductibility.

Personal Income Per Capita
Cumulative Growth 1997-2007 55.8% **Rank: 14**

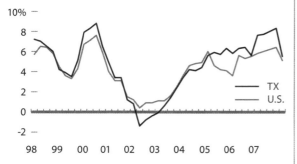

Absolute Domestic Migration
Cumulative 1998-2007 736,903 **Rank: 3**

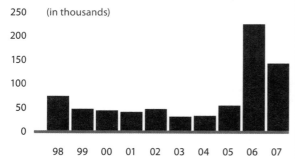

Non-Farm Payroll Employment
Cumulative Growth 1997-2007 20.3% **Rank: 8**

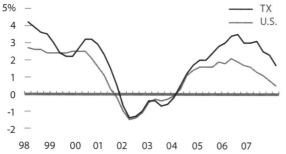

Historical Ranking Comparison
2008 ECONOMIC OUTLOOK RANK   **13**

Variable	Data	Rank
Top Marginal Personal Income Tax Rate	0.00%	1
Top Marginal Corporate Income Tax Rate	5.00%	8
Personal Income Tax Progressivity (change in tax liability per $1,000 of income)	$0.00	2
Property Tax Burden (per $1,000 of personal income)	$41.06	40
Sales Tax Burden (per $1,000 of personal income)	$23.31	27
Remaining Tax Burden (per $1,000 of personal income)	$18.12	24
Estate/Inheritance Tax Levied?	No	1
Recently Legislated Tax Changes (2007 & 2008, per $1,000 of personal income)	-$3.92	2
Debt Service as a Share of Tax Revenue	9.5%	43
Public Employees Per 10,000 of Population (full-time equivalent)	562.2	28
State Liability System Survey (tort litigation treatment, judicial impartiality, etc.)	56.8	41
State Minimum Wage (federal floor is $6.55)	$6.55	1
Average Workers' Compensation Costs (per $100 of payroll)	$2.61	34
Right-to-Work State? (option to join or support a union)	Yes	1
Number of Tax or Expenditure Limits (0= least/worst, 3=most/best)	1	13

Utah

22
Economic Performance
Rank: 2009

1
Economic Outlook
Rank: 2009

Economic Performance Rank (1=best 50=worst)

A historical measure based on a state's performance (equally weighted average) in the three important performance variables shown below. These variables are highly influenced by state policy.

Economic Outlook Rank (1=best 50=worst)

A forecast based on a state's standing (equally weighted average) in the 15 important state policy variables shown below. Data reflect state + local rates and revenues and any effect of federal deductibility.

Personal Income Per Capita
Cumulative Growth 1997-2007   45.6%   Rank: 43

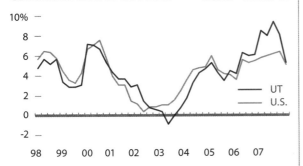

Absolute Domestic Migration
Cumulative 1998-2007   8,446   Rank: 23

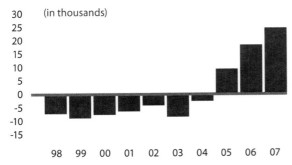

Non-Farm Payroll Employment
Cumulative Growth 1997-2007   25.9%   Rank: 5

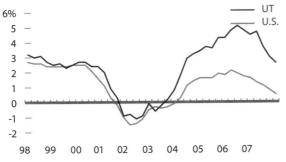

Historical Ranking Comparison
2008 ECONOMIC OUTLOOK RANK

Variable	Data	Rank
Top Marginal Personal Income Tax Rate	5.00%	17
Top Marginal Corporate Income Tax Rate	5.00%	8
Personal Income Tax Progressivity (change in tax liability per $1,000 of income)	$0.00	2
Property Tax Burden (per $1,000 of personal income)	$25.81	13
Sales Tax Burden (per $1,000 of personal income)	$26.38	38
Remaining Tax Burden (per $1,000 of personal income)	$16.62	17
Estate/Inheritance Tax Levied?	No	1
Recently Legislated Tax Changes (2007 & 2008, per $1,000 of personal income)	-$0.98	12
Debt Service as a Share of Tax Revenue	8.2%	33
Public Employees Per 10,000 of Population (full-time equivalent)	498.2	6
State Liability System Survey (tort litigation treatment, judicial impartiality, etc.)	68.6	5
State Minimum Wage (federal floor is $6.55)	$6.55	1
Average Workers' Compensation Costs (per $100 of payroll)	$1.63	6
Right-to-Work State? (option to join or support a union)	Yes	1
Number of Tax or Expenditure Limits (0= least/worst, 3=most/best)	1	13

Vermont

16
Economic Performance
Rank: 2009

49
Economic Outlook
Rank: 2009

Economic Performance Rank (1=best 50=worst)
A historical measure based on a state's performance (equally weighted average) in the three important performance variables shown below. These variables are highly influenced by state policy.

Economic Outlook Rank (1=best 50=worst)
A forecast based on a state's standing (equally weighted average) in the 15 important state policy variables shown below. Data reflect state + local rates and revenues and any effect of federal deductibility.

**Personal Income Per Capita
Cumulative Growth 1997-2007   61.2%   Rank: 8**

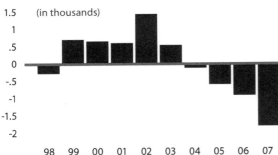

Historical Ranking Comparison
2008 ECONOMIC OUTLOOK RANK

Variable	Data	Rank
Top Marginal Personal Income Tax Rate	9.50%	48
Top Marginal Corporate Income Tax Rate	8.50%	33
Personal Income Tax Progressivity (change in tax liability per $1,000 of income)	$21.58	47
Property Tax Burden (per $1,000 of personal income)	$54.51	49
Sales Tax Burden (per $1,000 of personal income)	$11.88	7
Remaining Tax Burden (per $1,000 of personal income)	$29.42	47
Estate/Inheritance Tax Levied?	Yes	50
Recently Legislated Tax Changes (2007 & 2008, per $1,000 of personal income)	-$0.21	24
Debt Service as a Share of Tax Revenue	6.7%	14
Public Employees Per 10,000 of Population (full-time equivalent)	637.9	43
State Liability System Survey (tort litigation treatment, judicial impartiality, etc.)	67.6	8
State Minimum Wage (federal floor is $6.55)	$7.68	45
Average Workers' Compensation Costs (per $100 of payroll)	$3.14	47
Right-to-Work State? (option to join or support a union)	No	50
Number of Tax or Expenditure Limits (0= least/worst, 3=most/best)	0	29

**Absolute Domestic Migration
Cumulative 1998-2007   342   Rank: 26**

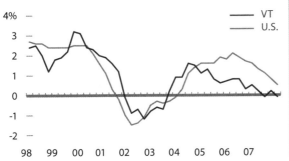

**Non-Farm Payroll Employment
Cumulative Growth 1997-2007   10.2%   Rank: 29**

Virginia

6 Economic Performance
Rank: 2009

4 Economic Outlook
Rank: 2009

Economic Performance Rank (1=best 50=worst)
A historical measure based on a state's performance (equally weighted average) in the three important performance variables shown below. These variables are highly influenced by state policy.

Economic Outlook Rank (1=best 50=worst)
A forecast based on a state's standing (equally weighted average) in the 15 important state policy variables shown below. Data reflect state + local rates and revenues and any effect of federal deductibility.

Personal Income Per Capita
Cumulative Growth 1997-2007   **56.4%   Rank: 11**

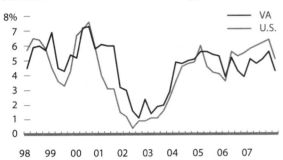

Historical Ranking Comparison
2008 ECONOMIC OUTLOOK RANK   5

Variable	Data	Rank
Top Marginal Personal Income Tax Rate	5.75%	24
Top Marginal Corporate Income Tax Rate	6.00%	15
Personal Income Tax Progressivity (change in tax liability per $1,000 of income)	$6.45	24
Property Tax Burden (per $1,000 of personal income)	$31.07	26
Sales Tax Burden (per $1,000 of personal income)	$12.65	9
Remaining Tax Burden (per $1,000 of personal income)	$21.37	33
Estate/Inheritance Tax Levied?	No	1
Recently Legislated Tax Changes (2007 & 2008, per $1,000 of personal income)	-$0.32	22
Debt Service as a Share of Tax Revenue	6.6%	13
Public Employees Per 10,000 of Population (full-time equivalent)	571.3	29
State Liability System Survey (tort litigation treatment, judicial impartiality, etc.)	68.4	6
State Minimum Wage (federal floor is $6.55)	$6.55	1
Average Workers' Compensation Costs (per $100 of payroll)	$1.43	4
Right-to-Work State? (option to join or support a union)	Yes	1
Number of Tax or Expenditure Limits (0= least/worst, 3=most/best)	0	29

Absolute Domestic Migration
Cumulative 1998-2007   **189,215   Rank: 11**

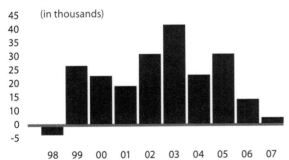

Non-Farm Payroll Employment
Cumulative Growth 1997-2007   **16.4%   Rank: 14**

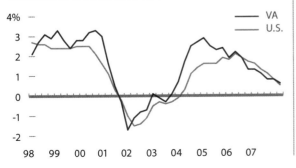

Washington

5
Economic Performance
Rank: 2009

22
Economic Outlook
Rank: 2009

Economic Performance Rank (1=best 50=worst)
A historical measure based on a state's performance (equally weighted average) in the three important performance variables shown below. These variables are highly influenced by state policy.

Economic Outlook Rank (1=best 50=worst)
A forecast based on a state's standing (equally weighted average) in the 15 important state policy variables shown below. Data reflect state + local rates and revenues and any effect of federal deductibility.

Personal Income Per Capita
Cumulative Growth 1997-2007   **55.8%   Rank: 13**

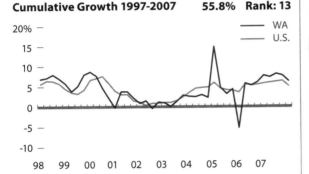

Historical Ranking Comparison
2008 ECONOMIC OUTLOOK RANK **30**

Variable	Data	Rank
Top Marginal Personal Income Tax Rate	0.00%	1
Top Marginal Corporate Income Tax Rate	0.00%	1
Personal Income Tax Progressivity (change in tax liability per $1,000 of income)	$0.00	2
Property Tax Burden (per $1,000 of personal income)	$29.23	22
Sales Tax Burden (per $1,000 of personal income)	$39.80	49
Remaining Tax Burden (per $1,000 of personal income)	$25.84	44
Estate/Inheritance Tax Levied?	Yes	50
Recently Legislated Tax Changes (2007 & 2008, per $1,000 of personal income)	$0.06	28
Debt Service as a Share of Tax Revenue	10.0%	45
Public Employees Per 10,000 of Population (full-time equivalent)	525.4	13
State Liability System Survey (tort litigation treatment, judicial impartiality, etc.)	61.5	26
State Minimum Wage (federal floor is $6.55)	$8.07	50
Average Workers' Compensation Costs (per $100 of payroll)	$1.98	14
Right-to-Work State? (option to join or support a union)	No	50
Number of Tax or Expenditure Limits (0= least/worst, 3=most/best)	3	1

Absolute Domestic Migration
Cumulative 1998-2007   **206,169   Rank: 10**

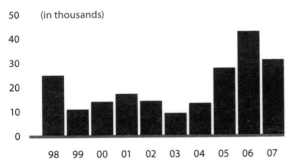

Non-Farm Payroll Employment
Cumulative Growth 1997-2007   **16.6%   Rank: 13**

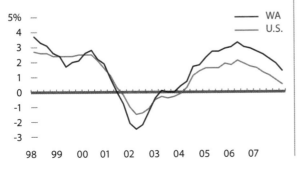

West Virginia

38
Economic Performance
Rank: 2009

33
Economic Outlook
Rank: 2009

Economic Performance Rank (1=best 50=worst)
A historical measure based on a state's performance (equally weighted average) in the three important performance variables shown below. These variables are highly influenced by state policy.

Economic Outlook Rank (1=best 50=worst)
A forecast based on a state's standing (equally weighted average) in the 15 important state policy variables shown below. Data reflect state + local rates and revenues and any effect of federal deductibility.

Personal Income Per Capita
Cumulative Growth 1997-2007   52.4%   Rank: 25

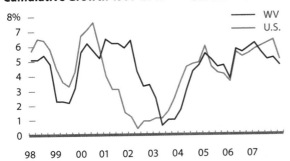

Absolute Domestic Migration
Cumulative 1998-2007   -7,979   Rank: 29

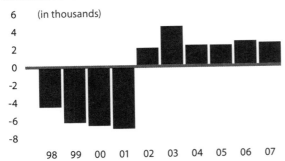

Non-Farm Payroll Employment
Cumulative Growth 1997-2007   7.0%   Rank: 41

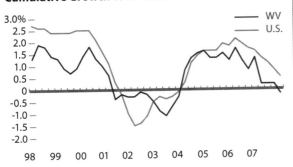

Historical Ranking Comparison
2008 ECONOMIC OUTLOOK RANK 38

Variable	Data	Rank
Top Marginal Personal Income Tax Rate	6.50%	28
Top Marginal Corporate Income Tax Rate	8.50%	33
Personal Income Tax Progressivity (change in tax liability per $1,000 of income)	$15.53	44
Property Tax Burden (per $1,000 of personal income)	$21.63	9
Sales Tax Burden (per $1,000 of personal income)	$20.24	16
Remaining Tax Burden (per $1,000 of personal income)	$30.18	48
Estate/Inheritance Tax Levied?	No	1
Recently Legislated Tax Changes (2007 & 2008, per $1,000 of personal income)	-$1.98	7
Debt Service as a Share of Tax Revenue	6.5%	12
Public Employees Per 10,000 of Population (full-time equivalent)	556.3	25
State Liability System Survey (tort litigation treatment, judicial impartiality, etc.)	42.4	50
State Minimum Wage (federal floor is $6.55)	$7.25	37
Average Workers' Compensation Costs (per $100 of payroll)	$1.86	11
Right-to-Work State? (option to join or support a union)	No	50
Number of Tax or Expenditure Limits (0= least/worst, 3=most/best)	0	29

Wisconsin

41 Economic Performance Rank: 2009

27 Economic Outlook Rank: 2009

Economic Performance Rank (1=best 50=worst)
A historical measure based on a state's performance (equally weighted average) in the three important performance variables shown below. These variables are highly influenced by state policy.

Economic Outlook Rank (1=best 50=worst)
A forecast based on a state's standing (equally weighted average) in the 15 important state policy variables shown below. Data reflect state + local rates and revenues and any effect of federal deductibility.

Personal Income Per Capita
Cumulative Growth 1997-2007   46.5%   **Rank: 42**

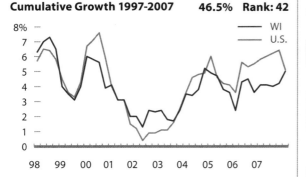

Absolute Domestic Migration
Cumulative 1998-2007   889   **Rank: 25**

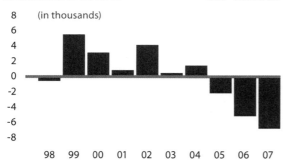

Non-Farm Payroll Employment
Cumulative Growth 1997-2007   8.5%   **Rank: 35**

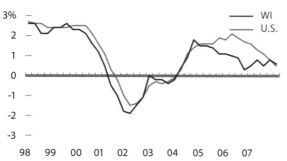

Historical Ranking Comparison
2008 ECONOMIC OUTLOOK RANK   33

Variable	Data	Rank
Top Marginal Personal Income Tax Rate	6.75%	29
Top Marginal Corporate Income Tax Rate	7.90%	30
Personal Income Tax Progressivity (change in tax liability per $1,000 of income)	$3.55	18
Property Tax Burden (per $1,000 of personal income)	$43.04	42
Sales Tax Burden (per $1,000 of personal income)	$21.55	21
Remaining Tax Burden (per $1,000 of personal income)	$16.38	14
Estate/Inheritance Tax Levied?	Yes	50
Recently Legislated Tax Changes (2007 & 2008, per $1,000 of personal income)	$0.18	30
Debt Service as a Share of Tax Revenue	7.6%	27
Public Employees Per 10,000 of Population (full-time equivalent)	502.5	9
State Liability System Survey (tort litigation treatment, judicial impartiality, etc.)	61.8	24
State Minimum Wage (federal floor is $6.55)	$6.55	1
Average Workers' Compensation Costs (per $100 of payroll)	$2.12	18
Right-to-Work State? (option to join or support a union)	No	50
Number of Tax or Expenditure Limits (0= least/worst, 3=most/best)	0	29

Wyoming

3 Economic Performance
Rank: 2009

6 Economic Outlook
Rank: 2009

Economic Performance Rank (1=best 50=worst)
A historical measure based on a state's performance (equally weighted average) in the three important performance variables shown below. These variables are highly influenced by state policy.

Economic Outlook Rank (1=best 50=worst)
A forecast based on a state's standing (equally weighted average) in the 15 important state policy variables shown below. Data reflect state + local rates and revenues and any effect of federal deductibility.

Personal Income Per Capita
Cumulative Growth 1997-2007 103.4% **Rank: 1**

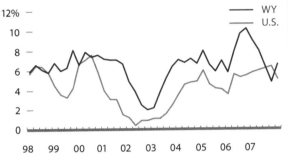

Absolute Domestic Migration
Cumulative 1998-2007 1,488 **Rank: 24**

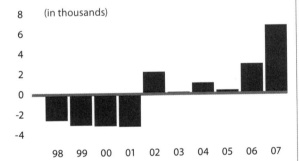

Non-Farm Payroll Employment
Cumulative Growth 1997-2007 28.3% **Rank: 4**

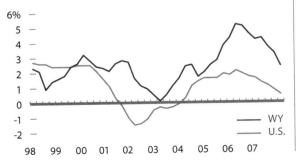

Historical Ranking Comparison
2008 ECONOMIC OUTLOOK RANK 4

Variable	Data	Rank
Top Marginal Personal Income Tax Rate	0.00%	1
Top Marginal Corporate Income Tax Rate	0.00%	1
Personal Income Tax Progressivity (change in tax liability per $1,000 of income)	$0.00	2
Property Tax Burden (per $1,000 of personal income)	$47.28	45
Sales Tax Burden (per $1,000 of personal income)	$27.24	40
Remaining Tax Burden (per $1,000 of personal income)	$13.34	4
Estate/Inheritance Tax Levied?	No	1
Recently Legislated Tax Changes (2007 & 2008, per $1,000 of personal income)	-$0.15	27
Debt Service as a Share of Tax Revenue	2.7%	1
Public Employees Per 10,000 of Population (full-time equivalent)	915.4	50
State Liability System Survey (tort litigation treatment, judicial impartiality, etc.)	62.1	23
State Minimum Wage (federal floor is $6.55)	$6.55	1
Average Workers' Compensation Costs (per $100 of payroll)	$2.06	15
Right-to-Work State? (option to join or support a union)	Yes	1
Number of Tax or Expenditure Limits (0= least/worst, 3=most/best)	0	29

Appendix A

2009 ALEC-Laffer Economic Competitiveness Index: Economic Outlook Methodology

Earlier in this book, we introduced 15 policy variables that have a proven impact on the migration of capital – both investment and human – into and out of states. The end result of an equally weighted combination of these variables is the 2009 ALEC-Laffer Economic Outlook Rankings of the states. Each of these factors is influenced directly by state lawmakers through the legislative process. The 15 factors and a basic description of their purposes, sourcing and subsequent calculation methodologies are as follows:

Highest Marginal Personal Income Tax Rate:

This ranking includes local taxes, if any, and any impact of federal deductibility, if allowed. A state's largest city was used as a proxy for local tax rates. Data was drawn from: CCH Tax Research Network, Tax Analysts and Tax Administrators.

Highest Marginal Corporate Income Tax Rate

This variable includes local taxes, if any, and the effect of federal deductibility, if allowed. A state's largest city was used as a proxy for local tax rates. In the case of gross receipts or business franchise taxes, an effective tax rate was approximated, when possible, using NIPA profits and gross domestic product data. Data was drawn from: CCH Tax Research Network, Tax Analysts, Tax Administrators and the Bureau of Economic Analysis.

Personal Income Tax Progressivity

This variable was measured as the difference between the average tax liability per $1,000 at incomes of $150,000 and $50,000. The tax liabilities were measured using a combination of effective tax rates, exemptions and deductions at both state and federal levels, which are calculations from Laffer Associates.

Property Tax Burden

This variable was calculated by taking tax revenues from property taxes per $1,000 of personal income. We have used U.S. Census Bureau data, for which the most recent year available is 2006. This data was released in July 2008.

Sales Tax Burden

This variable was calculated by taking tax revenues from sales taxes per $1,000 of personal income. Sales taxes taken into consideration include the general sales tax and specific sales taxes. We have used U.S. Census Bureau Data, for which the most recent year available is 2006. This data was released in July 2008.

Remaining Tax Burden

This variable was calculated by taking tax revenues from all taxes – excluding personal income, corporate income (including corporate license), property, sales and severance per $1,000 of personal income. We used U.S. Census Bureau Data, for which the most recent year available is 2006. This data was released in July 2008.

Estate or Inheritance Tax (Yes or No)

This variable assesses if a state levies its own estate or inheritance tax, in additional to the federal rate. We chose to score states based on either a "yes" for the presence of a state-level estate or inheritance tax, or a "no" for the lack thereof. Data was drawn from: Charles Fox, "2008 State Death Tax Chart," American College of Trust and Estate Counsel, April 2008.

Recently Legislated Tax Changes

This variable assesses static revenue estimates of recently legislated tax changes per $1,000 of personal income (in this case, 2007 and 2008). Laffer Associates calculations used raw data from Tax Analysts and other sources.

Debt Service as a Share of Tax Revenue

This variable shows interest paid on state debt as a percentage of total state tax revenue. This information comes from U.S. Census Bureau data.

Public Employees per 10,000 Residents

This variable shows the full-time Equivalent Public Employment per 10,000 of Population. This information comes from U.S. Census Bureau data.

Quality of State Legal System

This variable ranks tort systems by state. Information comes from the 2008 U.S. Chamber of Commerce State Liability Systems Ranking.

State Minimum Wage

This variable highlights the minimum wage enforced on a state-by-state basis. If a state does not have a minimum wage, we use the federal minimum wage floor. This information comes from the U.S. Department of Labor, as of July 2008.

Workers' Compensation Costs

This variable highlights the 2008 Workers' Compensation Index Rate (cost per $100 of payroll). Note: This survey is conducted by the Information Management Division, Department of Consumer & Business Services.

Right-to-Work State (Yes or No)

This variable assesses whether or not a state requires union membership out of its employees. We have chosen to score states based on either a "yes" for the presence of a right-to-work law, or a "no" for the lack thereof. This information comes from the National Right to Work Legal Defense and Education Foundation, Inc.

Tax or Expenditure Limit

This variable ranks states by the number of tax or expenditure limits in place. We measure this by 1) a tax expenditure limit, 2) mandatory voter approval of tax increases, and 3) a supermajority requirement for tax increases. This information comes from the National Conference of State Legislatures and the Cato Institute.

CHANGE IN METHODOLOGY FROM 2008

Last year's State Economic Competitiveness Index included 16 economic outlook variables. However, the authors determined the Education Freedom Index had to be removed because of data limitations. For proper comparison purposes, readers should use the 2008 Economic Outlook Rankings included in this year's book (see Appendix B) as a benchmark, as they were calculated using the 2009 methodology.

Appendix B
2008 ALEC-Laffer Economic Outlook Rankings

To ensure accurate comparability between the 2008 and 2009 Economic Outlook Rankings, the 2008 rankings have been updated below, using the 2009 methodology. For a detailed description of the 2009 methodology, please see Appendix A.

Rank	State	Rank	State
1	Utah	26	New Hampshire
2	South Dakota	27	New Mexico
3	Tennessee	28	Maryland
4	Wyoming	29	Kansas
5	Virginia	30	Washington
6	Arizona	31	Delaware
7	Nevada	32	Montana
8	Georgia	33	Wisconsin
9	Colorado	34	Nebraska
10	Idaho	35	Oregon
11	Arkansas	36	Pennsylvania
12	Indiana	37	Alaska
13	Texas	38	West Virginia
14	Oklahoma	39	Minnesota
15	Alabama	40	Connecticut
16	Florida	41	Hawaii
17	Michigan	42	California
18	North Dakota	43	Illinois
19	Mississippi	44	Kentucky
20	South Carolina	45	Rhode Island
21	North Carolina	46	Maine
22	Massachusetts	47	Ohio
23	Iowa	48	New Jersey
24	Louisiana	49	New York
25	Missouri	50	Vermont

Appendix C
ALEC Model Legislation

An Act Relating to Creating a Searchable Budget Database for State Spending

Intent Section
The Legislature finds that taxpayers should be able to easily access the details on how the state is spending their tax dollars and what performance results are achieved for those expenditures. It is the intent of the Legislature, therefore, to direct the [state budget office] to create and maintain a searchable budget database Web site detailing where, for what purpose and what results are achieved for all taxpayer investments in state government.

Short Title
This Act shall be known and may be cited as the "Taxpayer Transparency Act."

Definitions
"Searchable budget database Web site" means a Web site that allows the public at no cost to
1) search and aggregate information for the following:
   a. the name and principal location or residence of the entity/and or recipients of funds,
   b. the amount of funds expended,
   c. the funding or expending agency,
   d. the funding source of the revenue expended,
   e. the budget program/activity of the expenditure,
   f. a descriptive purpose for the funding action or expenditure,
   g. the expected performance outcome for the funding action or expenditure,
   h. the past performance outcomes achieved for the funding action or expenditure,
   i. any state audit or report relating to the entity or recipient of funds or the budget program/activity or agency,
   j. and any other relevant information specified by the [state budget office].

2) "programmatically search and access all data in a serialized machine readable format (such as XML) via a web-services application programming interface."

3) "Entity/and or recipients" means:
   k. a corporation,
   l. an association,

m. a union,
n. a limited liability company,
o. a limited liability partnership,
p. any other legal business entity including non-profits,
q. grantees,
r. contractors, and
s. a county, city or other local government entity.

"Entity/and or recipients" does not include an individual recipient of state assistance.

4) "Agency" means a state department, office, board commission, bureau, division, institution, or institution of higher education. This includes individual state agencies and programs, as well as those programs and activities that cross agency lines. "State agency" includes all elective offices in the Executive Branch of government and the Legislature.

5) "Funding source" means the state account the expenditure is appropriated from.

6) "Funding action or expenditure" shall include details on the type of spending (grant, contract, appropriations, etc.). This includes tax exemptions or credits. Where possible, a hyperlink to the actual expenditure document (in a format that is, at a minimum, as searchable as a searchable PDF format) shall be provided.

7) "State audit or report" shall include any audit or report issued by the [state auditor, inspector general, or comptroller], legislative auditor, legislative committee, or executive body relating to the entity or recipient of funds or the budget program/activity or agency.

8) "Director" means the Director of the [state budget office].

9) "Shall" means the obligation or duty to perform; no discretion is granted.

Searchable Budget Database Web Site Created
By January 1, 20xx, the Director shall develop and make publicly available a single, searchable budget database Web site including the required data for the [most recent state budget]. The Web site shall be given a unique and simplified Web site address. Each state agency that maintains a generally accessible Internet site or for which a generally accessible Internet site is maintained shall include a link on the front page of the agency's Internet site to the budget database web site.

Updates
The Director shall provide guidance to agency heads to ensure compliance with this section. "Effective [insert date], the searchable budget database Web site shall be updated as new data becomes available, if feasible, but no later than 30 days upon receipt of data from the agency."

By January 1, 20xx, the Director shall add data for the [previous budgets] to the searchable budget database Web site. Data for previous fiscal years may be added as available and time permits. The

Director shall ensure that all data added to the searchable budget database Web site remains accessible to the public for a minimum of 10 years.

Compliance with Act

The Director shall not be considered in compliance with this act if the data required for the searchable budget database Web site is not available in a searchable and aggregate manner and/or the public is redirected to other government Web sites, unless each of those sites has information from all agencies and each category of information required can be searched electronically by field in a single search.

Supermajority Act: An ALEC Model

Summary

Supermajority requirements are based on the premise that tax increases fuel excessive government spending. Therefore, to more effectively control the budgetary process, the ability to raise taxes or enact new taxes should be made as politically difficult as possible, require broad consensus, and be held to a high standard of accountability. This Act calls for a constitutional provision requiring all tax and license fee impositions and increases to be approved by two-thirds of all members of each House. It provides for an exemption if there are insufficient revenues to pay interest on the state's debt.

Model Legislation

"An Act concurring in a proposed amendment to the Constitution of the State relating to the imposition of taxes or license fees."

WHEREAS, an amendment to the Constitution of the State was proposed in the (session number) Legislature, being Chapter (number), Volume (number), as follows:

This Act may be cited as an amendment to the State Constitution relating to the imposition of taxes or license fees.

Be it enacted by the Legislature (two-thirds of all members elected to each House thereof concurring therein):

Section 1. Amend Article (number) of the Constitution of the state by adding a new Section thereto as follows:

A) Imposition or levy of new taxes or license fee.
1) No tax or license fee may be imposed or levied except pursuant to an act of the legislature adopted with the concurrence of two-thirds of all members of each House.

2) This amendment shall not apply to any tax or license fee authorized by an act of the legislature which has not taken full effect upon the effective date of this bill.

B) Limitation on increase of rate of taxes and license fees.

1) The effective rate of any tax levied or license fee imposed may not be increased except pursuant to an act of the legislature adopted with the concurrence of two-thirds of all members of each House.

C) Exemption to meet obligation under faith and credit pledge; allocation of public monies to meet such an obligation if revenues are not sufficient to meet such pledge.

1) Prior to the beginning of each fiscal year of the state, the legislature shall appropriate revenues to pay interest on its debt to which it has pledged its faith and credit and which interest is payable in the year for which such appropriation is made and to pay the principal of such debt, payable in such year, whether at maturity or otherwise. To the extent that insufficient revenues are provided to pay the principal and interest on such debt when due and payable, the first monies thereafter received by the state shall be set aside and applied to the payment of the principal and interest on such debt. To make up for such insufficient revenues, the legislature may increase the rate of taxes and fees without regard to the limitations of Subsection (A) and Subsection (B) of Section 1, hereof after the failure to pay when due the principal of and interest on such debt; and

WHEREAS the said proposed amendment was adopted by two-thirds of all members elected to each House of the (session number) legislature;

NOW THEREFORE, BE IT RESOLVED BY THE LEGISLATURE (two-thirds of all members elected to each House thereof concurring therein) said proposed amendment is hereby adopted, and shall forthwith become a part of the Constitution of the state.

Section 2. {Severability clause.}

Section 3. {Repealer clause.}

Section 4. {Effective date.}

Please contact Jonathan Williams, ALEC's Tax & Fiscal Policy Task Force Director, at jwilliams@alec.org or (202) 742-8533 if you have any questions or concerns about ALEC's model legislation.

ABOUT THE AMERICAN LEGISLATIVE EXCHANGE COUNCIL

The American Legislative Exchange Council (ALEC) is the nation's largest, nonpartisan, individual membership association of state legislators. With 2,000 members, ALEC's mission is to advance the Jeffersonian principles of limited government, federalism and individual liberty, through a nonpartisan public-private partnership of state legislators, the business community, the federal government and the general public.

Founded in 1973, ALEC is a 501(c)3 nonprofit organization that promotes free-market principles through "model legislation," developed by its public- and private-sector members in eight Task Forces:

Civil Justice

To promote systematic fairness in the courts by discouraging frivolous lawsuits, to fairly balance judicial and legislative authority, to treat defendants and plaintiffs in a consistent manner, and to install transparency and accountability in the trial system.

Commerce, Insurance, and Economic Development

To enhance economic competitiveness, to promote employment and economic prosperity, to encourage innovation, and to limit government regulation imposed upon business.

Public Safety and Elections

(Formerly known as Criminal Justice and Homeland Security)

To develop model policies that reduce crime and violence in our cities and neighborhoods; while also focusing on developing policies to ensure integrity and efficiency in our elections, and within our systems of government.

Education

To promote excellence in the nation's educational system, to advance reforms through parental choice, to support efficiency, accountability, and transparency in all educational institutions, and to ensure America's youth are given the opportunity to succeed.

Health and Human Services

To reduce governmental involvement in health care, to support a consumer-driven health care system, and to promote free-market, pro-patient health care reforms at the state level.

Natural Resources

To operate under the principles of free-market environmentalism, that is to promote the mutually beneficial link between a robust economy and a healthy environment; to unleash the creative powers of the free market for environmental stewardship, and to enhance the quality of our natural resources for the benefit of human health and well-being.

Tax and Fiscal Policy

To reduce excessive government spending, to lower the overall tax burden, to enhance transparency of government operations, and to develop sound, free-market tax and fiscal policy.

Telecommunications and Information Technology

To advance consumer choice in the dynamic and converging areas of telecommunications and information technology by furthering public policies that preserve free-market principles, promote competitive federalism, uphold deregulation efforts, and keep industries free from new burdensome regulations.